INDIGENIZING PHILOSOPHY
THROUGH THE LAND

Indigenizing Philosophy through the Land

A TRICKSTER METHODOLOGY
FOR DECOLONIZING ENVIRONMENTAL ETHICS
AND INDIGENOUS FUTURES

Brian Burkhart

Michigan State University Press | *East Lansing*

♾ The paper used in this publication meets the minimum requirements
of ANSI/NISO Z39.48-1992 (R 1997) (Permanence of Paper).

Michigan State University Press
East Lansing, Michigan 48823-5245

Printed and bound in the United States of America.

28 27 26 25 24 23 22 21 20 19   1 2 3 4 5 6 7 8 9 10

LIBRARY OF CONGRESS CATALOGING-IN-PUBLICATION DATA
Names: Burkhart, Brian, author.
Title: Indigenizing philosophy through the land : a trickster methodology for decolonizing
environmental ethics and indigenous futures / Brian Burkhart.
Other titles: American Indian studies series.
Description: East Lansing : Michigan State University Press, [2019]
| Series: American Indian studies series | Includes bibliographical references and index.
Identifiers: LCCN 2018050618| ISBN 978-1-61186-330-7 (pbk. : alk. paper)
| ISBN 978-1-60917-609-9 (pdf) | ISBN 978-1-62895-372-5 (epub)
| ISBN 978-1-62896-373-1 (kindle)
Subjects: LCSH: Indian philosophy—North America. | Epistemic logic.
Classification: LCC E98.P5 B87 2019 | DDC 970.004/97—dc23
LC record available at https://lccn.loc.gov/2018050618

Book design by Charlie Sharp, Sharp Des!gns, East Lansing, MI
Cover design by Erin Kirk New
Cover art is "Happy Iktomi," by Renelle White Buffalo, and is reproduced by permission of
the artist. All rights reserved.

Michigan State University Press is a member of the Green Press Initiative and is
committed to developing and encouraging ecologically responsible publishing
practices. For more information about the Green Press Initiative and the use of
recycled paper in book publishing, please visit *www.greenpressinitiative.org*.

Visit Michigan State University Press at *www.msupress.org*

CONTENTS

PREFACE

ktomi (the Spider Trickster) showed up to his class a bit late, as usual. He hadn't prepared, but felt confident that he could present Native philosophy in its truest light even if he didn't know much about Native people or Native epistemologies.

Iktomi knew Indians! He had been stealing food from Indians as long as anyone could remember.

But now he tried not to think about Indians as he stood before his class because Indians made him hungry, and he did not want his stomach to start growling because that stomach had been known to growl so loudly that it kept Iktomi from digesting his food.

Though Iktomi was generally confused and often hungry, he always looked sharp!

He was sharply dressed, especially for an eight-legged person—boy was it hard finding clothes that fit!

Today, Iktomi wore a sacred multicolored tweed jacket with beautifully beaded leather elbow patches and chicken feathers hanging from the shoulder pads and sticking out of his beautifully beaded black top hat. The beading on the top hat displayed tiny little images of Iktomi that circled all the way around the hat band.

Iktomi was not only sharply dressed; he was also a scholar.

Iktomi was a descendent of the grandfather of philosophy, the pre-Socratic philosopher Thales, and so had family rights to the teaching of the being of beings.

He told the story of his great-grandfather and how he would talk about that from which is everything that exists and from which it becomes and into which it goes. "That's substance," that old man would say. Iktomi was one of the few beings who could understand what that old man was talking about.

He was also a grandson of "the philosopher" himself, Aristotle. Those old men were his teachers. Those old men were his elders. Those old men were now the spirits that looked over them, but those spirits were very far away across the ocean and so have pretty much completely forgotten about Iktomi.

Iktomi began his lecture with the required discussion of Socrates. He said that that one knew that he didn't know. Iktomi thought that that kind of knowing was sacred.

Chickadee thought that Iktomi had stolen this from the Disney Pocahontas because she remembered the little cartoon Pocahontas saying to the little cartoon John that there was so much that he didn't know he didn't know. This didn't seem particularly insightful to Chickadee.

After several hours on Socrates, Iktomi started talking about the great white father of philosophy, Aristotle.

Chickadee was falling asleep.

Iktomi was not a good story-teller. He was an even worse relative, but he didn't care about that because Iktomi was an excellent philosopher.

Chickadee strained to keep her eyes open. She finally decided that she needed to say something, and so with the deftness and gentleness of the best Indian grandmother, she asked Iktomi, "Grandson, when are we going to start talking about Native philosophy?"

Iktomi could only laugh and laugh loudly. He laughed so loud and hard that he let out quite a fart and even urinated on himself a little.

"You are such a silly little bird," that one said.

"We are talking about Native philosophy. First you start with Thales, then Socrates, then Aristotle . . . then Kant . . . then Wittgenstein . . . then all of the European and Euro-American philosophers who are alive today, then in about 2,000 years, if we can get all the connections right, we will begin to bring in Native philosophy proper. Don't you see you silly little bird!"

Iktomi went back to lecturing. He continued lecturing and jumping and spinning as he lectured louder and louder. He spun. He jumped. He lectured.

He fell into a hole.

Chickadee thought perhaps she should say something about this Native philosophy. She began her lecture with a little dance. That one sang a little song. That one closed her eyes and swayed.

INTRODUCTION

I am a citizen of the Cherokee Nation of Oklahoma but with a patchwork mosaic of Native relationality that goes from the place of my birth and childhood in the Navajo Nation in Arizona to the hills of the Oglala Lakota Nation in South Dakota and many places in-between and beyond. This identity is not a "world" traveler self as Ortega (following Lugones) calls it (Ortega 2001; Lugones 1989). While the self of this book is not monolithic or nonpluralistic, it is also not an in-between in the sense of "new mestiza" (Anzaldúa 1987), not a "multiplicitious self caught in between the norms and practices of different cultures, classes, races, or 'worlds'" (Ortega 2001, 4). There are often feelings of despair or insecurity in growing up away from one's tribal community, in a big city or on another reservation, as I did, but these feelings and the ambiguities that come with an identity that is separated in some sense from one's tribal home, tribal homeland, organic connection to one's language and ceremonies, and so on do not give rise to a "mestiza consciousness"

(Anzaldúa 1987, 77). The self of this book is not caught between the city and the reservation or between one tribe or several and the people and the place of his Cherokee citizenship, because these ambiguities might give rise as they have for me to a consciousness of locality, both as a place that one is from but also a place that one can travel to but only through the land. This traveling is not a "world" traveling, at least not in an abstract sense; it is literally and figuratively a moving or traveling on the land and through the land as the very foundation of locality and Indigeneity itself.

Indigeneity has important ties to one's people and one's nation but cannot be reduced to these since Indigeneity, as I try to clarify in this book, is more importantly tied quite literally to land. Native identity insofar as it has a rooted in the land has no access to a single voice of culture or nation. My voice, as an author, is layered by the dynamic experiences of my identity in its locality (through the land). Native-ness, like all identity, is lived (in locality), while the concepts of Native culture and Native nationhood are abstractions that are constructed through delocality; they float free from the land. Native culture and Native nationhood, as concepts that float free from the land, have political and normative features that are not always functions of lived Indigenous experience as rooted and localized in the land. My effort to decolonize or localize my identity back through the land, to work through the layers of my identity as manifestations of coloniality, must follow the physical and conceptual layering of my locality and its geography and history. In other words, I cannot simply jump out of my skin (my locality and its geography and history) to abstractly identify with my Cherokee ancestors and my tribal citizenship. If that is my goal, I can only accomplish that goal in a step-by-step process from where I stand and have stood—my current locality that includes all of the dynamic layering of where I am and where I have been. This is why my journey back to the locality of the Cherokee Nation both in Georgia and Oklahoma (where my mother, grandfather, great-grandfather, and great-great-grandfather were born) is wrapped in the webs of the Lakota trickster-philosopher Iktomi, and has been wrapped in the wanderings of the Diné trickster-philosopher Ma'ii.

The journey through locality back to one's land is also why this book is in part about Vine Deloria Jr., but not about him in the traditional sense that one writes a book about a philosopher. I write about Deloria in this book in order to follow traces of my relationship with him as a mentor as they lead me toward the Cherokee homeland and however they carry me toward that goal. I met Leksi Deloria in April 2000 at the seventy-fourth annual meeting of the Pacific American Philosophical Association (APA) Conference in Albuquerque, New Mexico. I was a new philosophy graduate student, and he was the elder/mentor of the newly formed groups of the American Indian Philosophy Association and the APA Committee on the Status of American Indians in Philosophy. In my first conversation with him, I was talking about John Rawl's *Theory of Justice*, which I had just read in a graduate seminar. He told me that Rawls had it all wrong. He did not understand kinship. The kinship relationship a child has with an elder grandparent is different than kinship relationship an elder grandparent has with a child. There are different responsibilities one has based on who one is and how one is related, and these change over time, he said. Rawl's veil of ignorance cannot account for this difference, he chimed. This conversation at the APA conference in New Mexico was perhaps more important than any other in setting me on the road across the land to this particular place from which I currently am trying to speak and write in this book. Leksi Deloria became the outside adviser for my philosophy dissertation at Indiana University, and I worked with him on the possibilities and methods of Native American philosophy until he passed. This book is an attempt to situate myself in relationship to my elder as an expressive and creative rather than critical act. In order to complete this kinship relationship, I must now give something back from my own thoughts as a continuation of the teachings I received from Leksi.

Locality

Locality is being-from-the-land and knowing-from-the-land. I use "locality" as a term of art in this book as a way to reference the manner in which being, meaning, and knowing are rooted in the land. Locality as a root of being is a part of each of us and speaks through us and from our historical and geographical place in the world regardless of how our identity is constructed in relation to culture or nation. In that way, no one speaks with cultural or national authority even if he or she was born and raised in a vacuum of a single cultural reality. Cultures and nations do not speak, except as through the power of locality—or this book will try to show. No voice can truly be a voice of cultural or national authority—this is a transcendental notion or a notion born out of delocality itself. When my voice, as with any voice, is understood as a voice of cultural or national authority, either I am speaking for a people (I am taking their voice—at least unless I have been given the particular right and responsibility to speak for a people) or I am speaking abstractly about a people (I am removing their agency to speak). In addition, some voices (Indigenous ones in particular) are understood as only speaking ethnographically, that is, for their people. This contrast between the universal Euro-American voice and the ethnographical specific and collective Indigenous voice is a double-sided sword of coloniality. The reality is that cultural or national authorities of Native-ness, white-ness, or American-ness can only really be speaking from their own particular experiences of being human in the world, from their own locality in its present place. What we call cultural or national authority in the abstracted sense might arise from a cluster of experiences around a particular locality that is used to construct concepts of culture or nationhood, but to reify the cultural or national authority is to reify culture and nation beyond their social and political underpinnings. What allows us to conceptualize this reification of culture and nationhood is the delocalization of locality, which is the attempted unmooring of the roots of being, meaning, and knowing from out of the land itself, or the attempted breaking apart of being-from-the-land and knowing-from-the-land.

The attempt to turn words into being, to reify what we speak of into essences, is something that Ludwig Wittgenstein famously, or infamously perhaps, claims arises from "the bewitchment of our intelligence by means of language" (1953, §109). Language lays traps for us when we stop using it and start looking back at it from a perspective of delocality. Wittgenstein says these "confusions which occupy us arise when language is like an engine idling, not when it is doing work" (1953, §132). For example, we see that a single word or metaphor is used across multiple contexts and begin to suppose that there must be something underneath that word or metaphor that is also carried across all of these contexts, something like the essence or actual meaning of the word or metaphor. Wittgenstein thinks it is something about language itself that sets these delocalized, essence-seeking traps. In the context of locality, this "bewitchment" happens in part with the forgetting of our voice as a manifestation of being-from-the-land. Because language becomes associated with symbols, we forget the originary manifestation of language in the physical voice, in the speaking of words. We forget that our being is not human being in the sense that we understand that term as a delocalized, planetary humanness that floats free from the land. Our being is always first and foremost an originary and continual manifestation out of the land, being-from-the-land. Words, understood in the context of locality, are fundamentally not symbols but physically voiced manifestations of locality. Words are made with breath and have power in that movement of breath. It is through this physical voicing of locality that words are understood, in an Indigenous context, to have power and to arise, in the Diné landscape, for example, from a originary manifestation of language that is literally of the land, which is called *saad la'i*, where the first word and the capacity of speech are originary and continual manifestations of *nilch'i*, which is the air that is in motion or the wind that gives life to the *diyin dine'é* as well as the wind that carries their instruction on how to live to the people.

Locality is more than just the personalized human voicing of meaning. Locality is the way the human voice as the conveyer of human meaning arises from the voice of the land (knowing-from-the-land or meaning-from-the-land)—as in the manner of the Diné landscape whereby the wind gives rise to breath and makes the human voice quite literally an extension of the voice of the land. Locality is a way of conceptualizing place in Indigenous philosophy. It is more than place in the abstract, however. It is place as land. It is more than a concept; it is a materiality, but it is also a reconceptualization of materiality itself from the present perspective of delocality. Locality in this way is more than a backdrop or background context for being and knowing. Locality is the originary and continual manifestation of being, of knowing, of meaning. Locality is being-from-the-land, knowing-from-the-land, and meaning-from-the-land. Epistemic locality is more than the manifestations of knowing and meaning through locality because Indigenous locality is operated on by coloniality, which serves to laminate one locality (European) that has been delocalized onto another (Indigenous). The goal of coloniality in the first place is to erase the actual locality through delocality, which is to say the injecting of the unmoored European locality into the Indigenous land, and that can only be accomplished by removing the original Indigenous locality from the land itself. Epistemic locality is a framework of normative epistemology that creates an opening through which Indigenous locality can be freed from the blanket of European delocalized locality that attempts to hide and deny it as the original and true locality of this land. The problem with the colonial attempt to inject itself into the Indigenous land is that one delocalized locality (the abstracted European cultural reality) can never completely replace the locality it is laminated upon. Coloniality can never actually remove locality, so in the process of colonialism through delocality there always is left a remainder of locality—the Indigenous locality that coloniality operates upon through the force of delocality. Indigenous locality can never actually be removed; it can only be obscured. Indigenous being-from-the-land can never be completely erased as long as Indigenous people exist and as long as Indigenous land exists (there exists a remainder of being-in-the-land itself that survives the delocality of coloniality (being-in-the-land). Locality can only be hidden. Epistemic locality is then the framework of normative epistemology that opens a space for the original Indigenous locality to become known. This re-revelation of Indigenous being-in-the-land and Indigenous being-from-the-land opens a space for Indigenous liberation from the delocalized blanket of European delocalized locality.

To maintain the false locality of European coloniality in its attempt to obscure the Indigenous locality of the land, the narrative of colonial difference arises as a feature of the structure of coloniality. This narrative serves to create an Indigenous alterity that serves the European delocalized coloniality because it is not an alterity at all but rather a projection of difference from within the isolated (because delocalized) European locality. The narrative of colonial difference functions through and in service of delocality. The narrative creates a mirror of identity that only reflects coloniality (the abstracted European cultural reality). Seen through the reflection of this mirror of coloniality, Indigenous people can only be seen as either anticolonist or protocolonist. Indigenous people are either in binary opposition to the colonist (savage versus civilized) or they are backward versions of the civilized in the process of trying to reach the status of the civilized colonist. Epistemic locality, in the process of reconfiguring the obscured locality, must mark the divide of delocality that is laminated on top of the actual locality. The marking of this divide is, in Walter Mignolo's words, "the fact of colonial difference." He writes, "the limit of Western philosophy is the border where the colonial difference emerges, making visible the variety of local histories that Western thought, from the right and the left, hid and suppressed" (2002, 64). Epistemic locality, the process discussed and used in this book to, in part, mark the fact of colonial difference, makes clear that the relationship between locality and delocality through coloniality is ill-fitted, and not accidently so. The lack of fit of locality and delocality is a metaphysical fact, but the lamination of delocality onto locality is a colonial fact. Marking off the areas of ill-fittedness is an essential step in the methodology of epistemic locality. The narrative of colonial difference functions through delocality while the fact of colonial difference as revealed in the ill-fittedness of colonial lamination operates to uncover the locality obscured by coloniality. Epistemic locality is then the process of revealing the obscured Indigenous locality that is continually fracturing and seeping through the colonial mask that attempts to cover it.

The manifestation of the delocalizing force of coloniality in the narrative of colonial difference attempts to silence the Indigenous philosophical voice. Speaking with authority or questioning the authority of a voice in relation to a culture treats cultures as artifacts. But only Indigenous voices and cultures are treated as artifacts under the narrative of colonial difference. Andrea Smith points out that Indigenous voices "can only be read for their truth." We do not ask French philosopher Michel Foucault, she continues, "if he is authentically French" and if his philosophy authentically reflects French culture and nationhood. Smith points out that only Western philosophers "are granted rhetorical agency, analysis, and theory" (Smith 2014, 210). Foucault is understood as capable of speaking *the* truth rather than merely a cultural or national truth that can only be judged as an authentic or inauthentic expression of that culture or nationality. To see how strange this way of understanding Indigenous voices is, look at talk about science. Even though there is a vast diversity in science, no one speaks about different sciences or different cultural or national sciences. Even though the conceptualization of what science is within the field of biology as opposed to theoretical physics, we do not speak of the science of biology as distinct from the science of theoretical physics. We do not speak of diversity and authenticity in relation to the broad spectrum of voices of scientists because we understand science as arising out of something real, whereas we understand culture, religion, faith, spirituality (particularly as these relate to Indigenous peoples) as arising out of something fictional. One of the objects of this book is to reconfigure through locality the way we talk about is real and is fictional and so, by extension, how we talk about Indian voices and scientific voices as well.

Confusion regarding the distinction between the narrative of colonial difference and the fact of colonial difference through locality mires much of the efforts to decolonize academia, including Andrea Smith's controversial representation of herself as Cherokee. The result is that many efforts to decolonize through the rejection of the narrative of colonial difference only serve to further reify this narrative because the rejection is ultimately framed within that narrative because it does not recognize the fact of colonial difference through locality. Smith, in critiquing the manner in which Indigenous voices are only read for authenticity under the narrative of colonial difference, describes this containment of Indigenous truth as being "contained in their bodies." Given the particular operations of the narrative of colonial difference to create a mere material facticity for Indigenous peoples, it seems reasonable to disembody Indigenous peoples and reality as a rejection of the narrative of colonial difference. However, this obfuscates the manner in which delocality is maintained and so obfuscates the coloniality of the critique itself. While Smith is able to challenge the containment of Indigenous truth in Indigenous bodies, she is not able to see that a disembodied Indigeneity is a further operation of the narrative of colonial difference, which in this case serves to remove the being-in-kinship as an essential feature of Indigeneity in the context of locality. As Carol Cornsilk points out in the context of Smith's claims to be Cherokee, "Cherokee people . . . have always recognized their tribal members by their kinship" ("Cherokee Women" 2015). Kinship as understood in the framework of being-in-kinship is a function of locality and extension of the meaning of being-from-the-land. Marking the fact of colonial difference through locality can remove kinship from delocality and the narrative of colonial difference and reframe kinship as a function of being-from-the-land.

To break free of the delocal and colonial containment of Indigenous voices as authentic ethnography, I choose to reflect on those Native voices that are most contained in this way. I choose to listen to the words of Black Elk, Lame Deer, Chief Seattle, and others exactly because questions have been raised as to the authenticity of these words and their speakers. I choose to not allow the space for the authenticity of their words to be questioned. I choose to close that space in this text through a kind of extension of Audra Simpson's ethnographic refusal (2014). I am refusing to allow the space for the question whether these are authentic Indigenous words to even be asked. This is a form of ethnographic refusal because what it is refusing is ethnographic containment: Indigenous voices only have meaning as a form of ethnography, which would mean that the truth or value of their words is determined by the ethnographic authenticity of their words rather than truth or value in a broader sense. Perhaps only through this form of ethnographic refusal can the meaning of the words spoken by these Native thinkers be revealed in their locality.

Epistemic locality, as a process that reveals locality and coloniality as a function of delocality, is exceedingly challenging because of the fundamental normalization of delocality in Western language and thought. The semantics of delocality articulates any expression of locality through the lens of the narrative of colonial difference and the general delocalized structures of meaning. Thus, in what appears to be the normal understanding of a word, but is truly a function of the semantics of delocality, actual expressions of locality appear meaningless or nonsensical. This is because expressions of locality are almost always interpreted under the semantics of delocality as a generality floating free from the land, perhaps even a universal or an essence. Thus, insofar as the semantics of delocality frame the meaning of any word, there will always be a lack of clarity to any expression of locality. This is why I understand Western epistemology, in my essay "What Coyote and Thales Can Teach Us: An Outline of American Indian Epistemology," as an analogy to Coyote's trickster way of thinking and being. Just as Thales falls in a hole because he is not connected to the land upon which he is walking and instead is trying to grasp the nature of the stars in the abstract, so Coyote often forgets the locality of his relationships so that he can achieve an immediate and often selfish or petty end. Trickster methodology, as exemplified by Coyote, Jisdu (the Cherokee Rabbit Trickster), Raven, Iktomi (the Lakota Spider Trickster), and many other Indigenous tricksters, is a process that is much more than the naive reaching beyond locality as exemplified by Thales. Indigenous tricksters teach their relatives how not to act like Thales. Indigenous tricksters teach their relatives about the contours of locality and so help them put their feet back on the ground so that they do not continue to fall into the holes. Indigenous tricksters walk both sides of locality and delocality. Through humorous and creative failings Indigenous tricksters, like Coyote, Jisdu, Raven, and Iktomi, are able to deconstruct the epistemology and ontology of delocality from the inside. More simply, a trickster like Iktomi can lead you to spin and wrap yourself in the same webs that he spins around himself. As the Spider Trickster, however, he can do this in such a way that he will show you how you wrapped this web around yourself in the first place. This creates the space for you to be able to see how to get out of the web of your own making. In other words, the Spider Trickster's methodology is one of epistemic locality. Iktomi can mark off the fact of colonial difference in such a way that those who he works his trickster medicine upon are able to see the conflict between locality and delocality in a useful and meaningful way.

Iktomi brings a level of irony and frivolity that is often unwelcomed in an academic text though. Part of the reason that these acts of "play" are off limits in "serious" texts is that in "serious" texts the words themselves are supposed to convey a delocalized generic meaning, perhaps even universal meaning or essence. Indigenous philosophy, in my version, rejects this sense of meaning and seriousness of texts because meaning in locality is originary, is continually shaped by being-in-the-land and being-from-the-land. Meaning does not happen in disembodied, delocalized texts. Meaning is active and dynamic and carries all of the layers of the epistemic and ontological kinship of people and the land. Humor is perhaps the most powerful in creating and maintaining kinship, which means it is more important perhaps that the so-called "serious" language required in academic texts. Iktomi's stories are particularly poignant in this regard as they do not contain meaning in a mere delocalized arraignment of symbols. It is the act of being drawn into or putting myself into Iktomi's place—his attempts to find meaning—that allows me to create an intimate knowing kinship relationship to Iktomi and his stories. Seeing myself as Iktomi in his stories and in attempts to find meaning in my own life opens up a space for me to find the meaning that he could not as I am able to see in a deconstructive and first-personal way just what I/Iktomi have been missing in our search for meaning and understanding.

In a serious academic text, language must always be declarative and proclamatory. It must always proceed forward and directly to what we call truth and knowledge. Language in the trickster modality is seen, then, as frivolous and nonproductive because it moves backward and in circles in order to create a space for liberation, for creating new and maintaining or completing existing kinship relationships rather than simply spinning more webs around oneself and further removing oneself from the possibility of kinship. The framing of the academic enterprise within the boundaries of what can be taken seriously helps to maintain the existing, normative knowledge paradigms, which serves to block the entrance of decolonial philosophy from the academic enterprise. Often the criticism that one is not speaking seriously enough is another way of saying that one is not taking seriously the existing norms of what counts for knowledge and what counts as a method for producing such knowledge. The limiting of academic language to serious declarative proclamations is one way of removing the possibility of reflecting critically on the structures of truth and knowledge such declarative statements portend. What the trickster modality does that irritates the disciplinary structures of existing knowledge paradigms is to come to knowledge more freely, spontaneously, and creatively. Iktomi often creates knowledge unwittingly through his attempts to trick his relatives. This way of creating knowledge undermines the declarative power of an individual statement since Iktomi can create knowledge without even the intention to do so, much less a declarative and willful statement to that effect. The trickster modality is a real power and is a manifesting of knowing and meaning out of the land. The trickster modality is something that is often attempted for the sake of irony by what might be called hipsters, Bohemians, alternatives, or the like, but this modality is a manifestation of something real and powerful in Indigenous cultural epistemologies and so cannot be truly imitated. Tricksters are capable, in Indigenous story and history, of expressing the limits of existing knowledge paradigms and exposing the limits of those paradigms through creative and playful manifestations of knowing and meaning in locality. In this way, the trickster modality can undercut the coloniality and guardianship of Western academic philosophy as well as expose Western philosophy to itself. A trickster modality might reveal, for example, the contradiction in the story of Western philosophy: a tradition that now espouses only using written declarative statements when one of its supposed founders (Plato) writes in dialogue for the express purpose of never saying anything declarative and his most famous student (Aristotle) never wrote anything that we know of—his writings are nothing more than students' notes from his lectures.

Indigenous philosophizing is much more than this trickster methodology. The active relational dynamic of Indigenous language and knowledge transforms what ordinarily goes by the noun "philosophy" in English into "philosophizing" in an Indigenous context. Indigenizing philosophy is then, in part, making it more active and dynamic. Indigenous philosophizing is a verb, a kind of movement and action that is creative and originary. In the context of Indigenous decolonial philosophizing, the context of this book, this philosophizing movement is a movement back to the land, regrounding our language, being, knowing, meaning, and so on back in the land. This movement back to the land is not merely material as it is prematerial, reconfiguring our concepts and ways of thinking and speaking out of the land, out of locality, including our Westernized concept of land itself as well as materiality itself. The prematerial movement back to the land is required in order to reconceptualize the way we think about materially being of the land. Indigenous philosophizing, in this specific decolonial sense as well as in the broader sense in which philosophizing has existed in cultures of Indigenous peoples since time immemorial, manifests creative and original, sometimes even playful, reflective expressions of knowledge. One can see the creative and often playful expressions of knowledge in both Indigenous trickster stories as well as Indigenous stories of creation. Understanding philosophy as an original and creative act rather than as an analysis of texts or ideas that are delocalized from the originary creative act presents significant challenges for Western philosophy and Western academia. Western philosophy has become centered on the analysis and interpretation of ideas, texts, sometimes even the thinkers and the writers themselves. Whether the analysis is of texts, the thinkers who produce those texts, or some combination of the two, the analysis is delocalized and distant. There is no focus on creative and original reflections. The absence of a focus on original reflective thought is in part a result of the delocalizing of philosophical reflection—a fact that also serves to maintain the colonial structure of philosophical reflection. Adding to the structural pressure to maintain the colonizing, delocal framework of Western philosophy is the pressure to produce constant philosophical commodities as the practice of philosophy becomes ever more institutionalized within a capitalistic economy.

Beyond the commercial and colonial context of the production of philosophical texts that maintains a model of standardization and a limit or containment of Indigenous philosophy, the originary or creative aspects of the production of philosophy texts is almost always limited to the thinker herself and the idea that originally produced philosophical ideas might have some originary and creative aspects— although it is quite common to believe that even originally produced philosophical ideas are socially or historically constructed apart from the thinker herself. Few have seen the study of philosophical ideas, texts, and the philosophers who produce them as an originary and creative relationship. One exception is Gilles Deleuze, whose single manuscript studies of Hume, Kant, Spinoza, Nietzsche, Bergson, Leibniz, and Foucault are the opposite of what is expected in a twentieth-century study of a philosopher's ideas. Not quite in the context of the colonial containment of Indigenous philosophy, but in the general context of the history of philosophy in the Western academy, he sees this history as playing a "repressor's role" (Deleuze and Parnet 1987, 13). (Peter K. J. Park's *Africa, Asia, and the History of Philosophy: Racism and the Formation of the Philosophical Canon, 1780–1831* shows more clearly than ever the manner in which the creation and maintenance of the Eurocentric philosophical canon is a product of racism.) This most general containment of thought within Western philosophy that requires the reading of "Plato, Descartes, Kant and Heidegger, and so-and-so's book about them" creates "a formidable school of intimidation which manufactures specialists in thought—but which also makes those who stay outside conform all the more to this specialism which they despise" (Deleuze and Parnet 1987, 13). Deleuze saw the limitation of studying these Western thinkers and all of the texts written about them that try to articulate their thought abstractly and delocally (or apart from any relationship with the reader-thinker) as a historical shaping of "an image of thought called philosophy" that "effectively stops people from thinking" (Deleuze and Parnet 1987, 13).

This work does not follow Deleuze with any particular effort. It is important from the perspective of locality to reject the transcendent, or for Deleuze "transcendent organization" that "has always been the disease of the West" that "carries of forms and strips them of their indications of speed, which dissolve subject and extract their hecceities, nothing left but longitudes and latitudes" (1987. 94). And it is also true that understanding the locality of the land first requires an understanding of immanence or ground itself that does not already presuppose a concept of locality or materiality that is abstract and transcendental. The concept of locality itself must be sought as the ground of thought but also must be approached as thought or in thought itself. The creativity of thought is what allows it to approach the immanent ground of itself, not as a transcendent realm of knowledge or being but as the ground itself or the land itself in a premature sense. The earth or the land then becomes both the ground and the limit of thought and of being. The land or the earth cannot be thought of just as the planet or the human being cannot be thought of except through the imitating forms of delocalized thought in which what is thought is an imitation earth or human being. Indigenous philosophizing approaches the immanent ground of thought and being through creativity, which itself is manifest most clearly in the creating of new relationships or kinships. Indigenous philosophizing, as I express it in this text, studies the work of Vine Deloria Jr., Lakota philosophy, and the trickster methodologies of Iktomi through the methodological approaching of the locality of Deloria, Black Elk, Lakota philosophy, and Iktomi as a creative expression of new intimate knowing kinship relationships, relationships that produced (and simultaneously remade) this text. The Iktomi trickster modality also creates a capacity in the context of locality to approach locality from the inside out or from the trickster point of view where Iktomi can approach but also express the ground and limit of knowing and being through the creative and playing manifestations of knowing and being in locality.

This text focuses on Indigenizing philosophizing through epistemic locality. It reflects philosophically in a way that engages and critiques the delocalized epistemological structure of Western philosophy in both history and current practice and in the context of broader Indigenous philosophical practices. Some common Indigenous philosophical themes are these:

- Indigenous philosophizing works with and tells stories. See, for example, Shawn Wilson's *Research Is Ceremony: Indigenous Research Methods.*
- Indigenous philosophizing is original, innovative, creative, and active. Even basic human creation and creativity are on a continuum with creation and creativity on the most cosmic levels. Creation and Creator are power, movement, and energy in itself. See, for example, Gregory Cajete's *Native Science: The Natural Laws of Interdependence.*
- Indigenous philosophizing sees relationships as ontologically primary. One might see the nonbinary dualism of Indigenous logic as arising from the primacy of relationality.
- Indigenous philosophizing shows but does not present arguments *per se.* It opens up a space for readers/listeners to find meaning and understanding but does make or declare that meaning for them.
- Indigenous philosophizing respects the self-determination of all other living creatures and seeks to develop, in Jack Forbes's words,

"an attitude of profound respect for individuality and right to self-realization of all living creatures" (1998, 12).

- Indigenous philosophizing reads and speaks language, even the English language, in the manner of Indigenous languages: dynamic, multiple layers of meaning for every word. Action, process, and transformation shape the layers of meaning in any given word.
- Indigenous philosophizing focuses on meaning and understanding (which are relational and dynamic) rather than truth or proof (which is static and delocalized).
- Indigenous philosophizing focuses on all aspects of human understanding through a process of circularity. See, for example, the circle of the four directions of being in Black Elk (the heart, mind, body, and spirit), where understanding is both a momentary aspect of this circle and a never-ending movement of the circle itself.
- Indigenous philosophizing adapts stories and lessons to the hearer. It purposefully transforms ideas into those that can best be understood and most easily related to by the hearer. See, for example, Black Elk's stories and lessons to John Neihardt (Neihardt 1932), the story told to James Walker that was deliberately altered when told to Walker (Jahner 1983, 20), the White Buffalo Calf Woman story that was altered when told to the Jesuit missionary Eugene Buechel (Buechel 1978, 238–241), among countless others.

In addition to incorporating these Indigenous philosophical practices in the context of epistemic locality, this work is a work of Indigenous decolonial philosophy, which means that it will not be distracted by a

need to analyze or contextualize (even beyond the limits of such operations in the context of epistemic locality) just for its own sake. Indigenous
decolonial philosophy is always directed and focused on the creation
of philosophical tools for Indigenous liberation. It is from this place of
Indigenous decolonial philosophy through epistemic locality that I wish
to undertake creative and originary reflections on particular threads of
Western thought and culture regarding the human relationship to the
environment and the manner in which morality is constructed apart
from the land in order to being the work of marking of morality from
land that is a function of the fact of colonial difference. The layering of
European delocality onto Indigenous locality obscures the ontological
and epistemic relationship between morality and the land that arises in
locality. The obscuring of locality not only leads to particular patterns
of delocalized reflection that create Iktomi-like webs of confusion and
illusion, classic trickster circles that turn in on themselves, but also to
a disruption of earth morality, the creating and maintaining of kinship
relations with and through the land or the morality of locality. These
circles create a delocalized and imitation framework of reflection that
results in what appears to be intractable ethical and environmental
problems. Seen through an Iktomi modality, these intractable problems
that limit reflection about morality and the environment are self-cre-
ated through illusions of delocality. Confusions regarding locality or
illusions of delocality give rise to the dualistic binaries of real/fictional,
individual/collective. The process of untangling these Iktomi-like webs
is not easy, particularly if attempted from inside of the web-making
process. The misstep that often leads the internal attempt into its own
entanglement is not recognizing the point at which locality becomes
delocality or the context of coloniality, the point that the fact of colonial

difference becomes the narrative of colonial difference. Iktomi's trickster methodology can reveal how these seemingly intractable problems come to be in the first place in the context of approaching locality and the fact of colonial difference. Iktomi can reveal how the webs of binary thinking that entangle the discussions of intrinsic/instrumental value, anthropocentrism/nonanthropocentrism, moral realism/moral fictionalism, and natural/unnatural always arise from a forked path and a first choice between locality and delocality. Iktomi can show us the way back to that choice and that if we take a different path, the path to locality, the questions posed and the answers given regarding the human relationship to nonhumans are manifestly different and avoid these binary entanglements.

The patterns of delocalized thinking that arise in the context of the Western reflections on the relationship of humans to the land lead to these illusory binary entanglements: intrinsic/instrumental value, anthropocentrism/nonanthropocentrism, moral realism/moral fictionalism, and natural/unnatural. The dichotomy between what is real and what is fictional in the particular form of the opposition between moral realism and moral fictionalism arises out of delocality. Some write, as Joshua Green did in his work on moral realism, that moral realism sets the stage for a great deal of intolerance and so social and human ills. He suggests that a great deal of present and historical persecution and general human evils is founded on the idea that the moral beliefs of one's community, sect, self, or nation are as real and immutable as any scientific fact. He suggests that the rejection of moral realism and the taking up of a moral fictionalist position will result in more tolerance, less persecution, and fewer human evils (Green 2002). This appears to be false. Moral fictionalism seems to lead to the same sorts of ills, leaving us spun once again in a trickster web of our own making. The problem appears not to be moral realism or moral fictionalism but rather the way we think about reality apart from locality that leads us down a binary path between moral realism and moral fictionalism.

Another trickster entanglement that arises from delocality is found in the opposing dualism of anthropocentric and nonanthropocentric perspectives in ethics. Western environmental ethics arises through the attempt to deliberate morally using a nonanthropocentric perspective. Just like the discussion over the binary between moral realism and moral fictionalism, critics begin to raise problems with the possibility of deliberating nonanthropocentrically. The result is that moral deliberation pulls back to the pole of the anthropocentric perspective, resulting in moral deliberation only about humans, which reveals the self-centered core of human reason regarding reflection on the value of nonhumans.

Indigenous philosophizing through locality through a trickster modality will bring to light some important features of these ways of thinking about value and human perspective (about intrinsic versus instrumental value and anthropocentric versus nonanthropocentric perspective) that can be instructive in untangling from the delocalized thinking that gives rise to these binary entanglements in the first place. The creative and originary reflections of epistemic locality and the playful practices of the trickster modality can destabilize the binary entanglements of delocalized thinking and open a space for creating new ideas/relationships even without the removal of the delocalized framework in total. We can, through the injection of some locality back into the delocalized and colonialized framework, see the moral status of and our moral obligation to nonhumans realistically and nonanthropocentrically. This new way of seeing through the injection of locality can be useful even to Western philosophers who are immersed in the naturalized colonial attitude of delocality. Even a bit of locality injected into the conversation regarding morality and the land can create new ideas/relationships. It can begin to chip away at the naturalness of the colonial attitude of delocality. Through the perspective of locality, an understanding of morality and the land can be more comprehensive in the sense of the possibility of a general moral theory that is nonanthropocentric from the start and not an extension of a theory that primarily applies to humans, and more plausible in the sense that it does not require Western thinkers to accept the view that the nonhuman environment has intrinsic value. I do not intend to actually articulate any kind of Western moral theory in this text because, as will become clear, the basic framework of moral theorizing in Western philosophy is delocalized. As a decolonial philosophy text about moral locality in the land, I hope to provide, at minimum, a context for injecting locality into the epistemic and moral practices of Western environmental theorizing. Instead of providing just another delocalized Western environmental ethics, this trickster methodology opens a space for injecting bits of locality into the delocalized context of Western environmental ethics following the model of Iktomi where the injected locality provides a way of unseeing the naturalness of delocality but also of seeing how it becomes seen as natural in the first place. Some of these injected bits of locality are as follows:

- In locality, moral realism and moral fictionalism are not extremes and both true.
- In locality, nonanthropocentric moral theorizing does not require the claim that nonhumans have intrinsic value.

- In locality, morality can be understood as a feature of relationships rather than as founded on the value of things.
- In locality, the idea that morality is natural can be understood as an extension of the idea that morality is a feature of relationships rather than the value of things.

PART 1

The Coloniality of Western Philosophy and Indigenous Resistance through the Land

CHAPTER 1

Philosophical Colonizing of People and Land

Welcome to Settler Colonialism. The first rule of Settler Colonialism is: you do not talk about Settler Colonialism.

—Iktomi

T he power of Western coloniality, highlighted by the genocidal removal of Indigenous people from their lands as the foundational act of creating the United States, Canada, Australia, and New Zealand, is centered in land. It is no wonder, then, that given the manner in which coloniality must continually reposition itself philosophically and historically in order to cover up this genocidal relationship to Indigenous people because of their relationship to this desired land, deep philosophical reflection on the relationship between people and land is so underemphasized in Western philosophy. Environmental philosophy, specifically in the form of environmental ethics and more recently environmental justice, has only just become part of the Western philosophical landscape, and presently still exists in the far reaches of the periphery. Further, environmental philosophy is, as I will argue, structured around the coloniality of power in a similar manner to Western philosophy more generally. The Western philosophers who have reflected on land and place in relationship to meaning and being, and so on, are so scarce that they appear to be from another philosophical planet. This chapter attempts to show why land has this philosophical position in Western philosophy by articulating the manner in which coloniality operates on the land through concepts of temporality and subjectivity.

The reasons that Western philosophy virtually ignores discussions of land are multiple. One reason is that philosophy seeks the highest level of abstraction and universality, where land, just like race and gender, is seen as concrete and particular. Any reflection on land, race or gender serves as a distraction, at the very least, from the goal of reaching the highest level of abstraction and universality. The creation of the philosophical lacunae regarding land, as well as race and gender, arises most perspicuously through the process of coloniality, or in what Anibal Quijano calls the coloniality of power (2000). Coloniality of power describes the foundational framework of the modern world-system through the creation of race and racial hierarchies that structure modern economies, philosophies, and cultures. As Quijano makes clear, the development of what Immanuel Wallerstein calls the "modern world-system" of global capitalism that centers wealth and power in western Europe and North America cannot be understood apart from the creation of modern coloniality that arises from these same regions. Western Europe and North America, collectively constructed as the

West, become the center of global capitalism through the coloniality of power which allows the West to impose the coloniality of power as the foundational structure of the modern world-system or what it essentially constructed as a planetary system of power. The realization of this modern world-system through coloniality structures (for non-Western people) the internal (to each other) and external (to the West) relationships. A relationship to land is also realized through the manifestation of this modern world-system. As will become clear, the manifestation of this world-system as structured through the coloniality of power arises out of a cosmic reconfiguring of the foundational reality that exists in people (the nature of subjectivity) and the land (the nature of space and place).

The notion of the West and even the notion of Europe were constructed with a purpose. Before there was the West, before there was Europe, there were only Spain, Great Britain, Portugal, France, and so on. Coloniality is "a mode" through which "Europeans could develop their sense of European-ness" (Smith 1999, 22). As Quijano shows, the creation of Europe and even American national identity (conceptualized later as the West) goes hand in hand with the creation of non-Western identities such as Africa, Asia, and Oceania. These non-Western identities are further structured in relation to Indigenous "savages." For example, the East ("Orient") only exists as the inferior other to the West ("Occidental") in relationship to more inferior "Indian" and "black" others through the hierarchy of the coloniality of power (Quijano 2000, 540). Enrique Dussel marks this creation point as the "birth of modernity, when ... Europe could constitute itself as unified ego exploring, conquering, colonizing an alterity that gave back its image of itself" (1993, 66). Quijano puts the result of this birth as this:

The incorporation of such diverse and heterogeneous cultural histories into a single world dominated by Europe signified a cultural and intellectual intersubjective configuration equivalent to the articulation of all forms of labor control around capital, a configuration that established world capitalism. In effect, all of the experiences, histories, resources, and cultural products ended up in one global cultural order revolving around European or Western hegemony. Europe's hegemony over the new model of global power concentrated all forms of the control of subjectivity, culture, and especially knowledge and the production of knowledge under its hegemony. (2000, 540)

To see how the coloniality of power structures Western philosophy through its relationship to non-Western people and land (particularly Indigenous peoples) requires deeper examination of the concentration of power on the nature of subjectivity, culture, and knowledge. In particular, it is necessary to see how coloniality reconfigures the way people are able to conceptualize being and knowing in relationship to subjectivity itself as well as the earth around them, the land. The way Western philosophical coloniality manifests itself onto the land is deeply connected to the manner in which Western philosophical coloniality creates and maintains a subjectivity of domination.

Colonizers exercised diverse methods for reshaping the non-Western and Indigenous peoples' subjective as well as intersubjective relationships. One method is through a contradictory process of colonial logic that magically transforms the coloniality of power into the illusion of actual Western knowledge and progress. For example, while claiming that Indigenous people were the most backward and primitive examples of humanity, the colonizers expropriated the most powerful discoveries of these same peoples that were most apt to extend their power and profit while at the same time claiming them for their own—as Western discoveries, as Western knowledge. As Maori philosopher Linda Tuhuwai Smith puts it, "Indigenous . . . forms of knowledge" are "regarded as 'new discoveries' by Western science. These discoveries were commodified as property belonging to the cultural archive and body of knowledge of the West" (1999, 61). At the same time, the colonizers did as much as they could to eradicate Indigenous forms of knowledge and knowledge production. Quijano gives an example: "repression in this field [eradicating Indigenous symbolic forms of knowledge production] was most violent, profound, and long lasting among the Indians of Ibero-American, who were condemned to be an illiterate peasant subculture stripped of their objectified intellectual legacy" (2000, 541). Linda Martín Alcoff continues Quijano's thought by noting that claiming "there were no pre-Colombian books or forms of writing" is maintained by "raid[ing] and burning in heaps" any codices that could be found (2007, 87–88). The magical transformation of the coloniality of power into the illusion of something other than simple power happens at the level of federal Indian law in the United States. Lawmakers and judges claim the right to purchase Indian land while at the same time claiming that Indian people are mere animals who roam the land and have no legal title to it. Another method to transform Indigenous subjectivity and intersubjectivity while at the same time hiding the source of this transformation in the coloniality of power is to replace, by force as necessary, the existing culture and knowledge system with the culture and knowledge system of the dominant culture in whatever manner best suited the reproduction of that domination. Most often this replacement took the form of the culture and knowledge systems of Christianity. In particular, since the

Doctrine of Discovery (that all Indigenous property, including land and person, belong to the first representative of Christendom) was initially and then later functionally a Christian doctrine, the more Indigenous people were Christianized, the more they would, hopefully, support their enslaved and landless place in Christendom.

Another method by which colonizers reshape Indigenous subjectivity and intersubjectivity is through the narrative of colonial difference. This is not actual alterity but rather the constructed oppositional "other" that builds and maintains the ego of Western coloniality. This is the "other," from Dussel quoted above, that constitutes the European ego, existing as a mirror to reflect the European ego back upon itself. Indigeneity then is essentially tied to coloniality at every level in which narratives are created and maintained by the colonial state and modern settler state (ethnographies, histories, and so on) (Pagden 1987). The articulation of Indian difference is ideologically charged and structured. Narrating the colonial difference has the function of maintaining colonial order through the defining and knowing of Indian difference as a mirror of the ego of Western coloniality (Said 1978, 1994).

The Indian "other" is manufactured, in part, for the purpose of creating a salvatory ego centered in Europe that can innocently colonize a backward and savage other who if violently resists is seen as victimizing the original colonizers. Civilizing the savages or saving the heathens does not change the nature of Western ego, the subjectivity of domination. The path of continued domination, after civilizing and saving, threatens to reveal the bad faith of the civilizing and saving mission of colonization in the underlying reality of the mere coloniality of power. One response to this is to continually reposition the target of salvation: from religious salvation of Christianity to political salvation of Western civilization to economic salvation of global capitalism. This serves at one level to hide a form of what Enrique Dussel calls "the developmentalism fallacy," specifically through the denial that the states of being unsaved, uncivilized, and poor for non-Western subjectivities are dialectically connected to the states of being saved, civilized, and wealthy for Western subjectivities (1993, 67-68).

The civilizing mission of colonization is also a fallacy in the sense that it equivocates between notions of value in the first place. There is more hidden than just the dialectic connection of Western and Indigenous subjectivities. There is a trajectory of a subtler meaning to concepts of coloniality (civilization, freedom, and so on) from 1492 through the notions of freedom and liberty of the Enlightenment to the present. From the civilizing mission of colonization in America to Kant's freedom from immaturity through rationality to the bringing of freedom to the Iraqi citizens in Operation Iraqi Freedom, there is an equivocation between the way the Western subject thinks of the concepts of coloniality for himself and the way they are applied to those missionized. What freedom and civilization mean for Iraqis and Indians is really Western freedom and the coloniality of power. What George W. Bush meant when he proposed to save the Iraqi people by giving them freedom was to force them into global free enterprise, to be controlled by global capitalism and the coloniality of power. The real meaning of being savage, uncivilized, unfree, and so on is then determined by Eurocentrism, but not in the sense of Eurocentric values and so on, but simply in being European. It is, then, to lie outside of the scope of the coloniality of power and later global capitalism that truly marks the meaning of uncivilized and unfree. As Quijano puts it, the "coloniality of power" implies "the hegemony of Eurocentrism as epistemological perspective.... In the context of coloniality of power, . . . their new, assigned identities were also subjected to the Eurocentric hegemony as a way of knowing" (quoted in Mignolo 2000, 54). In other words, Eurocentrism is the epistemological perspective of modern Western philosophy. It is not an epistemological perspective that is then applied Eurocentrically to non-Western peoples; Eurocentrism *is* the epistemological perspective by which the concepts of being civilized, free, and so on are determined. Eurocentrism is also not used to define subjectivity, value, and so forth; Eurocentrism is subjectivity, value, and so forth. What is meant by freedom for the civilized is then the freedom to dominate through the coloniality of power, and freedom for the savage is the freedom to be dominated by the coloniality of power just like freedom for the Iraqi people is the freedom of free enterprise, to have their resources placed, through no choice of their own, on the open market to be purchased by the highest bidder.

The *Ego Conquiro* of Modern Philosophical Subjectivity

Modern Western philosophy seeks freedom from bondage, or what Kant calls "*Ausgang*" (a way out) from "*unmündig*" (a state of being unfree). It seeks, for humanity, a way out of doubt, a way out of immaturity. It seeks to actualize something, some sense of itself, of subjectivity, of humanity, and of European-ness. Kant defines the project of philosophy during his time as "the exodus of humanity by its own effort from a state of guilty immaturity" (1784). Freeing humanity from its self-imposed exile of immaturity actualizes the true, independent, mature humanity of modern civilization. Humanity is supposed to gain this independence, according to modern philosophy, through human subjectivity in the form of human reason. The underlying reality of this freedom is that independence is ultimately understood and dialectically engaged with actualizing dependence. There is a core of irrationality, then, at the center of the supposed rationality that is to free humanity from immaturity.

Enrique Dussel details in numerous works and on numerous grounds the coloniality of Western philosophy in the works of Kant, Hegel, and Descartes. Of Kant's claim that immaturity is a guilty state brought on by laziness and cowardice, Dussel asks, "Should all of these [colonized] subjects be considered to reside in a state of guilty immaturity?" (1993, 68). It is not with these thinkers, however, that Dussel finds the foundation of philosophical coloniality. They are but a mere second and third wave, continuing philosophically what has already become culturally established as the coloniality of power. Dussel discovers a prototype of the Cartesian *ego cogito* in the Spanish-Portuguese *ego conquiro* (I conquer) that carries coloniality to the Americas, and a prototype of Kant's immaturity in the *turditatum* (Latin meaning backward, slow, or stupid) that applies to American Indians in the sixteenth-century Spanish Valladolid (Dussel 2000). It is in the development of coloniality in the sixteenth century that Dussel finds the true roots of modern Western philosophy. It is in "the conquest of Mexico," he writes, that we find "the first sphere of the modern ego" (Dussel 2000, 471). Although gestating for some time, the modern European ego was "born" when it was in a position to place itself against an "other," and to transcend itself by creating and conquering that other (Dussel 1993, 66).

Ginés de Sepúlveda, Aristotelian student of the Renaissance philosopher Pietro Pomponazzi, exemplifies the *ego conquiro* in his contribution to the Valladolid (a debate regarding the ontological status of

Indigenous peoples in the Americas) in 1550, where he argues that the dominant culture grants the blessings of civilization to the fundamental backward (*turditatum*) Indians. He describes Indians as a new kind of barbarian, one that is not merely a heathen barbarian but a barbarian "with respect to our rules of reason." Reworking Aristotle's view of natural slavery (Aristotle claims that it is "in conformity with natural law that those honorable, intelligent, virtuous, and human men dominate all those who lack these qualities") onto a global scale, Sepúlveda claims that it is "in conformity with natural law that barbaric people be subjected to the empire of princes and nations that are more cultured and humane" (quoted in Dussel 2013, 11). Here Dussel sees expressed a form of the tautology equivocally embedded in the concepts of Western civilization and modernity: If you are not one of us (either European or at least supportive of the coloniality of power), you are against what is right and true. The tautology is constructed for Dussel through the equating of superiority with identity and that identity with truth and justice themselves. Europe and the West are then a priori superior. It is then simple logical consistency that requires whatever is discovered of Indigenous reality to be redefined in relationship to this superiority, and whatever is thought to exist in European reality must be confirmed to exist in oppositional superiority to Indigenous reality. All this happens as a matter of mere logic as defined by epistemological principle and concepts of subjectivity. As Dussel puts it, "the content of other cultures, for being different from [Europe], is declared non-human" (2013, 11). Sepúlveda, for his part, puts it most succinctly when he claims that it would be wrong to exercise violence against the people of America if they were found to worship "the true God," who of course is European and Christian (Dussel 2013, 12). Thus, the lack of civilization and humanity is not in relation to a rational ideal but rather simply in relation to being European and Christian. The equation of European and rational serves to expose the irrational core of the "rationality" that is supposed to bring Europe out of its guilty state of immaturity. The movement out of immaturity is then not achieved by rationality but simply by being European or approximating European subjectivity and culture. Sepúlveda gives philosophical merit to Eurocentrism and the religious claim of the Doctrine of Discovery initiated in the fifteenth century in numerous papal bulls–culminating in the Inter Caetera of 1493, which gave all the Indigenous land of the Americas to Spain and Portugal by right of discovery. This philosophical articulation also initiates through the *ego conquiro* a zero-point of subjectivity that becomes solidified in the *ego cogito*, which then serves as another layer of concealment of the Eurocentrism of modern philosophical subjectivity.

Descartes

When Descartes articulates his *ego cogito* almost a century later, it is in a world already consecrated by the *ego conquiro*. His zero-point of subjectivity that manifests itself through universality into the domain of truth hides Eurocentrism through the universalizing of localized history, religion, and experiences of European people. It also masks the coloniality of power through the raceless and genderless character of the zero-point of subjectivity. The *ego cogito* hides in its zero-point the white male center of humanity and subjectivity. The conceptualization of the *ego cogito* is also formed from Christian concepts and practices. A ten-year-old René Descartes entered the Jesuit school of La Flèche in 1606.

In this school, Descartes received a "modern" education that focused on the "rationalization" of practices of the Catholic Church. Dussel describes this education (from the autobiographical work of Father General of the Jesuits Ignacio de Loyola [1491–1556]) in this way: "each Jesuit constituted a singular, independent, and modern subjectivity, performing daily an individual 'examination of conscience,' without communal choral hymns or prayers as was the case with medieval Benedictine monks." The Jesuit training was to "withdraw into silence three times a day, to reflect on [one's] own subjectivity and 'examine' with extreme self-consciousness and clarity the intention and content of every action, the actions carried out hour-by-hour, judging these actions according to the criterion [of service to God]" (Dussel 2013, 6). These examinations were kept in a notebook that documented the errors made by the hour from morning to night. The philosophical codifying, justifying, and attempted universalizing of these practices in Descartes's work does not change their very particular local religious grounding and meaning.

There is a similar localized Christian meaning to Descartes's mind/body dualism. The soul and body stand in complex relationship in Christianity. The soul is saved, but the body is resurrected as the culmination of salvation. Thus, while there is sense of differentiation and primacy of the soul, there is also a mutual and necessary coexistence. During the peak of the Inquisition, as Quijano points out, "the body" becomes "the basic object of repression." Thus, "the soul" becomes "almost separated from the intersubjective relations at the interior of the Christian world" (Quijano 2000, 555). Descartes, for the first time, systematizes and "secularizes" this particular and local history of Christian thought. In addition, through the radical separation of mind and body brought about by this systematization, the "scientific" theorization of race and gender is made possible. Nature, animals, Indians, and sexuality are physical, and civilization, European humans, and rationality are mental/spiritual by definition before Descartes. Descartes only adds a layer of illusory philosophical universality to this local European and Christian ideology. Through the "objectification of the body as nature," writes Quijano, certain races that are associated with the body because of their non-European Christian reality can more clearly be "condemned as inferior for not being rational subjects." Because of their bodily and natural state, non-European people become "dominable and exploitable" and "considered as an object of knowledge" (Quijano 2000, 555). Indigenous people, because they are only bodily and natural, have no rationality since this resides solely in the mind. Indigenous people are then not capable of having knowledge but only being objects of knowledge because they are bodily and not rational.

There is a common practice in the justifying of colonial power to turn what is based in particular and localized religious points of view into something that is described as "secular." The description of "secularity" often veils coloniality of power and religious bigotry. The religious right of the pope to take all the property (including land and persons) of Indigenous people (legalized in the fifteenth-century papal bulls) becomes "secularized" as the Doctrine of Discovery in John Marshall's U.S. Supreme Court of the 1820s and 1830s, where the justifications primarily reference European discovery rather than Christian discovery and civilization rather than Christendom. Secularity is then often a way to conceal the religious bigotry embedded in the coloniality of power. Walter Mignolo put the relational structure of secularism, modernity, and coloniality like this: "Secularization was able to detach God from Nature (which was unthinkable among Indigenous and Sub-Saharan

Africans, for example; and unknown among Jews and Muslims). The next step was to detach, consequently, Nature from Man (e.g., Frances Bacon's *Novum Organum*, 1620). 'Nature' became the sphere of living organisms to be conquered and vanquished by Man" (2009, 87). Secularity then hides the particular religious function of the civilizing mission of "Man" conquering and civilizing nature/Indigenous peoples.

Descartes's *ego cogito* and Sepúlveda's *ego conquiro* are most fundamentally directed at "Manichean misanthropic skepticism," as Nelson Maldonado-Torres calls it. This skepticism "is not skeptical about the existence of the world or the normative status of logics and mathematics" but is "a form of questioning the very humanity of colonized peoples" (Maldonado-Torres 2007, 245). This skepticism is one of the foundational pieces of modernity. Originating in the Spanish Inquisition at the end of the fifteenth century, this skepticism seeks to find the "baptized men and women of Jewish or Muslim descent [who] were considered stained by ancestral heresies," to seek out the "enemy within"—those who had converted but were guilty of carrying "stained blood" (Silverblatt 2004, 31–32). Modern skepticism, according to Maldonado-Torres, then begins in the protoracism of the Inquisition. The *ego conquiro* overcomes this skepticism of the possibility of humanity but creates an *ego* that is undoubtable and unquestionable—relegating the other of this *ego* to the savage state, no longer doubtable or questionable (as in the Inquisition) but completely identified and known as the savage. The historical domination of this savage other by the *ego conquiro* solidifies or manifests the potentiality of the undoubtable and unquestionable *ego*. This domination is what brings this *ego* into physical being. Its potential or logical unquestionableness is manifested into an actual unquestionableness through the initial and continual domination of the savage other. It is through the coloniality of power that the *I am* of European humanity is fully actualized and the skepticism regarding the humanity of the Indigenous other is fully determined in the oppositional savage nonhuman other.

Hegel

Hegel picks up the thread of *ego conquiro*, on Dussel's account, when he discusses the achievements of reaching the stage of modern philosophy: "The human being acquires confidence in himself (Zutrauen zu sich selbst)....Man discovers America, its treasures and its people, he discovers nature, he discovers himself (sich selbst)" (quoted in Dussel 2013, 4). The key concept in Hegel's ontology is development (*Entwicklung*), which is, for him, the process by which what is potential becomes actualized. Development takes the form of the unfolding of subjectivity's inner potential into external actuality. The development of modern subjectivity, for Hegel, the unfolding of the Spirit, as well as world history, is "the development of the consciousness that the Spirit has of its freedom and the evolution of the understanding that the Spirit obtains through that development" (1975). The sovereign, rational individual subject of modern Western philosophy from Descartes to the present is, for Hegel, the result of a complex and extended historical process. The coming to be of subjectivity through this historical process is an action of actualization between the individual and the world. Put another way, a subject's acting on the world in a certain way allows for it to become aware of that action as *its* action and in so doing become a sovereign, rational individual subjectivity. Hegel put this process of development like this:

Reason becomes Spirit when it achieves the full consciousness of itself as being all reality. In the previous stage of Observing Reason it merely found itself in an existent object. From this it rose to a stage in which it no longer passively perceived itself in an object, but imposed itself more actively on the world, a stage as one-sided as the previous one. (1977, 483)

In Hegel's master-slave dialectic, subjectivity arises once again through the *ego conquiro*. In the master-slave dialectic, subjectivity arises through the conquering of another independent subjectivity. When a conquered subject is colonized his or her objectivity is appropriated—his or her land, resources, labor—for the benefit of the conquerors. This sets up the stage wherein the conquered people come to accept their subordinated place in the new subjectivity that includes conqueror and conquered but continue to seek rights and recognition within that new subjectivity. The interactive relationship between conqueror and conquered is one of an individual and the world, of mind and body, of subjectivity and objectivity. The conquered satisfy the subjective needs of the conqueror through their objective labor, land, resources, bodies, or nature. The mediation that creates subjectivity arises as the objective labor of the conquered subject mediates the subjective needs of the conquering subject. The objectivity of the conquering subject becomes the objectivity of the conquered subject (their labor, land, resources, bodies, or nature), while the subjectivity of the conquered subject becomes the subjectivity of the conquering subject (their mind, desires, culture, or civilization).

Through this mediation of conquering and conquered subjects the modern, rational, individual subjectivity arises. "Man" or the developing subjectivity "discovers America, its treasures, its people" or the underdeveloped subjectivity or more purely objective, bodily, natural existence. In doing so, "Man discovers himself" as an active, rational, conquering agent over and against this passive, nonrational, conquered subject cum object. This conquered subject is *other* and not fully human because it is seen as not capable of the self-actualization of the conquering subject. This explains why only the fully human subject, for Hegel, is capable of "creating (his) own history" (Smith 1999, 32)

Denise da Silva's *Toward a Global Idea of Race* makes the claim that this stage of the development of the Hegelian ego as *ego conquiro* is constitutive of the Western post-Enlightenment subjectivity. She argues that the rational, independent subjectivity comes to be by positioning itself against "affectable" others, which she understands as those who are subjected to "the 'laws of nature'" as well as the power of Western dominating subjectivity. Through the power to dominate others and the inability of others to dominate it, the Western subject comes to know itself (Silva, 117). The *ego* is defined by domination, and the *other* is defined by is affectability. The *other* is only affected by dominating Western subject but cannot affect any domination himself or herself, whereas the Western subject is not affected by other subjects but can only affect other "affectable" subjects.

The Western subject, however, in Hegel's master-slave dialectic, comes to realize that it is not totally free because it depends on the dominated subject for its subjectivity—it realizes that it exists only in relation to the subjectivity it dominates. Thus, the Western subject must sublimate the existence of the affectable subject (slave) it depends on for its effecting subjectivity (master). Andrea Smith (following Silva) puts it this way: "The anxiety with which the Western subject struggles is that the Western subject is in fact not self-determining. After all, nobody is actually able to exercise power without being affected by others. Consequently, the manner in which the Western subject addresses this anxiety is to separate itself from conditions of affectability by separating from affectable others" (2014, 208). The result of this attempt to sublimate the affectability of the dominated is the coloniality of power (racial hierarchies and so on) and the narrative of colonial difference (the construction of the history of the dominated as purely affectable in relation to the affecting colonizers). Hegel, for his part, conceals the coloniality of power, on one level, in the concept of "universal right." "The people that receive," he writes, "the configuration of the Spirit in the form of becoming" (history) are the "dominant people" and have "the absolute right . . . by virtue of being the bearer of the development of the World Spirit," against which "the spirit of other peoples has no rights." Hegel also conceals the coloniality of power in the concept of a "completed civil society," which by "the impulse to transcend itself that is proper to it . . . , it seeks to find ways to move about among other peoples that are inferior to it." "The development," he purports, "offers the means of colonization toward which . . . a completed civil society is compelled" (Dussel 1993, 10).

Colere Temporis: Colonizing the Land through Time

Enrique Dussel writes of the civilizing mission of coloniality that it produces violence with "a quasi-ritual character of sacrifice; the civilizing hero manages to make his victims part of a saving sacrifice." As examples, he not only references the colonizing of Indigenous people but also "the ecological destruction of nature" (Dussel 2000, 471). He does not make clear, however, the exact manner of the operation of the coloniality of power on nature or land such that nature and land become targets of "civilizing." In this section, I discuss some of the manner by which the land becomes a target of civilizing and colonizing alongside the people of that land as discussed in the section above. Part of the capacity to dominate the land as well as Indigenous people arises from a reconfiguration of history and time as floating free from the land.

Hegel is considered the father of the modern concept of history. Hegel's ontology, as we have seen, centers around the concept of development (*Entwicklung*), and development (of which history is an ontological manifestation, for Hegel) is geographically linear. This linear direction of development and the coming to be of history move through space: from east to west. Europe is the end of history, and Indigenous America is outside of history but is what the movement of history operates upon in order to realize itself, to become complete. Indigenous America is "a New World," and its newness is "absolute" (Dussel 1993, 66). In American geography, Hegel claims, we find fundamental newness, "enormous rivers that have not yet found their course," and "with respect to the elements that compose it, America has not completed its formation" (Dussel 1993, 69). Time and history are organized as the completion of world history (meaning Europe) that becomes so by operating on a fundamentally new America. America is seen as an open and unmanifest territory upon which the actualization of the European ego and delocalized history—a universal abstraction of the actual historical and physical processes of coloniality—can become manifest and mature. America, as an undeveloped landscape, can only be acted upon, and it is through such action (both on people and the land) that European subjects and European history as world history actualize their self-awareness and so become human subjects and world history.

History, on Hegel's accounting, is then not something "natural" or "divine" but something created by human (European) agents, even though, for Hegel, history is an abstract universality (Quijano 2000, 547). History itself (like the fully humans who can make it) acts on the passive and natural, including Indigenous people and Indigenous land. The relationship between essentially active old (developed) land and essentially passive new (undeveloped) land creates a separation between time and space, between history and land. The age of land is defined in relationship to coloniality of power as the age (development of history) of humans is so defined. America is, as Hegel says, "new absolutely: it is new in all of it aspects; physical and political" (1975, 199-200). The history (development) of the land and the history (development) of the people are bound up. This ties people to the land but not as a place in space but as a place in time (a racial place in human development), in the time of European world history and the coloniality of power.

Time becomes an agent of coloniality. Like European subjectivity that develops in modern philosophy, modern temporality becomes a center point for European domination of non-European spaces. Like the zero-point of *ego cogito*, time becomes delocalized and featureless. The zero-point of *ego cogito* is without race and gender but yet is still supposed to comprise a living subjectivity, which it can only in the sense that it is a European male ego. Time also, just as *ego cogito* is a European male, is not featureless; it is European time and European history as shaped by European subjectivity/identity. The absolute newness of America creates a necessary geographic shape to time and history in the direction of the colonization of America. As Quijano puts it, "the future is an open temporal territory" that is accessible through the colonization of the absolutely new American land (2000, 547).

To describe this idea of time and history as a featureless, zero-point of time, ironically, attempts to construct time without temporality at all, just as *ego cogito* attempts to construct a subject without subjectivity at all. Universal time, as in the absolute and finished (Eurocentric) world history, creates a sense of time without temporality. Kant attempts to deal with these antinomies of time by making time, not something found in experience, but a zero-point of experience. He defines time as one of the conditions of the possibility of experience. But if time is universalized in this way, as the universal conditions of the possibility of experience, then experience is universalized just as subjectivity was. The here and the now that feature in localized experiences and localized history are replaced with a vacuous temporality that erases these localized experiences and histories in the here and now just as it does for the stories of people here and now and of their experiences of the time before (history). There is, then, an antinomy of time and history that is not dealt with. This antinomy is between, as Dussel describes it, "abstract universality and concrete world hegemony" (2000, 471). Time and history are understood as abstract universals, but the very concepts and realities are created and maintained by the ideologies and concrete processes of coloniality.

A Spatial Point of View: Vine Deloria Jr. on Land and History

The key to understanding the way that coloniality of power manifests itself on the land through temporality can be seen in the separation that occurs between time and space, between history and land. As Vine

Deloria Jr. puts it in *God Is Red*: "Western European peoples (and of course later U.S. people) have never learned to consider the nature of the world discerned from a spatial point of view" (1994, 63). Deloria's statement not only represents an epistemological and metaphysical positioning but also reflects the manner in which time and history have been separated from spatiality, the way that time and history have been abstracted into something universal and so abstracted from the land. Without "a spatial point of view" time and history can be globalized and universalized. The particular needs, values, and history of a particular place can be universalized over all places through the coloniality of power. Particular needs, values, and knowledge can be universalized across time and space and forced onto people of other places at any time.

The operational philosophy of American Indian ideology, according to Deloria, is the importance of American Indian "land" or "place." "All their statements," he claims, "are made with this reference point in mind." The European colonizer, operating with the delocalized and universalized concepts of time and history, sees his movement across the ocean and "across the continent as a steady progression of basically good events, thereby placing history—time—in the best possible light" (Deloria 1994, 62). Deloria conceptualizes clearly the manner in which colonization requires a delocalized and universalized sense of time and history that is capable of operating developmentally (as a positive progress of time and history in the abstract) on a delocalized (which means in this instance that time has been removed from place) land. Deloria also conceptualizes clearly the "essence of Western European identity" in a linear progression of time that views the "unraveling of this sequence" as the manifestation of "the destiny of the peoples of Western Europe, and later, of course, the United States" (1994, 63).

The process by which this positive progression of time is conceptualized as the development of European identity and history itself Deloria understands not as an actual movement of time but as the colonization of space whose purpose is the tilling over of the "nonhomogeneous pockets of identity" that "represent different historical arrangements" in relationship to space, place, or land (1994, 65). This tilling over of diversity is mirrored, on Deloria's view, in the progression of time as conceptualized in the development of world religion. "Religion," Deloria writes, "has often been seen as an evolutionary process in which mankind progresses from primitive superstitions to logically perfected codes of conduct, from a multiplicity of deities to a monotheistic religion" (1994, 65–66). In contrast to this sense of progress, "monotheism," Deloria points out, "is usually the product of the political unification of a diverse society more often than it is the result of a revelation of ultimate reality" (1994, 66). The notions of European progress toward civilized society, world history, universal truth, and monotheistic religion can all be understood as the process of erasing a preexisting diversity in order to implant the singularity of European notions of society, history/time, truth, and religion onto non-European land and place. The spatial of place (the ontology of land itself) must be uprooted in order to implant these delocalized ideologies onto Indigenous, non-European localities.

The spatial point of view, Deloria expresses, as the contrast to delocality is exemplified in the statement: "truth is applicable to all places." Revelation is permanently tied to particular lands, from the spatial point of view. "Revelation," he writes, is "a continuous process of adjustment to the natural surroundings and not as a specific message valid for all times and place." Sacred places, whether they are "a river, a mountain, a plateau, valley, or other natural feature," Deloria argues, are "permanent fixtures in [Native] cultural or religious understanding." This permanence arises from a noncontingent sacredness that exists in the place itself, which is in contrast to the notion of "Holy Lands" that are "appreciated primarily for their historical significance" (Deloria 1994, 66–67). The holiness of these places is contingent, then, as the events that make them holy could have just as easily happen somewhere else. There is nothing in the place itself, the land, that is significant to its sacredness or importance. From the spatial point of view, the actual land and the particularity of that actual land matter much and function formatively and continually in the moral, epistemological, historical, and religious life of a people.

European Cultivating of Indigenous Land: Settler Colonialism in the United States

The term "coloniality" is used by many scholars to speak of the more abstract structure of colonialism beyond mere colonial periods. "Colonialism" refers to colonial situations that are enforced by the presence of an actual colonial administration, while "coloniality" refers to the more general colonial situation where actual colonial administrations no longer function in most of the modern world-system. Coloniality is the idea and ideology of domination, and colonialism is the practice of this domination. The term "colonial" comes from the Latin *colere*, which is "to till or cultivate" but also "to protect or nurture," even "to worship."

Coloniality and colonialism as historical practices and structures are imbued with agricultural metaphors. U.S. Commissioner of Indian Affairs Hiram Price, in his "Annual Report of 1882," describes "civilization" as "a plant" that needs to be "supplemented by Christian teachings" so that "our Indian population" can "speedily and permanently [be] reclaimed from the barbarism, idolatry, and savage life" (Newcomb 2008, 13). Colonizing can then be viewed as tilling the land in order to cultivate civilization in the form of European Christianity. Steven Newcomb, in *Pagans in the Promised Land*, put colonization in terms of "the steps involved in the process of cultivation: taking control of the Indigenous soil, uprooting the existing Indigenous plants (peoples), overturning the soil (the Indigenous way of life), planting new colonial seeds (people) or transplanting colonial seeds (people) from another environment, and harvesting the resulting crops (resources), or else picking the resulting fruits (wealth) that result from the labor of cultivation (colonization)" (2008, 14).

The cultivation process of colonization is complicated by colonial situations wherein the colonial administration has never ended. These situations are characterized by colonial power in the more literal administrative sense but also in the larger structural sense of coloniality. These situations arise in the United States, Canada, New Zealand, and Australia in particular and are characterized by what is called "settler colonialism." In settler colonialism, there is a more clear reference to the root *colo* of colonialism. *Colo* refers to the removing of "solids by filtering" (Newcomb 2008). Settler colonialism views Indigenous people as solid waste to be filtered from the land so as to acquire what is most valuable to settler colonists: the land itself. Settler colonialism seeks territory rather that resources to return to a home country—the process seen in standard external colonialism. This is because the fundamental goal of settler colonialism is to create a brand new nation-state upon the colonialized land after the genocidal removal of the Indigenous peoples of that land. The standard racial hierarchies of the coloniality of power will not do justice to this ultimate goal. The possible colonial benefit of the labor of racialized Indigenous peoples stands in conflict with the need to eliminate these Indigenous peoples in order to position the colonizers as the proper owners of the land they wish to form their new nation upon.

Settler colonialism, because of its ultimate desire to acquire and maintain possession of another's land, houses a constant genocidal impulse toward the Indigenous people of this land. This genocidal impulse takes many forms—many of them subtle and structurally attached to the very compositional fabric of the new nation-state created. One form this genocidal impulse manifests in the structure of settler colonial racism revolves around what Patrick Wolfe calls "the logic of elimination" (2006, 388). One example arises around the concepts of blood and race. Black people in the United States are racialized as slaves, and so they are labor resources for the state. Regarding blood, then, they are racialized as black by "one drop of blood," because the logic of elimination does not apply to them, only the general coloniality of power and the domination and even ownership of their labor as a resource. American Indians are racialized in the exact opposite manner because any benefit of their labor is mitigated by their ownership relationship to the land that is needed in order to create the new nation. Regarding blood, then, Indians are racialized as "half-breeds" and "white" with one drop of European blood. Being racialized as such, for Indians, has the effect of genocide through blood quantum. The one drop of black blood that maintains black racial identity and the one drop of white blood that erases Indian racial identity serve the function of the logic of elimination as it regards Indigenous peoples under settler colonialism.

The logic of elimination, while it serves genocide in this way, functions more broadly to erase the ownership and general relationship to their lands that any people would have to their homelands. Thus, the logic of elimination not only erases the history of Indigenous people in general, it focuses on erasing their history on the land and in every manner possible their relationship to their land. I would ask you to try this experiment: pick up any map of the United States that includes as many rivers, creeks, lakes, mountains, gorges, hills, valleys, and so on as possible. Now circle the inordinate number of these that are named after the devil (Devil's Tower, Devil's Lake, El Diablo Peak, Devil's Creek, and on, and on, and on). Now hold up the map with all the circled places and show your friends all of the Indigenous sacred places of the United States. It is very shocking and sad to realize just how reliable this procedure is. Often the renaming of the land happens in direct but demonized translation. Take Devil's Lake in Minnesota, for example. The Dakota name is *Mni Wakan* (sacred water). The settler colonial renaming is Devil's Lake. The procedure is often this simple: take the Indigenous sacred concept (*wakan*) and replace it with "devil." It then becomes rather difficult for Indigenous people to maintain their kinship relationship to this sacred place that now has been clearly marked by the settler colonial (European Christian) power as a place of the devil, which both removes the sacredness from the land itself but also replaces that sacredness with evilness as conceptualized by European Christianity.

One of the most remarkable features of settler colonialism is the level of maintenance and sublimation that it requires on the part of the settler colonial state, not only initially in erasing or removing the Indigenous people from their land and setting up the settler state but even more in maintaining it psychologically. The settler colonial state spends a lot of energy trying to justify the justice and rightness of its continued domination of supposed backward, heathen, uncivilized savages. The creation and use of racial and religious bigotry to push people toward the extermination or enslavement of a supposed lesser people is one thing, but continuing to justify those actions in history, in the court of public opinion, and in one's own mind on a daily basis is a much more difficult task. The result is a near schizophrenic level of bad faith in the very structure of the settler state. While claiming on the surface that the settler state is just and its relationship to the Indigenous people of the land it was built upon was and is just, everyone knows and the structural system of the settler state contains the truth that these lands and this state were created out of the genocide (literal, historical, political, philosophical, and so on) and removal of the true owners of this stolen land. That is quite an oedipal pill to swallow and impacts every aspect of the settler state and the settler psyche.

The bad faith nature of the settler state and settler psyche develops what Charles Mills calls an "epistemology of ignorance, a particular pattern of localized and global cognitive dysfunctions" that "precludes self-transparency and genuine understanding" and produces "an invented delusional world" (1997, loc 326 of 2,530). The particular epistemic practices that serve to conceal the bad faith of settler colonialism in the present are built upon epistemic practices that are designed to create the context of coloniality in the first place. In contrast to the ideas that time and subjectivity float free from space, Indigenous concepts of time and subjectivity tie both to particular places. Who I am, my history, and what I know are ontologically dependent on particular place-based relationships to mountains, rivers, valleys, forests, animals, and so on. These places-based relationships do not laminate onto ontologically prior absolute states of being and time but rather create real distinct histories, subjectivities, and realities. The real distinct histories, subjectivities,

31

and realities of this land must be contextually covered up by the settler colonial epistemologies of ignorance and the "invented delusional world" of land that floats free from itself and so can be reshaped in image of settler colonial histories, subjectivities, and realities.

Local Histories versus Global Domination: The Fact of Colonial Difference

The manner in which time operates within coloniality to dominate Indigenous space is the same manner in which time and history are abstracted from space (locality) so as to allow for the universalizing of local European time and history across nonlocal (for example, Indigenous) spaces. Just as civilization is defined as Western culture, history, experiences, and religion (for example, Sepúlveda's claim that Indigenous people would be civilized and free from domination if only they worshiped the European God), temporality is defined as the time and history of Western culture, history, experience, and religion (for example, Hegel's claim that America is essentially new in both time and space). In order for European time and history to be universalized, time and history must be disconnected from space or place, from land. In order for Hegel to define history as active and operating on a passive background of the natural as well as the temporal relationship between old, active spaces (Europe) and new, passive spaces (America), time and space must be separated and rearranged so that the time of one space (Europe) can be actualized on all other spaces (new America and timeless nature).

Walter Mignolo argues in *Local Histories/Global Designs* that the "I" of Hegel, Descartes, and Kant is meant to be "universal, isolated, detached from Europe's local history and global designs." These "global designs" that attempt to universalize local European history into a project of coloniality and also attempt to erase local histories of non-European spaces are "the very logic of coloniality, that moves the world, but it has to be disguised with the rhetoric of modernity, of salvation and progress." The erasing of local history as an act of modernity, salvation, and progress is "the two faces of the same coin—'modernity/coloniality'" (Mignolo 2000, xvi). This modernity/coloniality project is only possible if non-European spaces are conceptualized as out of time and only capable of being brought into time through European time and history, through colonization.

The replacing of the local history and time of non-European/Indigenous spaces with the time and history of modernity/coloniality is not automatic. It requires more than the simple act of so-called discovery to remove the local history from the land; it requires colonization as an act of cultivation to achieve the rooting out of the local history. It requires rigorous tilling (colonizing) of Indigenous land to root out its locality. It requires settler colonizing the land, cultivating, tilling the soil (removing the Indigenous people, history, knowledge), in short an attempted tilling out the locality of the land in order to supplant that locality with a delocalized European locality. The removal of this "waste" (*colo*) and attempting to supplant European locality onto this land creates the context for *ego conquiro* to manifest itself as *ego conquiro terra*, for European subjectivity of domination to manifest itself on Indigenous land. In this way the land itself is understood to be conquered; it is thought to become European land, as described by the names "New England," "New York," "New Jersey," and so on.

Sepúlveda claims, in his debate with Bart La Casa over the ontological status of Indians, that they have no idea of private property. He claims of the Indians of America that regardless of having "a republican institutional structure . . . , no one possesses anything as their own, not a house, not a field at their disposal to leave in their will to their heirs." Dussel claims that in Sepúlveda's expression we have a prototype of what is later concretized in the work of John Locke and Hegel as the idea that "private property is a precondition of humanity" (2013, 11–12). The concept of private property has a complex but foundational relationship with the reorganization of time and space as floating free from land that is necessary for the particular process of settler colonization.

Locke, Locality, and the *Ego Constituo* of Settler Colonialism

In 1689, John Locke wrote *Two Treatises of Government*, a work that presents what continues to be a major political philosophy of the modern world. Locke was extensively engaged in the colonial enterprise of the English colonies and their conceptual transformation into a settler state (the United States). Locke was secretary to Lord Shaftesbury, secretary of the Lords Proprietors of Carolina, secretary of the Council of Trade and Plantations, and member of the Board of Trade. As James Tully writes, "Locke was one of the six or eight men who closely invigilated and helped to shape the old colonial system during the Restoration" of the monarchy after 1660 (1997, 168). In fact, on March 24, 1663, King Charles II awarded the land of the Provinces of Carolina to eight noblemen who supported Charles in being restored as monarch. Locke was secretary to these Lords Proprietors and helped them rule this colonized land. When Locke writes the *Two Treatises*, he is "intervening," as Tully shows, "in one of

the major political and ideological contests of the seventeenth century"
(1997, 167). This contest is nothing more than the legal and moral justification of settler colonialism that can only come into being through the
appropriation of Indian land without consent. Appropriation without
consent is another way of saying theft, but Locke's project is to create a
justification for appropriation without consent of Indian land that can
be justified, at least in the context of settler logic, as something other than
outright theft. This project requires the use of the narrative of colonial
difference already greatly manifested in the work of John Winthrop and
other Puritan apologists but extended into a more sophisticated theory
of the universal nature of property and proper governance.

John Locke begins his philosophical articulation of the meaning of
private property with the European God. Both the European God and
European reason show us, he claims, that the entire earth is the property
of people in common (1821, II, 25). This first and seemingly innocuous
claim, in some ways, already creates, for Locke, the entire edifice of
settler colonialism through the delocality of humans and land—the
human being is a universal being that has no particular relationship or
manifestation in particular places or land. In order to fill in the complete
picture, Locke must separate the possible relationship to land into a form
that exists in Europe and a form that exists in America so as to protect
European land from appropriation without consent and to open up the
land of America to appropriation without consent. He does this through
the concept of the state of nature and the claim that America is "perfectly
in a State of Nature" (Locke 1821, II 14). It is only in this state of nature
that the entire earth is the property of all in common. For human beings
to acquire individual or private property, they must appropriate it from
the commons. However, in the state of nature, in contrast to civilized

Europe, the concept of property only applies to the actual products of labor in the commons—the actual apple that one picks from the common tree and never to the tree itself or to all the apples.

The idea of property, for Locke, starts with human beings; each person owns her own body and all the labor that can be created by it. Thus, when people add their labor, or their property, to some object, it becomes their property. An object becomes personal property when someone "hath mixed his labor with it" (Locke 1821, II 27). He uses the example of an apple: when I pick the apple (my labor), the apple becomes mine. When this theory is applied to land, what Locke imagines as original common land can become individual private property through that individual laboring on that land to make it more productive. An individual could clear a forest, till the soil, and cultivate crops, for example, to make an area of so-called common land "his" own. Once transferred from the commons, land can be transferred directly by the original owner to others, including heirs upon death. No more labor is required for ownership. The right of an individual to appropriate land from the commons to private holding comes from Natural Law, on Locke's view. In particular, this right arises from the duty that comes from Natural Law to perform actions that tend to preserve the human species. Because supposedly appropriating land from the commons makes possible labor that tends to preserve the human species, performing those actions is a duty and appropriating land is a right. The idea is that this labor and appropriating makes the use of the land more efficient and on this basis makes one a human duty and the other a right under Natural Law.

The problem is, of course, that Indigenous people in New England and throughout the Americas mixed their labor with the land through farming for 10,000 years. Thus, Locke, as Winthrop before him and

Chief Justice John Marshall after him, attempted to create a narrative of colonial difference that has Indians as hunters and gatherers rather than farmers. America is in a state of nature because the people have not developed much beyond the state of wild animals who hunt and forage for their food with no sense of a superstructure that governs these activities any more than the bear or the deer. The bear and the deer take the fish and grass as they please with no sense that these could belong to any other bear or deer. Locke picks through his extensive library on European travel in the Americas to shape a narrative of colonial difference in which the "savages" of the wild America will be understood as offenders of Natural Law. These offenders are "wild Savage Beasts," he writes, who "may be destroyed as a Lyon or Tyger" (Locke 1821, II 2, 16). As "wild Savage Beasts" "perfectly in a State of Nature," the actions of Indigenous Americans to simply protect their land are violations of Natural Law and so allow the offenders to be "destroyed as a Lyon or Tyger."

In this state of nature, what is hunted and gathered from the commons creates a property right to only those things that are hunted and gathered and only after they are actually in hand. Thus, in America there is "no reason of quarreling about Title, nor any doubt about the largeness of Possession it gave" (Locke 1821, II 51). Just like the obscuring of the 10,000-year Indigenous farming, the fact that Native people in the English colonies did in fact quarrel with the English about their appropriation without consent of what they obviously considered their land must be obscured or reconceptualized in order to maintain the "invented delusional world" of settler coloniality. The Mohegan Indians, for example, argued for sovereignty over their lands in litigation with the colony of Connecticut through the Privy Council in London that began in 1670 and lasted over 100 years. Even some Puritan leaders, such as Roger

Williams from Plymouth, argued that the English had no title to Indian land except as acquired through the instrument of international law, the treaty, which respected the mutual sovereignty of both the English and Native nations (Jennings 1976, 128–46).

In order to settle the dispute on the legal and moral status of settler colonialism and relegate the Native people of America to the status of beasts in a state of nature, all facts and experiences to the contrary, Locke constructed his theory of property with the particular target of justifying settler colonialism in North America. Tully demonstrates quite convincingly that Locke articulates his theory of property *in order* to justify European settlement on Indian land in America, in order to appropriate Indian land without consent. As Tully shows, "Locke constructed [his concept of property] in contrast to Amerindian forms . . . in such a way that they obscure and downgrade the distinctive features" of the Native system of property (1996, 167). Locke's *Two Treatises on Government* was written not truly as a general theory of property but specifically to defend England's colonial policy against the counterclaims of Indians. His theory was written with the particular purpose of justifying the dispossession of the American Indians of their land. Thus, Locke does not reference Indians by accident in his work on property, for it is particularly Indians of North America that are the target of his theory. In addition, Tully documents that Locke had significant personal investments in British settlements in North America as well as the enslavement of Native peoples. Tully claims that this brings into doubt "one of the major political philosophies of the modern world" (1997, 165). The extent to which Locke went to manufacture the rationality of his theory of property in relation to the savage Indian of the Americas further exposes the irrationality of the great freeing principle of rationality in modern philosophy. One way that we can see the irrationality in Locke's treatise on property is the way in which he picks through the already very limited and racially biased literature on American Indians at the time, picking items of support while purposefully leaving out anything from the literature that does not conform to his intent to justifying the dispossession of Indian land. Hegel does something similar with published African travel accounts, where he distorts the information "with systematic intent" in order to portray African people as "barbaric, cannibalistic, preoccupied with fetishes, without history" and "without any consciousness of freedom" (Bernasconi 1998, 63, 41). It is not surprising, then, that Hegel excuses the enslavement of Africans by Europeans and finds the European colonization of Africa to be a legitimate operation that brings civilizing benefits to African people (Bernasconi 1998, 55, 60). Truth, even in the particular epistemic practices of creating Locke's theory of property and Hegel's philosophy of history and theory of right, serves to maintain an "invented delusional world" of the coloniality of power (racial hierarchies and the appropriation of Indigenous land without consent).

An important question is why Locke defined the appropriating of property as individual labor mixing with the land. How does this particular definition serve the settler colonial interests? Locke is actually arguing against common law at the time. Until the seventeenth century, when Great Britain colonized America, the common understanding of property was defined by occupation or settlement. This definition did not serve the purposes of settler colonialism because it severely limited the European land claims in America due to the prior occupation of these lands by American Indians. In addition to prior and rightful land claims by Indians, there were all the prior European conquerors who claimed rights to Indian land by conquest. In this regard, Locke is arguing against

Hugo Grotius and the Spanish justification of appropriation of Indian land by right of conquest that makes all of North American Spanish land—legally documented in the papal bull of 1493. Locke is shifting the rights of conquest to rights of settler colonization, shifting the *ego conquiro* to the *ego constituo* (I settle), in order to justify the new form of colonization that Great Britain and America are initiating.

The change in attitudes toward Indian land that occurred in the latter half of the seventeenth century was a result of the change in Great Britain's colonizing mission—from trade and mining to settlement (Arneil 1992, 16). The historian Francis Jennings documents how the concept of property changes in order to accommodate this new settler goal (1971). The concept of private property, as we know it in the modern world, comes to be defined in relationship to the mission of settler colonialism in America. Wilber Jacobs, in *Dispossessing the American Indians*, identifies Locke's theory of property as the source of the American removal policies that are fundamental to U.S. Manifest Destiny and westward expansion in the early 1800s. Locke's handpicking from the limited and biased information on American Indians is in service of defining American Indians, in fundamental essence, as dispossessable. For Locke, seventeenth-century American Indians were living in an actual historical state of nature and were actual cases of so-called natural men. Indians are like idiots and children, Locke claims, in that their reason has not developed to the extent of that of the Englishman (1821, 48). The growth of reason that allows natural men to progress toward becoming civil men is accomplished through Christianity (Locke 1821, 50). In this state of nature and in this state of diminished reason, Indians have no property. All of America was common land owned by all of humankind. Indians, according to Locke's operations of the narrative of colonial difference and the invented delusional world that justifies settler colonialism, had no monetary system, had no government, and lacked the insatiable desire for wealth and unlimited possessions that are necessary for founding a civil society in his view.

Most of this understanding of American Indians generally or severally is utterly ridiculous and wholly manufactured by Locke within the already existing settler colonial imagination. These mythological constructions of Indian reality burden American Indian people from the moment of contact to the present, as they even play foundational epistemic roles in current Indian law and current Supreme Court decisions about tribal sovereignty. Even where Locke seems to be right about Indigenous locality—for example, Indians' lack of insatiable desire for wealth and unlimited possessions—his rightness is irrelevant in the purposefully and manipulated construction of dispossessable Indians because he defines this lack of infinite desire as the very feature that makes Indians savage and the insatiable greed that creates the need for laws to protect individual private property as a prerequisite for advancement to civilized society. The real question that remains is why, given his desire to construct Indians as dispossessable, does he choose or imagine what he does about Indians in this purposeful construction. How does his narrative of colonial difference result in a picture of Indians as dispossessable? Since the target is Indian land, the construction of Indian-ness also centers on land. Locke's intention is to define the land in a particular way as to erase the locality and make appropriation itself, defined by settler colonization, the most fundamental civilized human (humans no longer in the state of nature) relationship to land. The civilizing labor that creates a property relationship to land, however, is the labor of agriculture. So why, then, do Indigenous Americans, who quite literally invented agriculture as we know it, not count as owning the land they farmed? Indigenous Americans domesticated corn, squash, potatoes, and so on. Their agricultural technology was so great that at the time of Columbus's initial invasion, the Incas, as early as 9,500 years before, had through Indigenous technology invented 3,800 different varieties of potatoes. To deny this as agriculture labor requires redefining the very concept of agriculture through an epistemology of ignorance so that agricultural practices as obvious and great as the Incas' will be left out in an invented delusional world of coloniality and settler coloniality.

Redefinition is in fact the key to understanding the settler logic of Locke's definition of property. The actions that mark the appropriate civilized labor on the land are tilling, enclosing, and cultivating the land. It is not merely farming that is labor; it is a particular Eurocentric understanding of the relationship to the land that is actualized in that farming labor. What Locke's definition requires of the farming labor is that it removes locality from the land. In the first place, understanding land in a state of nature as the common property of all of humankind is itself an erasure of locality and part of the larger modernity mission of removing humans from the land and from nature, which is to say locality. After the locality of land is obscured, then an individual from Europe can come to America and re-create his or her European locality on this land. The act of appropriating land as property is identical with the act of settler colonizing itself. Hegel also defines Indian inferiority in relationship to land. He claims it is the natural state of American Indians that kept them from taming the American wilderness, thus making it unavoidable that they should disappear as a result of European settlement (Hegel 1975). Clearly, for both Locke and Hegel, it is not mere farming that is necessary to "tame" American "wilderness." It is the act of appropriating or removing the locality of land that allows it to become mine, for it to be incorporated into my human subjectivity or dominated by my subjectivity in some way—in a similar manner to which the Indigenous subjectivity is incorporated into European subjectivity or dominated by European subjectivity. Dominating and so possessing land, land that then can become mine in this very particular way, is what defines the proper civilizing acts of labor that Locke requires for land to become property.

The attempted erasure of Indigenous subjectivity into the singular agency of European subjectivity is necessary in order to create the power of coloniality, but it is not enough to complete the project of settler colonialism. The land has power. This power, just like the power of human subjectivity that is denied in the European creation of a pure affectable Indigenous other, is in locality. Power of the land is manifested in and through its locality. This is what allows particular places to be sacred. Just as removing the agency of Native subjects is an aspect of coloniality, removing the locality of land is an aspect of coloniality in the particular context of settler colonialism. The power of the land that exists in locality moves naturally through space but only continuously and contiguously and in contrast to the disjointed spatial power of coloniality. The life-giving power of a river, for example, in Cherokee is ᏴᏫ ᎬᎾᎯᏓ (*yvwi gvnahita*, or the long man), which moves through the mountains and valleys and speaks with the waterfalls and rapids, moves naturally across space without disrupting locality. This kind of extending of power through space must be differentiated from the settler coloniality of power. Settler coloniality of power moves through abstracted time and history, erasing locality so as to encircle or enclose space or land in order to settler colonize it. The settler coloniality of power attempts to disrupt the natural geographical power of locality and place in order to control space in order to dominate and to settle land. This settler coloniality of power is embedded in the modern concept of property as requiring subduing, enclosing, cutting off land, of people from land, all with the clear intention of removing the locality from the land (the power of the land) in order for colonizers to be able to settle it. Thus, just as coloniality tries to remove Indigenous human agency, settler coloniality tries to remove the locality of the land, which is its power or agency. The power or agency of land in the context of locality is a necessary feature of Indigenous morality in general and Indigenous relationship to land in particular as a manifestation of kinship. Indigenous environmental ethics, then, depend on an agent-to-agent relationship between humans and the land. This agent-to-agent relationship to the land expressed in locality marks Indigeneity in being, knowing, as well as moral relationships.

The sublimation of *ego conquiro* into *ego constituo* creates the sense of a kinder, gentler coloniality. Yet to settler colonize Indigenous land requires more than conquering (*ego conquiro*). To settler colonize, the subjectivity must become more than the mere undoubtable self of the conquering colonizer. To settler colonize, the subjectivity must transform the conquering power of the colonizer into an external force of truth and logic. One cannot create a home, a new nation, out of what is dominated pure and simple. The effort that conquering and dominating takes in its simple straightforward form is great. Pure force must be transformed into more ubiquitous and subtle forms of power. In reality, then, what appears to be a kinder and gentler colonialism is merely a subtler, more sinister coloniality. The focus on what seems like a natural process of erasing locality from land hides a darker logic of genocidal elimination of Indigenous people but also an ecocidal relationship to land through the attempted erasure of the power of locality that gives way to domination and enslavement of the land itself. The quasi-ritual sacrifice of the violence against Indigenous people in order to save them also operates on the land in order to root out the savage nature of land, its wildness, which is in reality nothing more than its power in locality than disrupts the capacity to settler colonize it.

The Narrative of Colonial Difference versus the Fact of Colonial Difference

The creation of the narrative of colonial difference in the context of epistemologies of ignorance and the invented delusional worlds of coloniality, as discussed throughout this chapter, is designed to erase the local histories as a function of obscuring locality itself from America in order to incorporate the Indigenous people and Indigenous land into a delocalized European subjectivity and European world history. This creates an intersection of Indigeneity and coloniality that makes it seemingly impossible to have one without the other, but this intersection is only a function of coloniality and the narrative of colonial difference. The narrative of colonial difference is created to conceal, in the structure of coloniality itself, a structure that Mignolo calls the fact of colonial difference (2002). The fact of colonial difference represents a deeper difference that the narrative of colonial difference is created in order to conceal. The narrative of colonial difference is not an actual difference. The narrative of colonial difference helps to create and maintain a constructed Indigenous "other" that acts as a mirror, Dussel argues, to constitute the European ego by reflecting European coloniality back upon itself.

According to Walter Mignolo, the fact of colonial difference underlies the narrative of colonial difference. The fact of colonial difference ties to indigeneity as well but with real roots rather than mere colonial roots. The fact of colonial difference is what modernity/coloniality operates upon to erase local history and replace it with global designs, to erase locality with universality. The universality of modernity/coloniality is false since it is really European locality. The fact of colonial difference is what creates the possibility of alienation for both Indians and colonists. If the narrative of colonial difference fully constructed Indigeneity, Indigenous people would not be aware of anything beyond this narrative. The sense of alienation that Indigenous people feel from their own temporality and on their own land is evidence of the failure of the narrative of colonial difference. It is only as a manifestation of the fact of colonial difference that Indigenous people imagine the real present as occurring somewhere else than where they live. This alienation occurs in postcolonial contexts as well, such as the alienation that Mexican people feel, as seen in the work of Samuel Ramos and Octavio Paz (Alcoff 2007, 85).

This is what modernism seeks for all people, according to Mignolo: alienation from their own temporal and spatial reality, from locality. Even settlers are alienated from their history and place, living in a foreign space and time but trying to make it their own through the colonial act of temporal displacement, cultivating a foreign land with foreign history and knowledge in order to reformulate it as the space and time from which they come, to make it a new Europe, to make it theirs. It is no wonder, then, that original settler colonists in America named their newly inhabited spaces with names like New England,

New Amsterdam, New York, and so on. It is no wonder that Luther Standing Bear claims that "the man from Europe is still a foreigner and an alien, . . . that he does not understand America." "The white man is still troubled with primitive fears" in a foreign land because he "has not yet grasped the rock and soil" of America (1978, ch. 9). The alienation has just as powerful temporal force as a spatial force, even though the temporal displacement is a secondary function of the displacement of time from space or from the land. Linda Martín Alcoff, in her study of Mignolo's epistemology, describes the alienation that occurs through the erasure of locality as temporal and spatial: "The temporal displacement or alienation of space, which causes the colonized person to be unable to experience their own time as the now and instead see that 'now' as occurring in another space, is the result of a Eurocentric organization of time" (2007, 87).

For some Indigenous thinkers, modernity, because of its literal reference to the now appears as the salvation from the alienation caused by feeling out of time. This is why Scott Lyons—for example, in *X-marks: Native Signatures of Assent*— expresses a desire for more modernity (2010, 12). Modernity cannot save Indigenous people or Indigenous land from this alienation, however, because it is the cause of it. It is ironic, then, that term for the manner in which the coloniality of power manifests itself on Indigenous people and Indigenous land with the express purpose of erasing locality and so the temporal context of now in the land itself is called "modernity." Modernity as a concept that references "the now" confuses those who only look superficially at modernity into thinking that by denying ourselves modernity, we are denying ourselves access to the here and now or even to what is new or the future. The reality is, in fact, the opposite. Modernity/coloniality operates to erase

Indigenous locality in the first place, thereby placing Indigeneity apart from the land and so outside of the present as a function of locality.

In response to the modernity/coloniality project and its attempt to erase Indigenous locality, Dussel creates the concept of transmodernity. Transmodernity signifies the discontinuity of locality that modernity operates over. It signifies the local history that underlies the attempted universalizing global design mission. Transmodernity as a project, Alcoff writes, "operates to displace the teleological and linear progression of modernity and postmodernity," since "even the most anti-Western postmodernist" is "complicit with the temporal concepts of colonialism that erased the colonial difference" (2007, 84). Thus, modernity must be transcended rather than rejected oppositionally through postmodernity. "The 'realization' of modernity," Dussel writes, will occur not in "the passage from its abstract potential to its real European embodiment," but in the present through "a process that will transcend modernity as such" (1993, 76). In Dussel's words, "trans-modernity (as a project of political, economic, ecological, erotic, pedagogical, and religious liberation) is the co-realization of that which it is impossible for modernity to accomplish by itself; that is, of an incorporative solidarity, which I have called ana-lectic, between center/periphery, man/woman, different races, different ethnic groups, different classes, civilization/nature, Western culture/ Third World cultures, et cetera." In order for this to happen, according to Dussel, "the 'other-face' of modernity . . . the Indian . . . must discover itself . . . as the 'innocent victim' of a ritual sacrifice, who, in the process of discovering itself as innocent may now judge modernity as guilty of an originary, constitutive, and irrational violence" (1993, 76).

Alcoff, in discussing Mignolo's epistemology of coloniality, puts his position on transmodernity as such: "Western epistemology systematically delocalized knowledge," and so its "hegemonic effects are tied to its denial of its own spatial locality" (2007, 89). Transmodernity can then functionally be seen as the reconfiguring of locality into history, temporality, and subjectivity, a configuration that has been obscured through the delocalizing process of modernity/coloniality. The constituting of locality, however, is inextricably tied with delocality (teleological and linear temporality, universal history, zero-point subjectivity). This constituting relationship of locality and delocality, of Indigeneity and coloniality, must be carefully considered and problematized in the process of transmodernity. Mignolo calls this consideration between Indigeneity and coloniality as "border thinking," which is "the necessary epistemology to delink and decolonize knowledge and in the process to build decolonial local histories, restoring the dignity that the Western idea of universal history took away from millions of people" (2000, x). The idea of border thinking must be separated from the narrative of colonial difference. As much as delocality/coloniality conditions the manner in which we reconfigure locality, it does not actually constitute locality, on my view, as locality always exists as a remainder in the delocalizing process of coloniality. Border thinking is not an attempt to find the obscured locality within a reality constituted by delocality. It is a thinking that attempts to clarify the manner in which delocality laminates itself upon locality. Locality is not constituted by the process of coloniality. It is merely obscured by the false universality of delocality. Confusion regarding the meaning and possibility of the fact of colonial difference results in much of the postcolonial and decolonizing academic work remaining stuck in delocality and the narrative of colonial difference.

Dussel understands transmodernity as disrupting the European locality that is abstracted into a universal or planetary delocality through modernity/coloniality. This is the reason for describing much of transmodern philosophy as postcontinental—because of the opening up the planetary scope of philosophy beyond the European continent. Planetary philosophy is a problematic concept, however, since it does not maintain a conceptual clarity of geographic locality and so seems itself to fall victim to the very delocalizing generalizations that give modernity/coloniality its illusion of power. Thinking planetarily without clarification can be equated with the same universality and delocality of modernity/coloniality that serve to disrupt the land itself as the ground and the limit to thinking. Thinking planetarily (thinking through the land) as tied to locality through the land is, alternatively, a powerful disruption of the delocality of modernity/coloniality.

Border thinking, as Mignolo describes it, can be a bit misleading as well. Transmodernity can be understood as a transcending of the binary between modernity and postmodernity and between modern and traditional. Border thinking is thinking beyond these binaries that are created by modernity/coloniality, but it must be made clear exactly what this border is that Mignolo suggests that border thinking can think on both sides of. It is not simply a border between the knower and the known that Mignolo sees this thinking attempting to transcend in the process of transcending hermeneutics/epistemology as the paradigms of knowledge in the modern/postmodern binary border. In or for border thinking to have the function that Mignolo wants it to have, the border in border thinking must be the border of locality/delocality–the geographical and conceptual space where ground of thought moves beyond itself, beyond the land. Border thinking, as a description, allows for too much ambiguity regarding the concreteness of locality in the face of the delocalizing process of coloniality/modernity. It allows too much room for postcolonial and decolonizing thinking to fall into delocality without being clear that speaking or thinking from the border only has the power it needs as a process of epistemic locality and not an actual reality in which Indigeneity exists in the face of coloniality/modernity through delocality. The particular resistance strategy, I propose, to the modernity/coloniality project, then, is epistemic locality. Epistemic locality is in keeping with the general project of transmodernity since it also seeks to disrupt the narrative of colonial difference with the fact of colonial difference. It seeks to disrupt the narrative of colonial difference through locality. Epistemic locality is resituating thinking in locality. Epistemic locality expresses the fact of colonial difference through its manifestation out of the land. Epistemic locality attempts to inject the alienating temporality with spatiality, which is to say it seeks to displace delocality with locality. The feature of epistemic locality that gives it power over other resistance strategies of transmodernity is that it goes beyond the clarifying of a border of colonial difference. Epistemic locality not only clarifies the fact of colonial difference but also makes room for thinking in locality beyond the lamination of European locality onto Indigenous locality.

As will become clear in the process of reading this book, epistemic locality necessarily illuminates the fact of colonial difference. This is because the fact of colonial difference is a dissonance of locality; it is a dissonance in the land. Since the lamination of European delocality onto Indigenous American locality is never complete and always needs to be maintained, there is always left a remainder—the remainder of locality. Stories of locality in America, then, will always appear out of tune in relation to the larger system of delocality. It is this dissonance that marks off the fact of colonial difference and allows the residue of locality to rise to the surface once more. Epistemic locality, then, can tune out the delocality of America in order to hear the Indigenous stories of locality as they actual are, manifested out of the land.

Indigenizing through epistemic locality does not seek to go back to some constructed Indigenous past any more than it tries to place itself in the "present" of modernity. The Indigenous past that often is sought in the act of decolonization is a "past" within the constructs of coloniality/modernity: it is a past without locality. To see ourselves, as Indigenous peoples, on a linear time line of past, present, and future in relation to the Columbus invasion is to accept our delocality. We are both here and now, and the here can never be separated from the temporality of now. When we are here, we are always now. We have always been here and always will be here when we express our existence through the land, on the grounds of locality.

Iktomi Tries to Fix Academic Philosophy's Diversity Problem and Meets a Naked Emperor at the APA

Iktomi decided to join the conversation on the nature and cause of the centering of American academic philosophy on the white male and white male perspectives. Iktomi thought he could fix the problem. It should be obvious to everyone, he thought, that the European male is not the only subjectivity with the capacity for philosophical reflection or that the nature of philosophical reflection should be determined by what the European male is wont to do.

Iktomi stepped up to the lectern to tell his own story to the American Philosophical Association (APA). Amy Ferrer, the executive director of the APA, had already made it clear that "philosophy is one of the least diverse humanities fields, and indeed one of the least diverse fields in all of academia, in terms of gender, race, and ethnicity. Philosophy has a reputation for not only a lack of diversity but also an often hostile climate for women and minorities" (Ferrer 2012). Iktomi had heard others point out that philosophy, "among the humanities, is perhaps the last relic of the good old days of academe, before the feminazis and the ethnics ruined everything," and that philosophy is "the last holdout" of inclusion practices that began in the 1980s in the humanities since philosophy "remains one of the whitest, malest fields in all of academia (worse, in fact, than most of the sciences)" (Schuman 2014).

Iktomi seemed to think that philosophy was actually rather proud of its "holdout" status. Back when Iktomi was a younger Spider Trickster, he had once taken a philosophy course with Alex Rosenberg, R. Taylor Cole Professor of Philosophy and chair of the philosophy department at Duke University, who told him that philosophy is the only humanities discipline that has not "lost faith with their callings as the bearers of a continuous cultural inheritance—a canon." He told Iktomi that philosophers did not view "the need to widen their curricula as a zero sum game, in which the entrance of more women, underrepresented minorities, nonwestern peoples has required the exclusion of more dead white dudes" (Rosenberg 2014). Iktomi pointed out to his professor that philosophy was not actually a holdout in the sense his professor described since that relies on inclusion of people in the first place, which then creates the supposed need for wider curricula and the "exclusion of more dead white dudes." Iktomi told his professor that if philosophy actually did have a significant number of nonwhite males, it too would have faced curricular-widening issues decades ago. His professor responded that because "philosophy has never surrendered its canon," philosophy's "continuous cultural inheritance" creates a curriculum that makes students feel right at home while the rest of humanities has a "curriculum their students find foreign" (Rosenberg 2014). Iktomi responded to his professor by saying that philosophy's lack of inclusion and its maintaining of its canon are two sides of the same coin and that those who "feel right at home" in philosophy's attempted holdout are not the diverse students that might become the future diversity of philosophers. Iktomi's conclusion: the canon impacts inclusion just as inclusion impacts the canon, which creates a two-headed snake against inclusion and diversity in philosophy. Iktomi hates snakes, so he left that university and moved to Canada, where he received a Ph.D. in Indigenous philosophy.

In Iktomi's dissertation he reviewed the ways that the colonial enterprise, as intertwined with the Enlightenment, centers modern philosophy around the goals of establishing systems of value, knowledge, and government based on the highest forms of rationality, which gives rise to the sense that this intellectual movement and its elite body of intellectuals were leading a world march toward progress out of irrationality and superstition. This sense that whatever European philosophers were doing was by definition the closest approximation to truth and that whatever anyone else was doing was by definition, at best, an approximation of what European philosophers were doing or, at worst, meaningless and backward nonsense created a structure of truth and history, Iktomi argued, that put European philosophy as the future, and everyone else was relegated to the past and their natural domain. Native people and philosophies were considered to be outside of this spectrum altogether, according to Iktomi's research. Native thought was considered by these supposed pinnacles of human reason as more akin to animal instinct. Western thinkers from the Enlightenment forward—which was only significant, Iktomi thought, because it was the first time that European people had any awareness or conceptualization of Native people (he thought the "Enlightenment" would have happened whenever Europeans discovered Indians whatever century that happened to be)—used the Indigenous people of the Americas as the most obvious examples of what they understood as irrationality and superstition. The great naturalist of the eighteenth century (along with Thomas Jefferson, who himself was a student of Locke and implanted Lockean ideology into nearly all of his policy-making), Comte de Buffon describes the Indian as having "no vivacity, no activity of mind." He continues: "The activity of the body is not so much an exercise of spontaneous motion, as a necessary action produced by want. Destroy his appetite for victual and drink, and you will at once annihilate the active principle of all his movements; he remains, in stupid repose, on his limbs or couch for whole days. . . . The bonds of the most intimate of all societies, that of the same family, are feeble; and one family has no attachment to another. Hence no union, no republic, no social state, can take place among the morality of their manners" (Chinard 1947).

Iktomi didn't think that sounded like any Indians he had known. It sounded more like a couch or some other piece of furniture rather than a human being of any sort whatsoever.

Iktomi began to see that Western philosophy conceptualized

itself as a form of Manifest Destiny in the thought of the Americas as well as the land. Locke and Hobbes both offer Indians as exemplars of the state of nature. The comparisons between modern civilized societies and modern uncivilized societies (Indians) confirmed the self-fulfilling prophecy of the progress of civilized society and the project of coloniality/modernity. As Adam Ferguson wrote in 1767: "It is in [the Indian's] present condition that we are to behold, as in a mirror, the features of our own progenitors" (Burrow 1966).

Iktomi was now ready to present his conclusions to the APA: the discipline of philosophy is characterized by alienation for both the Native and non-Native philosopher. The things the Native philosopher knows and experiences are barred from entrance into the conversation of Western philosophy. Thus, the conversation of Western philosophy will always seem foreign or alien to the Native thinker. In addition, the Native philosopher is always forced to perform a form of being and thinking that is alien in order to be recognized as capable or even merely rational by the philosophical community. The Native philosopher must always attempt to transcend her lived identity in order to assume the false identity of the dominant perspective. This transcendence and alienation from her lived experience and identity are necessary though in order for her voice to even begin to be heard.

Academic philosophy, on the other hand, Iktomi claimed, is alienated from its own contingent, corporeal, temporal, and material reality through the need to portray a universal perspective. This need to conceal its true contingent and temporal reality creates Western philosophy's vitriolic response to non-Western and feminist philosophies as well as non-Western and feminist philosophers.

Iktomi recounted the time he was chased with a hot fire poker when he tried to point out what seemed to be obvious bias against Native epistemologies. The Western philosopher slammed his fists on the table and proclaimed, "We have a right to be biased. It's just the truth." When Iktomi refused to submit, that's when the hot fire poker came out.

Another time, Iktomi was nearly squished under someone's shoe for claiming that Western philosophy should have a label like Native philosophy does rather than simply being called philosophy proper. The attack on Iktomi was a result of more than the fear of spiders on the part of the Western philosopher; it was from the fear of having any kind of label added to the supposed stand-alone term "philosophy." If what gets called simply philosophy is really European male philosophy, then what gets called philosophy is actually just one option among many rather than the only and therefore true version.

To make the connection clear to his audience at the APA, Iktomi recounted the story "The Emperor's New Clothes" from Hans Christian Andersen. Iktomi told them of the vain emperor who only cares about prancing about in the finest resplendency and is swindled into walking around naked by two tailors who claim to have made a suit so fine that it is invisible to the stupid and incompetent. After prancing naked through the town while the town's people play along—not wanting to appear stupid or incompetent themselves—a small child exclaims, "The emperor has no clothes," thus bringing the charade to an end. The emperor, who now knows that he is comporting himself naked through the streets, must continue to the end with head held high as to not appear anymore stupid and incompetent than prancing around naked has already made him (Anderson 1949).

Iktomi talked about how this story was about attempting to carry on in a way that everyone, including oneself, knows is false, while at the same time pretending that what is clearly false and known to be false by everyone is in fact true. When one is an emperor who has no clothes, then one must be well practiced in every number of behavioral and psychological tricks in order to carry on as normal. One of the things that an emperor cannot abide is the presence of too many innocent children. Iktomi pointed out that the naked emperor is Western philosophy's view of itself, and the innocent children are anyone who represents the rich diversity of experiences and voices that the traditional view of philosophy as a universal and singular voice serves to erase.

CHAPTER 2

Indigenizing Native Studies
Beyond the Delocality of Academic Discourse

V ine Deloria Jr. had a clear understanding of epistemic locality. His work is fundamentally structured around efforts to
decolonize the colonial understanding of Indigenous people
and Indigenous thought. His epistemology, his ontology, his study of
religion, and so forth are all grounded in articulations of the fact of
colonial difference. As Daniel Wildcat suggests, Deloria, unlike most of
the philosophers of his time, "did not view the Indian knowledge systems
. . . as artifacts or relics . . . [but] . . . rather as knowledges that should be
taken seriously for contemporary and practical purposes" (2005, 425).
But Deloria understood that the narrative of colonial difference and the
delocalization of thought have constructed "non-Western knowledge" as
"primitive attempts to explain a mysterious universe." The primitive label,
however, is a result of locality, the lack of the separation of Indigenous
knowledge from the land, or, as he describes it, "the failure" of tribal
people "to control nature mechanically." This failure to float free from

the land is also a failure to "conceive," as Deloria puts it, "abstract general principles and concepts," or what I have been describing as epistemic delocality (1999b, 41).

The almost universal misreading of Deloria's work as grounded in epistemic locality leads even Native scholars to interpret his thinking as overly simplistic, as Lyons charges in *X-marks*. The inverse is more likely: these scholars have oversimplified Deloria's thinking because their interpretations operate in a space of delocalized discourse. If scholars were to understand Deloria's work through the depths of its articulations of the fact of colonial difference and its contrary operations against the space of delocalized reason, then the discontinuity between the praise of Deloria and his work within Native studies and the power and impact of that work could be realigned.

In the last years before he retired, Deloria returned to the University of Arizona, where he began teaching in 1978 and established the first master's degree program in American Indian studies in the United States. It was during this time that he spoke to me of the awkward reception that he received from the new generation of Native scholars. They often joked about him behind his back, he said, claiming that he was the grandfather of Native studies but out of touch as a scholar and a thinker because, he felt at least, the new generation of Native scholars did not take their knowledge traditions seriously and could only hear expressions of locality in the delocalized space of reason, which, as I have shown, transforms these expressions into seemingly senseless gibberish. The new generation of Native scholars, as much as they honored Deloria's work and role in founding Native studies, could never follow him down the path of epistemic locality as they had become too conditioned by the delocalized discourse of the academy and too indoctrinated within their disciplinary paradigms, which are themselves constructed through delocalized epistemologies and as such cannot take seriously tribal knowledge since it is rooted in locality. This is the present and future Deloria worried about when he wrote "Philosophy and Tribal Peoples" during that time. He worried that Native scholars would have "virtually no experiences of the old traditional kind." What would matter for these present and future scholars, Deloria argued, would be the degree to which they took "their own traditions seriously and literally" (2004, 3–4). Native scholars without a grounding in epistemic locality create a deeper disconnect between Native studies/Native scholars and the Indigenous communities they serve, which often operate ontologically (identity), epistemologically (knowing), axiologically (values), and rhetorically (ways of speaking) through locality, as well as a disconnect between Native studies/Native scholars and the existence and power of Native land through locality.

Vine Deloria Jr.'s thinking through epistemic locality was so masterful that he could highlight the fact of colonial difference in a simple phrase. In one sentence, Deloria could construct powerful expressions of locality and the fact of colonial difference. One such example is the bumper sticker he made in the mid-1960s that read "Custer Died for Your Sins," which later became the title of his 1969 Indian Manifesto. Deloria explains that the original target of the bumper sticker was the National Council of Churches. The Custer slogan originally "referred to the Sioux Treaty of 1868 signed at Fort Laramie in which the United States pledged to give free and undisturbed use of the lands claimed by Red Cloud in return for peace." "Under the covenants of the Old Testament," Deloria continues, "breaking a covenant called for a blood sacrifice for atonement. Custer was the blood sacrifice for the United States breaking the

Sioux treaty" (1969, 148). This phrase masterfully and subtlety presents the fact of colonial difference in the manner that European locality in the form of Christianity is laminated upon the land of Red Cloud and the Lakota. Deloria pushed back against that dislocated reality by putting Custer, the attempted European conqueror, into the position of Christ and his sacrifice for Christian people.

Breaking of the delocalized Christian covenant/treaty that made promises over the Lakota locality (the land) created a delocalized European savior (Custer) to shed blood to redeem the broken covenant. Making Custer the sacrificing savior for European immaturity (breaking of a covenant) reverses the coloniality relationship of the European savior who sacrificially sheds the blood of the immature savage in order to save him from his sins. This reconfiguring of the foundational myths of coloniality reveals the manner in which delocality creates immaturity and violence over Indigenous land that is born from that immaturity.

The manner in which Custer is re-created as a hero/savior/martyr of European coloniality with his death at Greasy Grass after his failed invasion of Lakota land as then configured in the "Custer Died for Your Sins" slogan reveals the locality of the Lakota people fighting for their land (which is not "theirs" as a possession, as something owned through domination and possibly lost through further dominations, but as something of which the Lakota people are a part) against a colonial and so delocalized invader who sees the land as a rightful possession and anyone who stands in the way as an invader. Custer, then, can be seen as the necessary martyr of delocality and coloniality, in Deloria's slogan, that is created through the dissonances that delocality creates upon the land.

Situated Knowledge versus Epistemic Locality

Misunderstanding of the epistemic locality of Deloria's work is only the topsoil of problems that arise in academic Native studies regarding locality and delocality. Mignolo reflects on these problems in the duality between modernism and postmodernism/poststructuralism, between epistemology and hermeneutics. Having reflected deeply upon the relationship between modern epistemology and coloniality, Mignolo turns to what many see as the solution to the problems of modernity/coloniality in poststructural philosophy and hermeneutics. Alcoff, in promoting the hermeneutic option to Mignolo, portrays hermeneutics as "the science of interpretation that focuses on understanding rather than mere propositional knowledge . . . , the other of epistemology, its more expansive sibling, or its gentler, kinder face." Hermeneutics is such, Alcoff claims, because of the recognition of the "interpretive step involved in all understanding." With the possibility of "pluralized meaning, many see hermeneutics as less prone to imperialism than epistemology proper." Hermeneutics, in contrast to epistemology's insistence on a unsituated ego that battles the fear of skepticism and relativism, "the situated-ness of knowers, what Gadamer calls 'prejudgement' and Heidegger calls 'foreknowledge' that works to situate both knower and known in time and space, is a precondition of knowledge and not the sign of its demise" (Alcoff 2007, 88). Mignolo rejects hermeneutics "as vigorously as he rejects epistemology," and, given his claim that "epistemology's hegemonic effects are tied to its denial of its own spatial locality and delocalization of knowledge," one might wonder, as Alcoff does, why he rejects hermeneutics with such vigor (Alcoff 2007, 89).

Alcoff claims that Mignolo sees hermeneutics "as the corollary of epistemology, not its true other. . . . Both domains . . . are represented without the colonial difference" (2007, 89). Modernism and postmodernism/poststructuralism, epistemology, and hermeneutics are all delocalized constructions of knowledge because they lack an appreciation of the fact of colonial difference. Any situating of knowledge is thus only superficially so as it does not penetrate beyond the delocalized situating, the layering of delocality onto locality. As much as scholars try to situate knowledge in poststructural thinking, this situating fails because it is still delocal situating; it is situating in concepts of history, time, culture, self, and gender that are themselves constructed delocally.

Examples of thinking that attempts to situate being and knowledge but fails are some of the discussions around gender and gender identity. As much as work is done to situate gender in context, to critically reflect upon how gender is constructed, often this work fails to actually situate gender because it does not contextualize gender in epistemic locality. Gender is human gender, gender as it regards the human species across the planet. The reflections are on human biology, human sex, human societies, and human construction. Even in the most postmodern or poststructurally situated context, the situated-ness is only into the human community and never into the depths of locality, into the land. If gender discussions were manifested through epistemic locality, they would reflect the continuum from gendered locality to human gender. If the discussions were to reflect the relationship of gender in one locality, they would reflect stories of Mother Earth and Father Sky, in many cases, or maybe the male and the female substances that climbed out of the place of emergence in Dinétah, the Diné (Navajo) homeland. Also, discussions of gender would not speak of gender in terms of the *ego conquiro* that in the case of gender manifests itself as I conquer myself or I determine myself: I determine my gender. This is the construction of gender through delocalized human subjectivity, in terms of which this subjectivity is able to determine her gender by removing herself from her locality. This does not mean that alternatively a subjectivity's gender is determined in the abstract or floating free from the land. Gender is not a function of abstract reality, but neither is it constructed or situated by human determinations. Gender in locality is an expression of being-from-the-land.

Cherokee scholar Sean Teuton claims in *Red Land, Red Power* that poststructural thought is a "rejection of our human capacity to make normative claims to knowledge" (2008, xvi). Audra Simpson and Andrea Smith, in the introduction to *Theorizing Native Studies*, point out that poststructural thinkers claim that "the fact that all knowledge . . . is socially situated . . . does not mean that valid knowledge is impossible." Their position is that the claim that truth is relative is merely the flip side of universal truth: both assume a capacity to "escape the grid of intelligibility one lives in" (2014, 2). While it is true that relativity and universalism are two sides of the same coin, they are two sides of the same coin in the same way that realism and fictionalism is. As I try to make clear through this book, situated-ness and universalism, as with realism and fictionalism, are two sides of the same coin because they are both born out of delocality. Thus, claims to fully situated knowledge without attempts to "escape the grid" are not better off than those that do. Simply embedding knowledge in a "regime of truth" does not produce epistemic locality, and often, insofar as it operates in a realm of truth that is disconnected from the land, from locality, this situated knowledge is just as guilty of reproducing the delocalizing operations of the coloniality of power as the classic Western epistemologies.

It seems wrong to say, as Simpson and Smith claim in contrast to Teuton, that situating knowledge in a regime of truth does not destroy the context of knowledge. Attempts to situate knowledge without the power—however artificially constructed—of universal truth or without epistemic locality do, in fact, unhinge truth and knowledge as those are understood in the context of delocalized claims to truth and knowledge. In addition, placing the worry of relativity with universal truth as an escape from context does not free poststructurally situated epistemologies from falling into relativity. The distinction that Simpson and Smith miss is between relativity as a practice of truth and the meta-claims about that practice. The argument that Simpson and Smith give applies only to meta-claims about relativity as a practice of truth but not to the actual practice. The practice need not make the meta-claims about truth that require an attempted escape from the grid of intelligibility and so not fail to be unsituated in that way while still practicing a relativity of truth that does, in relation to Teuton's claim, severely undermine any capacity to talk about truth and knowledge as delocalized practices.

Another way to look at this is from the point of view of universal truth. It seems fairly clear, in part from the articulations of the last chapter, that universal truth, as much as it might claim to be unsituated, is in fact very clearly situated in a context of European male identity and the complex of modernity/coloniality. Worries about claims to be unsituated for universal truth or relative truth are not the issue, then, because claims to be unsituated in either case seem to be mere attempts to conceal the actual situated-ness of their epistemic practices. The concerns regarding both universal truth and relative truth ought to be the actual nature of the situated-ness of their epistemic practices relative to delocality. It is really through delocality that both universal truth and relative truth destroy the possibility of producing knowledge and making knowledge claims, and it is through delocality that so-called situated knowledge remains unmoored from the only thing that can truly situate: locality in the land.

One of the ways that the epistemic practices of situating knowledge in poststructuralism actually fail to produce knowledge and truth in relation to locality is through the conventionalizing of knowledge and truth—this is similar to the manner in which moral fictionalism creates moral conventionalism and so fails to produce moral knowledge. The epistemic practices of conventionalized truth and knowledge make it impossible to conceptualize Indigenous epistemic practices in relation to land. The thinker under such circumstances is left searching for one convention in relation to another that floats free from epistemic locality and so finds herself at sea in relationship to actual Indigenous epistemic practices that rely on locality in the land. In contrast to Stanley Fish's claim that "relativism . . . is not a position one can occupy," thinkers who immerse themselves in ideas of conventionalized truth and knowledge begin to conceptualize their own epistemic practices and formations of belief as mere convention, creating alienation from one's own beliefs and particularly the epistemic locality of knowledge and belief, just as those who conventionalize morality begin to conceptualize their own moral beliefs as mere convention and are alienated from their own values and value in general.

I provide the following anecdote as a far too often seen example of the inability of practitioners of situated knowledge to grasp Indigenous epistemic practices of locality: A few summers ago I took a trip with some students and colleagues to my home on the reservation where I grew up. On the journey, I was describing to a colleague some of the things I needed to do upon arriving on the land where I was born, the things I needed to do in order to take care of my relationship to that land and to the spirits and ancestors who are a part of it. He asked me the puzzling question, "Who told you to do that?" Upon interrogating this question a bit more, I discovered that my Indigenous colleague only understood Indigenous epistemic practices as conventions, which of course are created by people. My Native studies colleague could not fathom any practices that were more than convention and so could not fathom how any practices could arise from the actual land upon which we were standing. My colleague could not find meaning in any epistemic practices of locality because in his poststructural reality, truth and knowledge were situated in human communities and human conventions, which without epistemic locality also float as free from the land in almost exactly the same manner as the delocalized universal truth. Indigenous epistemic practices in relationship to the land are then incomprehensible because the conventionalization of truth and knowledge cannot conceptualize epistemic locality, expect insofar as it could be a contingent convention of humans or human communities. The human situating of knowledge floats just as free from the land as the abstract universal claims to knowledge do. The locality of knowledge can neither be a human construction nor a feature of objective reality, as both float free from the land. The locality of knowledge must arise from locality itself as a manifestation of the land in a prematerial sense.

The Semantics of Locality

One way to begin to conceptualize epistemic locality is through examples of epistemic practices of locality. One such example is in the operations around the Lakota phrase *mitakuye oyasin* and the Lakota term *tiyospaye*. *Mitakuye oyasin* is translated as "all my relations." Lakota wisdom-keeper David Swallow Jr. says in the documentary *Lakota Wisdom Keepers*, "*Mitakuye oyasin* is the whole wide world. We are all connected. Vertically and horizontally, we are all connected. I am related to the tree here, the sun, the sky, all the human beings and to the earth right here." A superficial look at this phrase and what Swallow says might lead one to think this phrase represents a delocalized, universal concept of interconnectedness. A closer look at the manner in which Swallow speaks of this concept will show something different. He begins his description of *mitakuye oyasin* with the very particular tree that is next to him, actually pointing to it. He then points to the sun and speaks of the sun, waves his hand across the horizon and speaks of the sky, spreads both arms out wide and speaks of all the human beings, and finally puts his finger right into the dirt in the ground in front of him and speaks of the earth right there in front of him.

Swallow's particular manner of describing is not accidental. It is an important way to express the concept of *mitakuye oyasin*. He describes the concept in this manner because it allows him to express it through epistemic locality. *Mitakuye oyasin* is a concept, like all concepts under epistemic locality, that is rooted in the dirt right in front of Swallow and, like the roots of the tree he points to, only has meaning insofar as it spirals out from the locality and only insofar as the tree can grow while keeping its roots solidly in the soil. Even the most inclusive concept (the interconnectedness of everything) is only meaningful and expressible in relationship to a concrete—in other words physical—land base. Practices of epistemic locality are quite literally grounded in the land in this way and spiral out through interconnected meanings without ever losing their umbilical cord in the land. The Lakota term *tiyospaye* expresses this grounded spiral of meaning and relationships that arise out of epistemic locality. It expresses the semantics of locality. *Ti* is a short form of tipi, which means dwelling. *Ospaye* refers to the circle of circles, the circle of tipis that form an encampment. The full concept is then the grounded spiraling relationship that extends from one's own tipi and tipi family to all of one's extended relatives, even through *Hunkakaga* (the ceremony for making of new relatives) and extending through *mitakuye oyasin* as a regulative ideal.

These concepts of epistemic locality match much of actual rhetorical practices and even epistemic practices of Indigenous peoples. One simple but enlightening example is the way elders often use the word "Indian." This way of speaking fills the pages of Luke Lassiter's *The Power of Kiowa Song* (1998), a book that includes pages and pages of narratives from Kiowa elders such as Billy Evans Horse. Throughout the book these elders speak of Indian ways, Indian songs, and so forth, leading someone immersed in delocalized rhetoric and epistemic delocality to possibly charge these elders with essentializing their own experience into all Indian or even Kiowa reality. Upon closer examination of the narrative, it becomes clear that throughout the book "Indian" means Kiowa or even sometimes just the individual speaker and her experiences. My Lakota friend's *unci* (his grandmother) spoke this way as well. She spoke of loving to go to the Indian center in Los Angeles because there was another elder woman there "that she could speak Indian with," by which of course she meant the Lakota language since she knew better than anyone that there was no Indian language in general. She referred to herself as "an Indian," when she meant Lakota, and she asked some singers once if they were going to sing her anymore "Indian songs," when they came to sing her a Lakota birthday song. In every single instance where she used the word

"Indian," she actually meant Lakota in general or something even more specific to her as a Lakota *wiyan* (woman) or even to her very specific experiences.

Why does this cause so much confusion for non-Native people? As a professor of Native American studies and director of a Native American studies program, one of the most common things I am asked is for help in clearing up all the confusion on what to call Native American people: Indians? American Indians? Native Americans? Indigenous? First Nations? The general American and academic public seems consternated by the fact that Native people will not just clear all this up for them. This *tiyospaye* semantics of meaning (the rhetoric of epistemic locality) is confounding to those immersed in rhetorics of epistemic delocality and semantic delocality. In the semantics of delocality, words and meaning are abstracted from their originating context in the land, which always starts with here and now and in the dirt in front of me, as Swallow describes it. Words and meaning that remain grounded in their originary manifestation and never leave the horizon of that originary manifest are either ignored as anomalies or translated into delocalized or generalized meaning in order to be seen as meaningful at all. This is what creates the confusion around the uses of "Indian" by the elder in my example or in the pages of Lassiter's book. These elders are either speaking unclearly or incorrectly when they use the term "Indian" in a way that under the semantics of delocality can only be understood as either overgeneralizing Kiowa or Lakota reality to the entire hemisphere or undergeneralizing Indian reality to only contain Kiowa or Lakota reality. The more obvious answer though is that the term "Indian" is used under the semantics of locality, by which the meaning of this term is determined by relation to the dirt in front of the speaker and only extends to the contiguous horizon of the speaker and has no function in delocality and so no confusion caused by attempted interpretation under delocalized semantics.

It is often this misapprehension concerning the rhetorical status of the word "Indian" that gives rise to worries regarding essentialism. The same can be said for more specific tribal names, even, such as Jalagi (Cherokee), Diné (Navajo), Lakota, and so on. Words come from a particular speaker or writer, but if we understand those words and their meanings to carry beyond the locality of that speaker, then we move into the realm of the semantics of delocality. Language that is delocalized expresses another *ego conquiro* through the idea that a word can carry and even force meaning and reference beyond locality and across localities. The *ego conquiro* of language is the idea that words and meaning have a universal determination that can be carried across localities and forced upon distant people and distant lands. Finding the meaning of a word means perhaps tracing a movement across an abstract, linear development of the history of the word (etymology) divorced from any concrete locality. Or finding the meaning might simply mean looking at a dictionary that gives a definition that is one-dimensionally and universally applicable to all speakers of the language across all localities. There is never any reference to the actual speaker of the word and the horizon of locality from which her voicing of the word arises, a locality that both creates and limits the meaning of the word. The loss of this originary and horizonal context of meaning is a result of the operations of delocalized subjectivity and history as operating on language and meaning. "Indian" and "Lakota" are understood as generic terms of reference that refer abstractly to every single member of a class of people who fall under the category of that term. Contrastingly, if we understand the use of these words under the semantics of epistemic locality, through the *tiyospaye* spiral of grounding meaning in locality that never allows that meaning to stray too far from its originary manifestation, then the entire context of worries about essentialism disappears. If words are never allowed to carry meaning beyond the horizon of the experience of the speaker as the carrier of that meaning's originary manifestation on the land, then there is no possibility of the general or the essential, as essence is just a particular kind of general property.

Beyond Authenticity: Ontological Entrapment and the Locality of Identity

"Authenticity," "identity," and "assimilation" are another interconnected set of terms that create worries for Native studies scholars. Progress made by these scholars on these issues is limited by a lack of understanding of the fundamental delocality that underlies the problems in the first place. Andrea Smith argues against what she calls the ethnographic entrapment of Native studies. She grounds this worry in "the presumption that the problems facing Native peoples is that they have been 'dehumanized,'" without recognizing that "the human" is a project that "can only exist over and against the particularity of 'the other'" (Smith 2014, 209). The first problem is, as was made clear in the previous chapter, that becoming a fully human subject requires the domination of an "other." This ontological entrapment, the irrationality of the freeing project of modernity, means that freedom for dominated subjectivities—not considered fully human—requires becoming a dominating subject oneself, dominating an "other," taking away freedom from others, or putting others in bondage. Ethnographic entrapment arises from the sense that a "dehumanized" subject can "be granted humanity if they can prove their worthiness." The sense is, Smith writes, that "if people understood us better, they would see we are human just like they are, and they would grant us the status of humanity." This puts our humanity-seeking projects into ethnographic entrapment since in order to "demonstrate our worthiness" of being granted the status of self-determining subjects we must reveal ourselves as "objects of discovery, unable to escape the status of affectable other" (Smith 2014, 209). Audra Simpson, in *Mohawk Interuptus*, and on the basis of very similar reasoning, concludes, "If we take this historical form of ethnological representation into account, we might then be able to come up with techniques of representation that move away from 'difference' and its containment" (2014, 97). What both of these perspectives miss is the real nature of the underlying ontological entrapment and the possibility that revealing something of ourselves is often marking off the fact of colonial difference in relationship to our being-in-locality and thereby disrupting the very foundation for the more superficial ethnological entrapment in the underlying ontological entrapment. In the case of *Mohawk Interuptus*, for example, regardless of the expression of ethnographic refusal that attempts to move away from "difference" and its containment, the book functions through the fact of colonial difference, as the book is an authoritative history in locality of Kahnawà:ke that exposes, through epistemic locality and the fact of colonial difference, a uniquely Kahnawà:ke conception of community that transcends national and ethnographic prescriptions created and maintained by the narrative of colonial difference. The point is that it is not speaking to colonial difference itself that is the problem but the narrative of colonial difference and the way that speaking to colonial difference is often entrapped within the narrative of colonial difference. We disrupt the ontological entrapment not by ethnographic refusal, at least most clearly and directly, but by marking off difference in the context of locality as the fact of colonial difference.

Another way of looking at this is through the primacy of the ontological entrapment. Once it is shown, as Andrea Smith does, using Silva's work, that the concept of humanity that bars colonized people is a humanity of domination against a merely affectable other, the project of gaining humanity in the first place becomes unintelligible immediately. There is no need to articulate a fuller level of entrapment that arises out of that entrapment. Also, once we are in the ontological entrapment, we can never reach the ethnographic entrapment since we can never prove our humanity outside of manifesting ourselves as dominating subjectivities. The ethnological entrapment is merely a diversion from the real ontological entrapment. The project of gaining humanity is already completely unintelligible at the level of ontological entrapment. Expressing the worry of ethnographic entrapment as more than a superficial lamination on the more primary ontological entrapment does reveal confusion about the nature of the ontological entrapment in the first place, as shown in the failure to recognize the expressions of the fact of colonial difference in many ethnographic projects designed to tell our "truth." Projects that mark off the fact of colonial difference in the process of epistemic locality disrupt the status of an affectable "other" that is created through delocalized subjectivity and history in a way that any project that seeks to circumnavigate ethnographic entrapment (the representations of difference or the narrative of colonial difference) cannot since it is delocality that produces the entrapment in the first place.

Andrea Smith and Audra Simpson both rightly see, at least at one level, how the delocality of subjectivity and the narrative of colonial difference give rise to worries about authenticity. A constant question that surrounds Native texts is whether they are authentic. Nearly all the life-story, biographical, and autobiographical literature of Native peoples has at one time or another been surrounded in controversy regarding its authenticity. Maria Josefina Saldana-Portillo studies the controversy regarding the authenticity of Rigoberto Menchu's autobiography (2003). Andrea Smith, referencing that work, claims that Saldana-Portillo shows "how Menchu is imagined only as a container of truth that must be revealed to the Western subject—who in turn is deemed responsible for adjudicating truth" (Smith 2014, 210). The Indigenous subject's lack of the capacity to make choices and strategies toward self-articulated goals makes it impossible for the Western reader to understand Indigenous writers or speakers outside of binary lens of authenticity or inauthenticity. It is the only kind of question that can be asked of the voice of the pure affectable "other." Just as when one studies an ecosystem or a pride of lions, one can only ask: "Is it or is it not?" One can never ask what it desires to be and what strategies it has taken to fulfill that desire. In the same way, one can only ask of Indigenous writers or speakers: "Are they or are they not?" Their existence as an authenticity vessel of truth for the Western subject is the only framework by which Indigenous voices are made intelligible under the structure of subjectivity and history in the coloniality of power. Audra Simpson's response to this naturalizing of Indigenous voices is to ask us to "consider that maybe [we should be] engaged in a rhetorical strategy that determines what [they] want to say, what not to say, and to whom," to consider "whether [they] actually owe us the truth"

(2014, 210). This kind of rhetorical strategy is framed as "ethnographic refusal": "a calculus ethnography of what you need to know and what I refuse to write in" (Simpson 2014, 105).

While it is correct to question the construction of authenticity in relation to Native writers and speakers as an aspect of dominating subjectivity that silences the Native voice beyond mere truth or falsity, responded to this silencing with ethnographic refusal—at least by it-self—does little to disrupt the dominating and delocalizing subjectivity and temporality that create the silencing in the first place. Unless our calculus that determines what to say or refuse to say is in service of marking off the colonial difference in the context of epistemic locality, then our refusal may temporarily disrupt the narrative of colonial difference (simply in the sense of not speaking) but do little to disrupt the power structures of coloniality that give that narrative life. An example of the limitations of responding to ethnographic entrapment without a clear sense of locality and the fact of colonial difference can be seen in Andrea Smith's discussion of the contrasting reading for mere truth of Native authors but not Western ones. She points out that Native "stories can only be read for their truth. Is this person's depiction true? Are they authentic? Yet we don't read Michel Foucault asking if he is authentically French. Western writers are granted rhetorical agency, analysis, and theory—the ability to tell truths that are not contained in their bodies" (Smith 2014, 210). This is a very poignant expression of the way that Native voices are viewed as mere containers of truth while Western voices have agency and self-determination. The problem with this analysis is that it is only half of the equation and so only represents the narrative of colonial difference and not the fact of colonial difference. The fact of colonial difference can be seen in this: perhaps in the Western academic world no one asks Foucault to tell his own story—who he is not foundational to his work—but Indigenous people probably would ask him to tell his story and would imagine that who he is would be foundation to his work. One of the most common questions I hear in Indigenous communities is "who are your people?" Indigenous people ask this question, I believe, in order to ground their dialogues and relationship in epistemic locality through an understanding of kinship. The fact that one does not ask Foucault who his relatives are is a function of the delocality of Western agency and subjectivity. Unless the framing of these questions and the nature of the subjectivity involved is viewed from the perspective of locality, the concern as it is raised and addressed by Smith seems to call for a similar delocalized agency for Native authors as for Foucault rather than to address the underlying problem in the very nature of agency and subjectivity through delocality—not just granted to Foucault and withheld from Native authors by the narrative of colonial difference, but as a subjectivity and agency that attempt to float free from the land in the first place. Audra Simpson's ethnographic refusal and Andrea Smith's concerns about ethnographic entrapment seem to focus on moving beyond the narrative of colonial difference but without a clear sense of the fact of colonial difference in the context of locality that has the power to truly disrupt this narrative insofar as it is not simply forced upon Native people and withheld from Western subjects, but as construction of the nature of Western agency and subjectivity as floating free from the land in the first place.

Territorial Power or Power over Territory:
Sovereignty through Locality

Sandy Grande argues in "American Indian Identity and Intellectualism" that obsessions with identity theory and formation work to deny the critical difference of American Indians as tribal peoples of distinct nations with sovereign status and treaty rights. Her claim points to the often interconnected discussions of Native identity and sovereignty that dominate work in Native studies. In this essay, she attempts to reconfigure the modes of identity theory to match the concerns regarding sovereignty and self-determination that center American Indian intellectualism (Grande 2000). Conversations regarding identity and sovereignty in Native studies often do not recognize the deeper structure of modernity/ coloniality (particularly in the form of delocalized subjectivity and history) that shapes these obsessions with identity theory in Native studies. Scott Lyons, in *X-marks*, employs the metaphor of the "x-mark" to speak about what he calls the "Indian assent to the new." His book tries to remove Indigeneity from the binary of assimilation and resistance to such. He tries to unseat the binary between traditional and modern because it is his "conviction that the original x-marks were pledges to adopt new ways of living that, looking backwards, seem most accurately described as modern." Binary thinking is one of the classic forms of epistemic delocality, but Lyon's work against this particular binary serves to reinforce epistemic delocality rather than disrupt it. In part, this is because his description of traditional is in the worse possible light in which that term can be seen, and his description of modern is in the best possible light in which that term can be seen. Clearly from the manner in which he formulates the x-mark, Lyons's effort is to create a positive space in Native culture, history, future, and so on for the modern as a way of thinking about the new. This sense of modernity as an innocent present is quite naive though and creates an inverted straw-man argument in favor of modernity—constructing a position that is rather easily defendable but not at all fair or accurate, where the straw-man constructs an easily defeatable but not at all fair or accurate position. Lyons says of modernity: "I follow Jürgen Habermas in seeing modernity as neither inherently negative nor positive; it is, rather, 'an incomplete project' that 'still depends on vital heritages, but would be impoverished through mere traditionalism'" (2010, 12). Lyons then begins his attempt to dislodge the binary of modernity and traditionalism with the assumption of a deep-seated binary between the two, undercutting the very project from the start. Lyons also does not seem aware that Habermas is following Hegel in this description of modernity. Habermas is citing Hegel when he writes that "the historical events that are decisive for the implantation of the principle of subjectivity are the Reformation, the Enlightenment, and the French Revolution" (Dussel 1993, 11). Habermas follows Hegel's Anglo-Eurocentric view also in denying a role even for Spain in the origins of modernity. Habermas mentions the discovery of America in passing but claims it is not important to the development of modernity. For Habermas, as for Hegel, the development of modernity is essentially Anglo-Eurocentric, and it is only in the playing out of that essentially Anglo-European development that the undeveloped backdrop to modernity—for example, Indigenous America as mired in traditionalism—is operated upon by modernity. Lyons's attempt, then, to unseat the binary of traditional and modern is undermined by the sense that his solution is to turn modernity into something positive and traditionalism into something negative. The constructed binary—constructed and maintained by Lyons in the context of the narrative of colonial difference—then becomes rather easy to unseat since Lyons constructs it not as expressions of locality and the attempted constructions of delocality but simply as a generalized and innocent old and new. It reasonable then for Lyons to say of modernity, as simply an innocent new, that he "want[s] more of it, not less" (2010, 12). However, if Lyons want more modernity, following Habermas, then he wants more Europe and Eurocentrism, which means, in this way, that he has resolved the supposed binary between modernism and traditionalism through a reaffirming of Eurocentrism. There is no binary any longer because all is Europe.

The delocality of Lyons's analysis also shows up in the claims that he makes about Indian identity in the service of unseating the binaries of traditional/modern and traditional/assimilated. He claims, "Indian identities are always historically produced; constituted in writing and laws, on tribal rolls and employment forms, through social relationships and perceptions of phenotype and of course in the inner recesses of one's sense of self" (Lyons 2010, 37). What Lyons seems to ignore—as with the coloniality of power that undergirds the very concept of modernity in the first place—is, as Christopher Bracken points out, "that the concept of identity is itself historically produced," and produced under the delocalizing force of modernity/coloniality that frames the production of the more particular identities that Lyons features (2014, 126). The creation of identity as a way of framing subjectivity is part of the attempt to manifest being through delocality (the universality of sameness over difference) and operates in service of erasing Indigeneity, not as just another delocalized identity but as a seat of locality that must be obscured in the process of colonializing this land. As much as the binary of traditional/modern needs to be unseated, if it is attempted through delocality, or worse through the valorizing of delocality, as the correct way to move beyond mere traditionalism, as Lyons does, the true seat of the binary is never even exposed, which is in the very processes of modernity/coloniality and the creation of a delocalized subjectivity and history that gives shape to the conception of identity itself that can be manifested as either traditional or modern.

It is Locke who creates the modern notion of identity. At the same time that he comes up with the property concept of settler colonialism (Ricoeur 2014), Locke borrows the empty logical/mathematical property of sameness—hence the use of the name "identity," which describes the logical property of sameness—to construct a notion of the human self that is pure delocality in the form of universal sameness. Locke claims that identity is an attribute of anything that is "the same with itself," which is perhaps the most vacuous concept ever imagined, at least in relation to something as concrete as a human person. Identity as sameness is a clear example of delocalized thinking and the naturalness with which delocalized thinking is taken up, but with little regard for its vacuity. Identity for a person, according to Locke, is the sense of being the same subjectivity in diverse places and times, "the same thinking thing in different times and places" (Locke 1975, 335). As Ricoeur notes, this creation of identity as an aspect of modern subjectivity and personhood marks the victory of sameness over difference (2014, 104). Identity is sameness, and so identity as the framework of subjectivity and personhood is a creation of subjectivity and personhood in the context of sameness (delocality) over difference (locality). This victory of sameness over difference is exactly the same attempted victory of coloniality/ modernity as an operation of colonialism itself upon Indigenous locality (both land and people), an attempted victory of locality (difference) over delocality (sameness). Subjectivity in the context of locality is not identity (sameness) but difference. The manifestation of subjectivity in the context of locality is a manifestation of difference as such and not the obscuring of difference through delocalized sameness.

The other side of Grande's critique of the obsession with identity in Native studies is the importance of sovereignty both politically and in Native scholarship in the form of intellectual sovereignty. Indigenous intellectuals are in what Robert Allen Warrior calls "a "struggle for sovereignty." He describes this sovereignty as "a way of life," which is "not a matter of defining a political ideology. It is a decision, a decision we make in our minds, in our hearts, and in our bodies to be sovereign and to find out what the means in the process" (Warrior 1992, 18). Audra Simpson grounds her work in the interruption brought about by Indigenous people's sovereignty: "the sovereignty of the people we speak of, when speaking for themselves, interrupts anthropological portraits of timelessness . . . that dominate representations of their past and, sometimes, their present" (2014, 97). Use of the term "sovereignty" is so ubiquitous within Native studies that it is often difficult to understand its meaning in so many various contexts. The foundational context of the term "sovereignty" is political, as its modern meaning is shaped by the same delocalizing operations of modernity/coloniality in creating the shape and power of the modern nation-state, which is also a piece of the creation of the settler-state. In his 1576 treatise *Les Six Livres de la République*, Jean Bodin argued that a sovereign must be "absolute . . . the sovereign . . . must be able to legislate without his subjects' consent, must not be bound by the laws of his predecessors, and could not, because it is illogical, be bound by his own laws" (1576, 25). During the Enlightenment, Thomas Hobbes, in *Leviathan* (1651), borrowed Bodin's definition of sovereignty, creating the first modern version of the social contract theory, arguing that to overcome the "nasty, brutish and short" life in a state of nature that people must join in a "commonwealth" and submit to a "Soveraigne Power" that is able to compel them to act for the common good. For Hobbes, a sovereign could have no conditions or outside arbitrator in order to be the final authority in his territory (Hobbes 1651).

When the state or commonwealth becomes sovereign, it, just like the sovereign, gains this absolute and final authority over its territory. The rise of the nation-state and the coloniality of power are coextensive and come into being cocreatively. It is understandable, then, that Indigenous people would turn to what is given to the colonizing entities and not to the colonized in the nation-state/coloniality of power complex: sovereignty. The reasoning within that paradigm is that if the United States, Great Britain, Spain, and so on are considered sovereign nations that it is only fair that the Cherokee, Mohawk, Diné, Lakota, and so on would be considered such as well. This equality of sovereignty (just like the equality of agency that Andrea Smith seeks with Foucault) then seeks to disrupt the hierarchy of power that is required for the operation of coloniality. The problem is, just as with agency and identity, that there is not enough evaluation of the way that these terms are shaped, and they frame a delocalizing form of being or power that operates as tools of the coloniality of power. Just as with subjectivity and its ontological entrapment, sovereignty creates a coloniality of power entrapment, particularly as it forces Indigenous peoples and nations to operate with a concept of power that is founded in delocality and floats free from the land. The concept of sovereignty is itself quite clear about this: "sover" means "to come from above," and "reign" is "to have dominating power over."

Speaking of self-determination rather than sovereignty raises similar problems, as the concept of self-determination is founded in the *ego conquiro* of delocalizing and dominating human subjectivity. To have self-determination is to have constitutive authority over oneself. Self-determination is a capacity to dominate but to not be dominated oneself. The uses of the concepts of sovereignty and self-determination are so complex and various within Native scholarship that it seems clear that many thinkers attempt to reconfigure and perhaps even relocalize sovereignty and self-determination as Indigenous rather than as concepts of the nation-state/coloniality of the power complex. For example, Jack Forbes views intellectual sovereignty as an aspect of self-determination, which includes "living a self-determined life which respects the rights of self-determination of all other living creatures." This way of life emphasizes "the development of an attitude of profound respect for individuality and right to self-realization of all living creatures," and to "not impose [our] will on other [people]" (Forbes 1998, 12). This way of understanding intellectual sovereignty and self-determination seems to purposefully exist in opposition to the *ego conquiro* of delocalizing and dominating human subjectivity.

Deloria understands sovereignty mainly through a responsibility (rather than a power) "that sovereignty creates," which "is oriented primarily toward the existence and continuance of the group" (1970, 123). The way that Indigenous people use sovereignty, on Deloria's view, is to confront the false consciousness of individualism in the United States, which then confronts the individualism of nationhood in the idea of nation-state as sovereign. Tying sovereignty to individuals through intellectual sovereignty or through Audra Simpson's "people's sovereignty," Deloria worries, means that "Indians are not going to be responsive to Indian people, they are simply going to be isolated individuals playing with Indian symbols," which is another way of saying that Indian intellectuals will be operating through delocality. "Tribal societies," he argues, "were great because . . . people followed the clan and kinship responsibilities, took care of their relatives, and had a strong commitment to assisting the weak and helpless. Those virtues need to be at the center of our lives as actions and not somewhere in our minds as things we believe in but do not practice" (Deloria 1998, 28). Deloria's assertion of tribal values should not be confused with unchanging traditionalism and the binary opposition that Lyons struggles with between traditional/modern. Tradition, according to Deloria, must be created and re-created as a part of the life of a community as it struggles to exercise its sovereignty. The power of tradition, he claims, is not in its form but in its meaning and adaptability to new challenges. We must be careful, he points out, not to reify tradition and fail to understand the true power of it. "Truth," he writes, "is in the ever changing experiences of the community. For the traditional Indian to fail to appreciate this aspect of his own heritage is the saddest of heresies. It means that the Indian has unwittingly fallen into the trap of western religion, which seeks to freeze history in an unchanging and authoritative past" (Deloria 1999a, 42).

Deloria is framing truth, tradition, and sovereignty in relation to community as a process of epistemic locality through kinship. The contrast between kinship-based identity and individualism is meant to mark off a site of the fact of colonial difference as a part of a process of reframing and regrounding the concepts of sovereignty and self-determination in locality. Deloria, in "Philosophy and Tribal Peoples," raises important questions about epistemic locality in relationship to the concepts of kinship identity and intellectual sovereignty. His concern here is with the manner by which "Indian thought" and "Indian identity" will be related. He ponders the fact that as "American Indians . . . request entrance into this professional field [of philosophy], the vast majority will have virtually no experiences of the old traditional kind. The majority of them will begin in the same place as non-Indians wishing to write on American Indian philosophy. The difference will be in the degree to which Indians take their own traditions seriously and literally" (Deloria 2004, 3–4). The literalness that Deloria references here, which even Native academics often ignore in their scholarship and will become a highlighted feature throughout the rest of this book, is locality as it occurs in the epistemic practices and narratives of Indigenous people and communities. "The old traditional kind" of "experience" does not reference some special pathway to a constructed past that only old and nonassimilated Indians have access to or can carry on; it is the experience of locality that, in contrast to the manifestation of coloniality and delocality, arises out of and is maintained through an originary physical and spiritual relationship to the land. When the concepts of tradition, identity, and sovereignty are removed from their context in the narrative of colonial difference and the coloniality of power, then they can become useful and even powerful concepts for reestablishing locality in relationship to the workings of knowledge, being, polity, and so on.

Part of what drives Indigenous scholars and sometimes Indigenous peoples and communities to construct their own identity and polity in the context of delocalized sovereignty is the attempt to control or protect territory—just as becoming a fully self-determined human allows abject people to gain a sense of control over their own agency and subjectivity.

Sovereignty works to grant the absolute authority over territory to the sovereign of that territory—just as becoming fully human allows for the dominating authority necessary to determine oneself. The problem with reaching for these concepts of power and control is that they trap Indigenous identity and politics in the structure of the coloniality of power that dominated these territories in the first place and created the need to escape this domination. Indigenous identity and politics, just as with the ontological entrapment of human subjectivity, can come to operate and manifest these same structures of power that attempted to deny them power in the first place. The key to unraveling this entrapment is in the concept of territory and territoriality and, as Deloria claims, in not ignoring the literalness of Indigenous narratives regarding land and people.

Chief Luther Standing Bear claims that understanding America requires being connected to "its formative processes," which is another way of saying connected to the land through locality. In order to find or understand "the roots of the tree of [one's] life," which he also describes as "grasp[ing] the rock and the soil, . . . men must be born and reborn to belong. Their bodies must be formed of the dust of their forefather's bones" (1978, loc 3636 of 3934). Standing Bear, in these words, provides a clear expression of being and knowing in locality. Standing Bear's expression also clarifies the fact of colonial difference in relationship to both relativism and universalism. Locality is a process, not an abstract limit. The movement of a river is not defined with some abstract limit and boundary, but its progression across the land, where it will lead and end, is always a contiguous movement through locality, touching each part of the land that it crosses with the intimacy of kinship.

In another expression of locality, Young Chief, a Cayuse, refused to sign a treaty because he felt the land was not represented in it. He worries that no one asked the ground what it thought. If we listened to the ground, it would say:

> It is the Great Spirit that placed me here. The Great Spirit tells me to take care of the Indians, to feed them alright. The Great Spirit appointed the roots to feed the Indians on. The water says the same thing. . . . The grass says the same thing, Feed the Indians well. The ground says, . . . it was from me man was made. The Great Spirit, in placing men on earth, desired them to take good care of the ground.

There are many reasons that Native academics virtually ignore these literal expressions of locality. For one, they seem to express a traditional or religious perspective that many academics feel cannot be taken seriously in the academy because the academy is modern and secular. As I have argued, the forced focus on the secular masks the religious hierarchy that is built into the coloniality of power in such a way as to make meaningless any religious perspective other than Christianity, which is embedded into the delocalizing core of Western epistemology, metaphysics, politics, and so on from the start. The forced focus on the secular, then, is just another way to silence the voice of the colonized. If we speak from locality, as do Standing Bear and Young Chief, then we are understood as speaking from an inappropriately religious or premodern perspective—inappropriate for the modern and secular academy; but if we secularize and modernize our understanding of these words, we lose their locality and we gain the delocalized Christian religious perspective that is implanted as the epistemological, metaphysical, and logical foundation of what is called modern and secular. Another reason these words are ignored is, as

Andrea Smith expresses, the colonial entrapment of authenticity that places Indigenous voices in the realm of nature, only capable of being an authentic or inauthentic expression of particular Indian-ness and not capable of having meaning apart from this. Many Native scholars then pass over these words with the same ridicule that serious modern and secular scholars of truth and knowledge ought to of texts that are premodern, religious, and only readable for their ethnographic truth.

If we confront these words, as Deloria suggests, on the terms of the speakers and not under the framework of secularity and authenticity, then new layers of epistemic locality are revealed. It becomes clear that people do not create territory, as the structure of sovereignty suggests; territory creates a people. If people create territory, then territoriality exists as a human convention. It makes territory a contingent choice of people. This makes the land of a people a mere human political or social convention that floats free from the land itself. This is not how territory works through epistemic practices of locality or in the narratives of Indigenous people regarding their relationship to land. I do not choose the land; the land chooses me. The land is what makes me who I am. It is not a convention. It is a part of my ontological makeup; it is part of my spirit. There also is power in land so understood. There is power that flows from my originary and continual locality in the land that disrupts the coloniality of power. It is, in fact, this very power in the land that settler colonialism and Locke's creation of private property are meant to disrupt. Private property and territory in the context of sovereignty are meant to cut Indigenous people off from locality, their prematerial relationship to land and the power that arises from such.

Indigenous people refer to this locality of their identity in the land in a myriad of ways. Black Hawk (Sauk) says that "land cannot be sold.

The Great Spirit gave it to his children to live upon" (2008, 56). Black Hoof (Shawnee) says that "each nation of Indians was made by the Great Spirit, in the skies, and when they were finished he brought them down and gave them a place upon the Earth" (1939, 61). Standing Bear says that he belongs to the land in the same way the wild sunflower and buffalo do. This way of speaking about the locality of Indian identity in the land carries into the present. In the 1980s, a group of tribes met in Ottawa to adopt the Declaration of the First Nations, which begins with the following: "We the Original Peoples of this land know the Creator put us here" (Flanagan 2008, 75). In 2000, the Treaty Elders of Saskatchewan, in describing Indian sovereignty, said things like "it is the Creator that put us here on this land," and "we were put here by the Creator on this Earth to live with a certain purpose" (Hilderbrandt and Cardinal 2000, 30). Native people have been speaking these words of locality since time immemorial, but little meaning or credit is given to these words except as religious or primal Indian notions that no longer have meaning or should be taken seriously. Even Native academics often ignore these references as religious or "primitive" expressions that are supposed to remain outside of the purview of objective, scientific academic work. It seems clear to me that these expressions are not religious—at least not any more so than any other expression might be. They are merely the attempt to convey in English the epistemic practices of locality, the relationship that people have to land that is not constructed by people but constructs the people or, as the Treaty Elders say, constructs their "language, spiritual practices, and way of life" (Hilderbrandt and Cardinal 2000, 30).

If we understand ourselves, our relationships, our power (even political power such as sovereignty) as originary manifestations of the land, then we are able to maintain a relationship to the power of the land that only exists in locality. We are not cut off from our locality as we are when we understand ourselves as sovereign nations that hold rightful power over that land. If we understand sovereignty as a function of locality, then the power of sovereignty arises from the land and truly disrupts the delocalizing power of coloniality in a way that much of the talk of sovereignty by Native scholars cannot. The power of sovereignty in locality is in the land. It is the same power by which a river carries itself across multiple territories without disrupting the locality of those territories, without operating on those territories as an externalized, delocalized, dominating force. The power of a river creates a fact of colonial difference in contrast to the power of coloniality. Coloniality carries itself across multiple territories only through the disrupting of locality. Further, if we understand identity in locality, subjectivity as a manifestation of difference in locality rather than as delocalizing sameness, then we truly and likely for the first time begin to unseat the variety of notions of Indian identities and their binary constraints in terms of assimilation, tradition, race, nation, and so on. If we understand the power of sovereignty in locality, then we can unseat the power of delocalized sovereignty through coloniality and begin to understand ourselves politically and intellectually as arising out of the locality of the land and true, natural sovereignty—the sovereignty our ancestors and current elders have been speaking of in their expressions of locality.

CHAPTER 3

Refragmenting Philosophy through the Land

What Black Elk and Iktomi Can Teach Us about Locality

Epistemic locality has to fragment knowledge in order to re-tune our understanding to the land, just like the valley fragments the mountains and the river fragments the valley.

—Chickadee

Stories go in circles. They don't go in straight lines. It helps if you listen in circles because there are stories inside and between stories, and finding your way through them is as easy and as hard as finding your way home. Part of finding is getting lost, and when you are lost you start to open up and listen.

—Tafoya 12

Iktomi was the size of an ordinary man. His body was big and round like a bug. His legs and arms were slim like a bug's. His hands and feet were large and long.

—George Sword

Iktomi was the first thing made in the west that matured. He invented language. He saw all animals when they were made and watched them grow. So he gave them their names. He was very wise in many things, and very foolish in many other things. He delighted in playing jokes on everything. He would fool men and spirits to get something from them and would cheat and lie to them. He was like a man, but he was deformed.

—George Sword

Iktomi stirs up strife among the Four Winds when he can so that he can have fun watching them fight.

—Red Rabbit

Iktomi Farts Himself into Space (Rosebud Sioux), *transcribed by Richard Erdoes*

One day, so they say, Iktomi was digging up timpsila (wild turnips) to make into soup. The timpsila told him: "You better watch out, if you eat us, you'll fart a lot."

"Farting is very pleasant. It makes everybody laugh. It makes me feel good."

"Have it your way," said the timpsila. So Iktomi ate them. He became very bloated. His belly swelled up like that of a pregnant woman in her ninth month. "Oh, oh," Iktomi whined, "I have a belly ache. I am about to burst. It will tear me apart. This will kill me!"

Then Iktomi began to fart thunderously. He farted so loud that people miles away said to each other: "A thunderstorm is coming."

Iktomi came to a village. He was still farting. The stench was so bad that the people called: "Ow, ow, we are suffocating!" People fainted. One old feeble person was stunk to death.

Iktomi's farts were powerful. Each time he broke wind, it lifted him up—one foot, two feet, three feet. "Ow, ow!" he cried. "These farts are shredding my onze (anus) to pieces. Ow, ow, I am farting my guts out! I should have listened to those timpsila. Onze yugmuza, I must keep a tight hole back there."

But he could not keep it tight. A buffalo bull came charging up behind him. Iktomi's farts blew the buffalo away—far, far off.

Then Iktomi let out a very powerful fart, and it lifted him up to the top of a very tall tree. "Oh, my, how will I ever get down from here?" Iktomi wailed. But there burst out of him the mightiest fart ever farted. Iktomi tried to hold on to the treetop. He held on to the tree so that he uprooted it. Up, up, up went Iktomi and the tree together. Iktomi had to let go of the tree. The mightiest fart was also the longest. It lasted and lasted. It wafted Iktomi high into the sky, high above the clouds. At last, this fart's final burst blasted Iktomi right out of this world. He has not come back yet (Erdoes 2012).

Iktomi and the Ducks

Iktomi's stomach growled when he woke up. He always woke up hungry. Besides sleeping, Iktomi spent most of his time being hungry. Iktomi wasn't a very good hunter. In fact, no one in their right mind would call Iktomi a hunter at all. With his trickery, he could live off those around him. He was really very good at that. He rubbed his eyes from sleep as he looked around. His stomach was still growling. It was a beautiful summer afternoon with the cottonwood leaves singing in the playful breeze.

Iktomi didn't care about anything that wasn't easy for him to eat.

After wandering around for a while, he thought he heard laughter. He was so hungry and tired that this laughter just made him angry. He followed the small buzzing laughter sounds. As he got closer he heard splashing mixed with the laughter. Iktomi let out a little chuckle himself when he saw a large flock of ducks laughing and splashing on a small shallow lake. They were so busy having fun that they didn't even hear Iktomi's loud stomach. Iktomi gathered a large bundle of sticks that he tied together and hoisted on his back. He approached the ducks bent over as if he were carrying a very heavy load. He walked straight past the ducks without ever glancing in their direction.

As he knew, one of the ducks cried out, "Iktomi! Look out!" Iktomi took no notice and kept walking. The ducks all gazed at the strange sight of Iktomi marching by bent under a bundle of wood.

Iktomi soon passed the ducks and began to walk away from the lake. It was more than the ducks could take. "Iktomi!" one of them called out. Iktomi kept walking. "Iktomi!" they called out in one voice. Iktomi paused and looked around, acting surprised to see the ducks. "Hello my relatives," he called out. "What are you doing?"

"We are dancing in celebration because it is such a good day," they told him. "I am happy for you!" Iktomi called back, turning to leave. "Wait!" the ducks called. "What are you doing? Why are you carrying all that wood?" Iktomi seemed anxious. "It is not wood, you see," he told them. "These are songs, very sacred songs that I am taking to a celebration over there by the river, and I have to get over there."

"Don't leave!" the ducks shouted. "We want to hear one of these songs!" Iktomi was hesitant. "These songs are very sacred," he said. "Oh please!" begged the ducks. They climbed out of the water and waddled up the bank to gather around Iktomi.

He had to use all of his willpower not to grab one of those tasty ducks right then. "Ok," Iktomi sighed. "But you have to follow my instructions very carefully. These songs are very sacred. When I begin to sing you must hold your eyes very tight." He bent over the sticks to examine them carefully. Picking up each one, he closed his eyes and hummed softly. When he found the heavy stick he was looking for, he rose. "Here is the right one," he said. "Now remember! This song is so powerful it will be very dangerous if you open your eyes while I am singing it." "We will keep our eyes closed," the ducks promised.

Iktomi cleared his throat and closed his eyes. He began to sing, "Heya hey, heya hey, hey ya hey hey ya hey hey ya hey hey hey ya." The song was beautiful, and Iktomi was a grand singer. With eyes closed, the ducks swam and danced in the little lake. Iktomi poured his heart into the song, but only because his stomach was so empty. The ducks splashed and swayed with eyes held tightly closed. Iktomi peeked with one eye. The ducks were so engrossed in the song and their dancing that they did not notice Iktomi creeping slowly into the water. He walked back and forth in front of them so that his voice would come from several directions.

Soon Iktomi was right in the middle of the fat juicy ducks nearly slobbering on their heads with his drool. He splashed along with the ducks while raising his heavy stick over his head. With a swift skillful swing, Iktomi smashed one of the ducks. But with all the splashing and singing, no one seemed to notice. Iktomi swung again and clobbered another duck. Soon seven ducks were dead. So many ducks were dead that the splashing became much softer. One of the ducks opened his eyes. "Fly! Fly! My relatives. Iktomi is killing us," he cried. Other ducks opened their eyes and saw what had happened to their relatives and fled to the sky. Iktomi's song became a song of glee and laughter as he gathered the ducks that did not escape and began a fire with the bundle of sticks he had gathered. He roasted so many ducks that he could not even eat all of them. Soon he had to crawl off to find a place to sleep.

—liberal retelling from Joseph M. Marshall, *The Lakota Way* (2001)

These stories belong to the Spider (Iktomi tawayelo) . . .

Localizing Ontology

Joseph Marshall, in his book on Lakota stories, recounts another story of Iktomi (the Spider Trickster) tricking Mato (the bear) by playing on the latter's honor and honesty. Marshall opines, "our current method of choosing leaders reminds me too much of Mato's loss at the hands of the clever Iktomi. . . . As a society we reward arrogance and 'attitude,' and our heroes tend to be loud and brash sports figures, millionaire developers, movie stars, and the like—those kinds of people who don't know, or don't want to know, what humility is." What Marshall is speaking of is a general conditioning toward an Iktomi mentality, which is a way of thinking that supplants locality with delocality in the construction of values, relationships, identity, knowledge, and so on. Iktomi mentality is centered in the practices of delocality. One of the ways that Iktomi can teach us about locality is through his contrary understanding of himself as a delocalized *I*. It is in Iktomi's sense of self, the delocalized *I*, that the most constructive understanding of the practices of delocality in contrast to epistemic locality can be found. Iktomi's sense of identity (*I*) bristles up against a more nuanced (*I/We*) identity of kinship. Iktomi's sense of self does not allow for the humility and gratitude that are necessary for kinship identity, as the grounding of identity in locality. Iktomi's sense of self has little room for the respect and reciprocity necessary for being a good relative. Simply put, Iktomi lacks an understanding of kinship, which is the foundation of value and knowledge in locality. It is often his focus on himself that sets him in contrast to the ideals of kinship. But his lack of understanding of kinship is not mere ignorance or accident. Iktomi constructs himself as an *I* in a contrary way to kinship identity. Iktomi's lack of an *I/We* identity of kinship—as much as he protests through his constant use of kinship terms in his stories—frustrates his capacity for relationships and reciprocity and gives him the delocalized "knowledge" that it is appropriate to take what he wants from his relatives, to trick Mato or the ducks or eat too much timpsila without any sense of the impact beyond his own selfish desire. Iktomi's identity and positionality in epistemic delocality give rise to living, thinking, and constructing knowledge in binary dualisms. One way this trickster positionality gives rise to binary dualism is through one of the most basic dualisms of all—*me/you*. Because the trickster identity is so simply framed around a singular *I*, everything outside of the delocalized *I* is a *you* or an *it*. This construction of an *I* is made possible by the very same delocalizing concepts of human subjectivity that European identities and histories are able to construct for themselves through domination of the Indigenous *other*. The Indigenous *other* becomes the *you* or *it* by which the European *I* is constructed as a singular *I* and upon which the *I* dominates in order to produce its agency or sense of self-determination.

In post-Enlightenment Western philosophy, the zero-point of subjectivity is often understood as simply the basic requirement of objective or scientific knowledge. This zero-point is almost never conceptualized as an attempted conformity of the diversity of experience and identities into one single mono-experience and identity that are essential European experience and identity abstracted from their locality in order to become delocalized and manifest across diverse localities. This zero-point is almost never seen in the light of its operation in the coloniality of power. The *ego cogito* is rarely understood in terms of its foundation in the *ego conquiro*. In this section, I leave aside the foundation of the zero-point of subjectivity in the coloniality of power for the moment in order to bring to light important layers of the manifestation of delocality that can be observed by focusing on Iktomi's binary *I/you*.

One of the layers of delocality can be seen in the manner by which "things" are established as foundational in Western ontologies and epistemologies. Just as Western languages, particularly English, are noun-based (there is relatively little complexity in conjugating verbs, and a great deal of the communication power in the language comes from creating and sharing the words that name things), Western philosophy focuses almost exclusively on the being of things and establishing the being of things and the relationships between things as a foundation of knowledge. The notion of truth as correspondence is an example. In in its simplest form, the idea here is that a claim is true when it corresponds to states of affairs in the world. The idea is often credited to Aristotle in the *Categories* (12b11, 14b14), where he indicates that there are underlying things that make statements true, which is to say that states of affairs like the cat being on a particular mat underlie the statement "the cat is on the mat." Also particularly influential is Aristotle's claim that thoughts are "likenessess" (*homoiomata*) of things (*De Interpretatione* 16a3). The truth of statements, the content of thoughts, and so on are understood to be things in this primary intuition of Western thought that the primary building blocks of reality must be static things that can exist across time and space (an idea that might be called substance metaphysics). Substance metaphysics is, however, as should be clear, a delocalized view of the world. The substance metaphysics intuition is so embedded in the thinking and practices of Western philosophy that thinking this way or seeing the world this way is almost a precondition of doing philosophy in a Western key. Concepts of human subjectivity (*I*) and the relationality of human subjectivities (*I/You*) are framed by, almost inextricably so, substance metaphysics—in subjectivity as well as intersubjectivity.

René Descartes is one of the founding fathers of modern Western thinking about subjectivity. Of course, as we have seen, Descartes codifies the Jesuit practices of "examination of conscience," "withdraw[ing] into silence . . . to reflect on [one's] own subjectivity," and "'examin[ing]' with extreme self-consciousness and clarity the intention and content of every action," judging in accordance with service to God and recording these meditations in a notebook. In addition, there is a localized Christian meaning to Descartes's mind/body dualism. During the peak of the Inquisition, as we have seen, "the body" becomes "the basic object of repression." Thus, "the soul" becomes "separated from the intersubjective relations at the interior of the Christian world." Descartes, for the first time, systematizes and "secularizes" this particular, even peculiar, history of Christian thought, through which he creates an "objectification of the body as nature." The bodily and natural state of non-European people allows them to be "dominable and exploitable" and "considered as an object of knowledge" (Quijano 2000, 555). Descartes's methodological skepticism leads to a metaphysical dualism, a binary of mind and body, of *I* and *It*. In Western philosophy, this dualism creates the context for the study of consciousness. Philosophically consciousness is, following Descartes, a state of being characterized by subjectivity, senescence, and agency. In this way, consciousness is in binary contrast with the purely physical. Rock, trees, stars, and the like are nonconscious. They are nonconscious because they are thought to lack subjectivity, senescence, and agency.

The concept of subjectivity, in particular, is a multidimensional and nearly ubiquitous concept in Western thought, and the having or lacking of such docs great philosophical work throughout the discipline. Subjectivity, on one hand, is a capacity for experience that is inner to the experiencer. Subjectivity is a what-it-feels-like-from-within dimensionality of a thing. The key concept for this meaning of subjectivity is "experienced interiority"—although experience is often another way of describing subjectivity, which indicates the difficulty in even of speaking of subjectivity in a noncircular way. Subjectivity is also described through the notion of perspective, having a point of view. Subjectivity, experience, and perspective all are thought to be importantly interior. Subjectivity, then, creates internal relations beyond the mere external relations of objects. I can be taller than you (an external relation of two bodies), but I can also feel puzzled about why I am feeling anxious to meet you (an internal relation between two experiences within a subject).

For Descartes, however, this interior is not just important, it is fundamental. Absolute and private interiority is an essential feature of subjectivity and experience for Descartes. Subjectivity is the domain of a wholly private and independent *I* or ego. But the interiority of subjectivity, in contrast to Descartes's thinking, does not necessarily result in a wholly private and independent ego. The interiority of subjectivity and the exteriority of objectivity need not result in a dualistic separation between the two. In fact, it is possible for subjectivity to be interior and shared rather than private. This possibility of shared subjectivity gives rise to notions of intersubjectivity.

Intersubjectivity is also a multidimensional concept. One way that we can think about intersubjectivity is psychological. Private egos interact with each other within a reliable background that is created by empathy, rapport, and so on. Through the nonphysical presencing of empathy and the like, independent subjects create participation and agreement that condition the various experiences of those independent subjects. Intersubjectivity, in this sense, has no ontological status apart from the being of the independent subjects and arises only in relation to these subjects as things. A stronger way to think about intersubjectivity is to see the *I* as opening up into a wider sphere of shared space. The interiority of subjectivity does not ontologically isolate the subject from a shared space of being with other subjects. Subjectivity itself is interdependent, which does not mean the subject, *I*, or ego, is not distinct. A distinct subject exists in an ontological relationship to other distinct subjects through a shared and cocreating nonphysical presence.

The first psychological sense of intersubjectivity arises from Cartesian subjectivity (private egos). In this sense, the private ego subjectivity is ontologically prior to intersubjectivity. Individual private egos come into relationship with other such egos through external signs of communication that create a context for agreement and consensus. In the stronger sense of intersubjectivity, the subjectivity itself is in relationship with other subjectivities. Intersubjectivity is a cocreation of individual subjectivities, and so relatedness is ontologically foundational and primary. All individual subjects coemerge from a holistic field of relationships. The being of any one subject is ontologically dependent on the being of all other subjects, and so each is ontologically dependent on the being of relationship between subjects prior to any individuating subjectivity. Intersubjectivity, in this sense, precedes Cartesian subjectivity.

This stronger sense of intersubjectivity and weaker subjectivity make things very difficult for conventional Western philosophy and science. Western philosophy and science are based on an ontology of substance that is seriously challenged by truly relational subjectivity. In a Western philosophy and science of substance, preexisting things are always prior to relationships and so to intersubjectivity. Preexisting relatum are then necessary conditions of relationships in the first place—this is just another form of the basic intuition of substance metaphysics, which takes in this form the idea that for there to be relationships, there first has to be *things* to have these relationships. There are few Western thinkers who even address the topic of relational ontologies because relational ontologies deny the basic intuition of substance metaphysics and allow relationships to exist before and as primary to things. The few examples of Western relational ontologies are from outliers in the farthest reaches of Western thought, such as Alfred North Whitehead and Martin Buber. Non-Western ontologies, on the other hand, are quite often relational. In addition to Indigenous relational ontologies, one finds, for example, that Buddhist ontologies are often founded in process rather than things. *Pratītya-samutpāda* metaphysics (classically in Nagarjuna and the Madhyamaka school of Mahayana Buddhist philosophy) propounds *anatta*, the doctrine that entities have no essence or own-being (*svabhāva*), but rather are configurations of relations that arise within the context of preexisting relationality (Eckel 1992). Also see, for example, Joanna Macy's *Mutual Causality in Buddhism and General Systems Theory: The Dharma of Natural Systems* for more examples of Buddhist relational ontology.

Martin Buber is one of a small handful of Western philosophers—and perhaps only because he exists on the edge of that tradition—who seems to grasp the issues that Iktomi struggles with in his frustrations regarding kinship and being-in-relation. Buber asserts that human beings only become problems to themselves in times of social and cosmic homelessness. It is only in this space of Iktomi-styled groundlessness and homelessness that humans ask the question "What am I?" The question of what is a person cannot be asked in the "visual image of the universe (*Weltbild*)" realized by Aristotle "in unsurpassable clarity as a universe of things, and now man is a thing among these things in the universe." In this picture of the universe, the Aristotelian human is "given his own dwelling-place in the house of the world" (Buber 2014, 127). Delocality unsettles this dwelling, for Buber, in the form of the inability to comprehend "the edge of space, or its edgelessness, time with a beginning and an end or time without beginning or end," which leads Buber to "seriously [think] of avoiding [the danger of madness] by suicide" (2014, 136). Kant creates an opening for finding a way out of his homelessness, for Buber, by transforming the "hostile and terrifying . . . mystery" of the "space and time" of the world, or "comprehension of the world," into "the mystery of your own being" (2014, 137). It is then in Kant's attempted escape from self-imposed immaturity that Buber finds the first real asking of the question "What am I?"

Buber is not satisfied with Kant or Hegel's addressing of this question though. Buber claims that the self-banishment of solitude must be overcome in order for humans to know themselves. The self-imposed immaturity of Kant's enlightenment project is then, for Buber, a project of false-consciousness that arises not out of immaturity but out of self-imposed banishment from our home, from a kind of locality. Hegel, Buber also asserts, diminishes the wholeness of the concrete human person and human community in exchange for universal reason. Buber claims that human beings and human communities will always be lost in the Iktomi-styled homelessness of Hegel's world of universal reason. Humans cannot return home through the very project that reifies the choice to leave home in the first place. For Buber, the overcoming of solitude comes from the realization of relatedness. Human solitude is created by removing relatedness from its ontological primacy, in favor of the delocalizing and isolating subjectivity against a background of nonconscious, nonfeeling, and passive things. Human solitude then oscillates between absorption in the self (solipsism) and absorption in the all (collectivism). In either case, a singularity of *I* or *We* is posited that removes human beings and human communities from primary relatedness.

The human search for release from solitude is not only blocked by the search for perfection in universal reason, according to Buber, but also by the notion of history itself, as exemplified by Hegel. History, in this sense, is perfection in time rather than in space. Placing perfection in the future, as a necessary or possible outcome of history and time, separates humans from the lived experience of relatedness in the present. It is our spatial present through which we are related and connected. Buber is remarkably clear about the destructive power of delocalized human subjectivity and history as manifested by the project of coloniality/modernity. He charges delocalized history—which not only removes time from history in the sense of actual lived experiences of relatedness in the present but also removes space from history in the form of relatedness itself—with blocking the human release from the solitude that is self-imposed by these very processes of delocality. The focus on a binary between a singular *I* and a singular *We* without a primary relational context creates a self-imposed solipsism that cannot be overcome without reattaching the *I* to locality, or what we might call ontological kinship. For Buber, overcoming solitude can only come when we realize that we are selves-in-the-presence-of-other-selves. Relationality is ontologically prior to the individual self or other selves. The self is a part of reality only insofar as it is relational. It is the binary between *I* and *We* that hides our identity in relational locality. For Buber, the question "What am I?" is not found in reason, self-determination, sentience, or agency. It is found in "man's seeing that which he confronts, and with which he can enter into a real relation of being to being, as not less real than himself, and through it not less seriously than himself" (Buber 2014, 167–168).

Buber develops his relational ontology further through two modes of existence: *I-Thou* and *I-It*. The *I-Thou* relation between two entities is a relation between whole and unique beings that produces knowledge without subsuming that knowledge or those beings under a universal, which is to say that it produces knowledge and being only in a kind of locality. The *Thou* of this encounter is not subject to classification or reducible to particular characteristics that remove it from locality or embodiment within the encounter. The *I-It* mode is characterized by the duality of sameness and difference and always is subsumed under a universal definition. The *I-It* relation is an experience of a detached thing. This thing is fixed in time and space, which is to say that it exists out of time and space, out of locality. The *I* that experiences this *It* is then also fixed and delocalized as an *It*. The *I-Thou* mode, in contrast, understands the *I* and the *Thou* as participants in a dynamic, living process of locality. The *We* that is created through an *I-It* modality is then also fixed and delocalized as an *It*. It is only a *We* that is created through the *I-Thou* modality that is a true *We*, on Buber's account. Buber claims that "the person who is the object of my mere solicitude is not a *Thou* but a *He* or *She*. The nameless, faceless crowd in which I am entangled is not a *We* but the 'one.' But as there is a *Thou* so there is a *We*" (2014, 175).

This isolation even in community, even in a *We* of community and even in the appearance of the context of kinship, is the source of much of

Iktomi's frustration and confusion. Iktomi does not understand himself; he does not understand who he is because he tries to comport himself in the mode of an *I-It*. He sees himself as an *I-It* that constructs his identity as a mere thing among other things. Iktomi's dualism of *I/You* arises from the core of his identity as an *I* and his inability to construct a *We* of kinship that arises from a relational *I-Thou*. The world of mere things in which Iktomi exists, which allows him to use his relatives only to his own advantage, arises from the delocality of being and subjectivity that creates a world of solitude and control for the subjectivities in it. Iktomi as an *I-It* can only choose between controlling and being controlled, of being a subject or an object. In being a subject in relation to objects, Iktomi creates the solitude that all of his attempted dominations are meant to escape.

Iktomi is the contrary of his locality, the Lakota land centered around He Sapa (the Black Hills) or *Wamaka Og'naka Icante* (the Heart of Everything that is), which is "a wizipan, a repository from which [Lakota people through *Lakol wicoun*, or "the Lakota way of life"] can draw physical and spiritual sustenance" (Howe et al. 2011, loc 163). In the context of He Sapa, the air, the valleys, the trees, the plants, the animals, the water all are part of the *Lakol wicoun* and intertwine with the Lakota people in a material as well as more than material sense, such that "stones and rock formations intricately sculptured against the sky are part of [the people] too. In *Lakol wicoun*, this is *Mitakuye Oyasin*. They are all our relatives, and we are all related. All of this we know and hold in our hearts" (Howe et al. 2011, loc 171). It is in the context of the locality of *He Sapa, Lakol wicoun*, and *Mitakuye Oyasin* that Iktomi is criticized for his self-centered *I*; his stories teach powerful lessons to his people, the people of this locality. His stories and his actions warn of the danger of succumbing to the false consciousness of Western individualism, as Deloria describes it, but also of the danger of reifying the concepts of culture and nation into a delocalized individualism of an *I-It/We*. The web that Iktomi traps himself in creates the appearance of a natural tension between the individual and the group, a natural tension between subjects and objects. But in his locality the *I/You* and *I/We* are not in binary opposition. At the core of his *I* is a nonbinary dualistic intertwining of the individual and collective. The nonbinary intertwining of the particular and general is part of the very nature of locality and being in locality.

In Lakota philosophy or *Lakol wicoun*, the smaller individual things or parts of things are intertwined with what is more general. In the Lakota language, we see it in the terms *nagi* (spirit) or *nagila* (little spirit) and *nagi tanka* (big spirit). Good Seat says that "anything that moves or does anything has a spirit" (Walker 1980, 72). Everything has a *nagila*, except for human beings and the *Taku Wakan* (the sacred relatives, like *Wi*, the sun; *Maka*, the earth; *Iyan*, the rock; and *Tate*, the wind); they have *nagipi* (spirits). These spirits (*nagipila, nagipi*) are not properly in the rocks, wind, trees, or humans that they associated with, which is in contrast to the inner ego of Descartes's secularized rendition of the Christian concept of soul. In fact, *nagi* is actually a spirit that has never been a part of a human being. A *nagi* that becomes a part of a human being becomes *wanagi* (a *nagi* that has once been in a human being) and will remain *wanagi* after the human dies. *Wanagipi, nagipi*, and *nagipila* are not a part of the things they are associated with, says Good Seat. A person's "*nagi* is not a part of himself. His *nagi* cares for him and warns him of danger and helps him out of difficulties. When he dies, it goes with his *wanagi*" (Walker 1980, 70–71). All beings or things have multiple sides: there are all of the invisible parts that are vital (*woniya*: the life or breath of life, and *sicun*: influence) and nonvital (*nagi*: spirit), and then there are the visible parts (the physical body, manifestation of physical breath in smoke or steam, the physical manifestation of influence). These invisible and visible aspects or connections to a person or a thing are two sides of the same relationality that we might call a person or a thing. Every visible thing has an invisible side, and every invisible thing has a visible side. Energy in general has these two aspects: visible and invisible. The power by which a thing or the energy of a thing is transformed from the visible to the invisible or vice versa is *tun* (sometimes written as "*ton*," as in Walker 1980). Even life and death are two aspects of the same thing because one is the visible aspect of the other and vice versa. The complexity of the invisible and visible within or around a person or thing also is within or connected to a larger complexity in the relationship between individual *nagi* and *nagila* and *nagi tanka*, or the individual spirits and the big spirit. Individual persons or things have this complex multiplicity as well. The one that is small and specific (our own individual spirit) is intertwined inseparably with another that is big and more general (big spirit) (the intertwining of our own spirit with the big spirit). The *nagi tanka* is itself, though, not separate from the individual *nagi* or *nagila*, which is why Good Seat says, "there is no *Nagi Tanka*," by which he means that there is no *nagi tanka* per se as something that exists apart from the specific (something that exists out of locality) in a general or universal way.

Within the context of *He Sapa, Lakol wicoun*, and *mitakuye oyasin*, what might seem like a tension between the individual and the group, the particular and the general, is really just a manifestation of the relationality of being in locality, and it is this relationality as *mitakuye oyasin* and the *tiyospaye* spiral of meaning that found *Lakol wicoun* and the Lakota practices of locality. *Mitakuye oyasin* (all my relations) conceptualizes an *I* of relationality. I am my relations. Those relations, however, as David Swallow Jr. specified, are not delocalized in a universal concept of interconnectedness. *Mitakuye oyasin* is grounded in locality. It begins and ends with the trees and the dirt that one can touch. *Mitakuye oyasin* (the interconnectedness of everything) is only meaningful and expressible in relationship to locality both as a concrete land-based but also a prematerial understanding of the very nature of land in the context of locality. The *tiyospaye* spiral of meaning extends this interconnectedness from the ground like the roots of the tree that Swallow points to but does not extend beyond the contiguous horizon of locality.

This relationality and spiral of meaning indicate the nature of ego in the Lakota locality as well. This relational ego that Iktomi flaunts is embodied, grounded in prematerial as well as physical locality but also spiraling inward toward interconnected relatedness. The Lakota ego can discover the already deeply relational *other* or *Thou* not through external conflict or recognition but through the relational spiral of her own ego. The *nagi* and *nagila* of the Lakota ego not only indicate a kind of individual essence in the *nagi* or spirit but also the relational spiral of the *nagila* to the *nagi tanka*, the little spirit to the big spirit, that spirals from inside of her like the roots of a tree that spread out to the leaves. Even in the deepest recesses of the Lakota ego, one finds an individual subjectivity but not one that is essentially inner or isolated. The individual Lakota subjectivity is intertwined within itself and beyond itself through relational interconnectedness and nonbinary interactive dualism.

Black Elk

Black Elk recounts the story of Pte San Win (White Buffalo Calf Woman) bringing the calf pipe to the Lakota. He concludes the telling of this story like this:

> Then she gave something to the chief, and it was a pipe with a bison carved on one side to mean the earth that bears and feeds us. . . . "Behold!" she said. "With this you shall multiply and be a good nation. Nothing but good shall come from it. Only the hands of the good shall take care of it and the bad shall not even see it." Then she sang again and went out of the tepee; and as the people watched her going, suddenly it was a white bison galloping away and snorting, and soon it was gone.
>
> This they tell, and whether it happened so or not I do not know, but if you think about it, you will see that it is true. (Neihardt 1932, 1–5)

Localizing Epistemology

Vine Deloria Jr. reads this last line from Black Elk not as a statement of faith but as "a principle of epistemological method" (1999b, 44). The epistemological method that Black Elk is describing is a way of coming to know that is centered in a kind of lived experience, a being in relationship to one's locality that is characterized by epistemological and ontological kinship. In the heart of this method for coming to know, as Black Elk describes it, is an individual "seeing," but an *individual* seeing and a *seeing* that is fundamentally relational. The idea that truth is found in seeing means that knowing is essentially bound up in experience in a very intimate way. The individuality of this seeing is the individuality of the *I-Thou*, and the seeing is the seeing of a *Thou* in the context of an *I-Thou* kinship. Structurally, seeing truth means that knowing cannot be extrapolated out of the intimate experience that it is bound up in, out of locality, just as the *We* of *I-Thou* cannot be subsumed under a universal. The way that Black Elk states it, knowing is not something that can be extended or even shared beyond the lived experience itself. "If you think about it, you will see that it is true" means that seeing truth or coming to know is something that *you* must do for yourself. In "What Coyote and Thales Can Teach Us: An Outline of American Indian Epistemology," I discuss the emphasis on propositional knowledge in Western episte-mology and Western thought in general. Propositional knowledge is the kind of knowledge that is contained permanently in true statements or propositions, the kind of knowledge that requires universality beyond the *I-Thou* kinship relationship. In that essay, I discuss the difficulties that non-Western traditions have in communicating their focus on non-propositional knowledge (as in Black Elk's and Deloria's epistemologies) to Western thinkers who are engulfed in the epistemological world of propositions or statements. Western thinkers find it nearly impossible to see, given their most basic values and assumption, that propositions could be superfluous to knowledge from the perspective of locality (Burkhart 2004).

I will not attempt to defend Indigenous philosophizing against the view that knowledge can only be found or even is primarily found in true propositions or statements. However, it should be clear that the traditional Western relationship of knowledge to statements arises out of delocality, out of the need to create an *I-It* relationship of knower to known—a binary relationship between subject and object. Beyond the framing of this issue in the context of delocality, it is important to reflect on the values in Western thought that come out of delocality and produce the sense of naturalness of the view that delocality is necessary for knowledge. It is worth reflecting on how these values are created and sustained in Western culture and thought, in contrast to the locality of Indigenous epistemology. Some of what seems to maintain the trajectory of these Western ideas about knowledge is the emphasis placed on the values of the absolute, the eternal, the unchangeable, and the rational. The motivation for reaching toward the absolute or valuing what is absolute is understandable. There is a feeling of security that comes when knowledge embraces the absolute, eternal, and unchangeable. This security, however, like the false release from solitude in understanding one's subjectivity through others, reason, and history, is false security. The sense of security that is achieved by absolute, eternal, unchangeable knowledge is gained by delocality, which provides an illusion of removing the originary manifestation and context in knowing and meaning in order to maintain universal consistency across all places and times. The rationality of Western knowledge is also achieved by irrationality, through delocality and coloniality. The irrationality underlying Western knowledge is the savagery that underlies civilization in the form of coloniality and Western knowledge's core power as the coloniality of power. This irrationality lies, as Dussel puts it, "in the confusion between abstract universality and the concrete world hegemony," which means that the Western construction of universality helps to create world hegemony and then world hegemony extends the constructed universality toward a global universality and global hegemony (2000, 472). The false absolute of Western knowledge is the Eurocentric bubble that creates a mirror of itself across all localities with the false impression of universality. The Eurocentric bubble creates a mirror of itself backward onto the ancient Greek locality and forward onto the Indigenous locality (Dussel 2000, 472). The irrationality and false absolute seek themselves through the proposed rationality and absolutism, as Nietzsche puts it (1954). The focus on rationality within the context of the actual Western practices of rationality obscures the underlying irrationality, and the focus on an absolutism serves to hide the underlying false absolute of Western knowledge. Thus, Western knowledge, in claims to being absolute and rational, turns in upon itself even by its own best lights.

In Indigenous stories, those who focus on the concepts of the absolute, eternal, and unchangeable appear foolish. Reaching for such is common behavior of Iktomi, Coyote, Rabbit, Raven, and other tricksters. In their stories, this reaching is seen as akin to childish wanderings—like the Kantian immaturity that is supposed to be overcome through eternal and absolute reason expect in this case it is the striving for eternal and absolute reason that is the cause of the immaturity. The absolute and unchangeable are those sorts of things we reach for, in the context of Indigenous tricksters, before we really come to know ourselves or our world, before we have found our home in a world grounded in a relational kinship of *I-Thou*. The world is, if "seen" in its locality within the context of relational kinship, fragmented, dynamic, and in constant motion and change. Instead of a focus on propositional knowledge, then, in Indigenous epistemologies we find lived, experiential, and embodied knowledge achieved through kinship. Lived knowledge is knowledge that is a part of us as humans and a part of the movement and dynamic changeability of the journey of our lives through kinship within a dynamic and ever-changing locality. In "What

Coyote and Thales Can Teach Us"—where I explore the fundamental trickster modality of Western epistemology—I write, "In contrast to propositional knowledge, which seems to be designed to outlast us, to take on a life of its own, to be something eternal, [lived knowledge] is the kind of knowledge we carry with us" (Burkhart 2004, 20). This lived knowledge is not knowledge we carry with us out of locality or freely across localities and out of the land. It is knowledge we carry with us as a function of being with the land.

Knowledge is created by truth in the Western context. Regardless of whether one talks about correspondence theories or coherence theories of truth, the basic assumption of Western epistemology remains the same. If a statement is false—does not turn out to be true in all localities—then there can be no knowledge. And knowledge is contained in statements or propositions (knowing is knowing a statement or proposition). The idea is that unless the statement that is contained at the heart of a piece of possible knowledge is true, then the possibility of knowledge is destroyed. This truth cannot be temporary or local because, if it turns out later that the statement is shown to be false but seemed to be true in one place or at one time, then the claim to knowledge is invalidated even at the time or place that it appeared to be true. For example, it might seem reasonable to say in English that "everyone knew that stress caused ulcers, before two Australian doctors in the early 80s proved that ulcers are actually caused by bacterial infection" (Hazlett 2010, 501). It is seemingly uncontroversially accepted that people know that stress causes ulcers, but the statement that stress causes ulcers is false. One cannot know that stress caused ulcers because it turned out that ulcers were caused by bacteria. In another sense, Newtonian physics is Western scientific knowledge, but Newtonian physics turned out to be false. Any claims about knowledge in relation to Newtonian physics are voided by the future falsity of the theory.

This most basic and now normalized assumption of Western epistemology exposes the fundamental flaw in operations regarding knowledge. If knowledge requires truth over all places and times, over all localities, then knowledge must manufacture continuity over localities, which requires knowledge and even being to be removed from locality, to float free from the land. In Western epistemic practices, human rationality attempts to abstract a core of delocalized truth that is continuous across all localities. As Deloria puts it, "the whole process of Western science is that of finding common denominators that can describe large amounts of data in the most general terms, rejecting anything that refuses easy classification as 'anomalous'" (2001, 4). But this continuity is manufactured through delocality. Attempting to abstract out the locality—which is the reason for the constant presence of anomalies from the start—in order to construct a delocalized "world" is the necessary precondition of the entire edifice of the Western knowledge system. In locality, there are no anomalies because there is no attempt to manufacture continuity across localities through delocality or to try to produce knowledge that floats free from the land. Deloria puts this as the "fundamental premise" of Native epistemology (that there are no anomalies in knowledge through locality), "that we cannot 'misexperience' anything" (1999b, 46). The only kind of continuity that exists across localities is the power of locality itself, which moves through and across localities *through* locality, in the way a river carves its course through a mountain—the river is not all rivers; the mountain is not all mountains; and their relationship is created and maintained only through locality. Knowledge in locality is similarly produced through the land, and its continuity across localities is one that exists through locality. This knowledge must move across the land in the way a river does and can never remove itself from the land in order to float free from the land even for a moment without losing its truth. Continuity as a function and power of locality, rather than floating free from the land that exists through delocality and so can be created abstractly and at any place and time, cannot be created at all, much less be manufactured in delocality. Continuity is a power in and of the land that disrupts delocalized knowledge and manufactured continuity. Continuity is a power in the land that disrupts sovereignty as a manufactured power of people and nations in delocality. Continuity is a power in the land that creates knowledge through locality that arises in first-person experience in the act of "seeing" through relational kinship.

The manufacturing of continuity in Western epistemic practices is achieved through delocality or through finding abstract, delocalized "connections." However, in being delocalized, these "connections" are not actually connected at all, except in the ideas themselves and in the minds of the people "connecting" them, both of which float free from the land and so are not connected through foundation conduit of connectivity, which is the land as the ontological and epistemic capacity for kinship. The locality of the things, ideas, beings, meanings, and so on must be removed in order to manufacture this continuity in abstraction. Alfred North Whitehead recognizes the delocality of Western "scientific materialism" as a "fixed scientific cosmology which presupposes the ultimate fact of an irreducible brute matter, or material, spread through space in a flux of configurations." He claims that "in itself such a material is senseless, valueless, purposeless. It just does what it does do, following a fixed routine imposed by external relations which do not spring from the nature of its being" (Whitehead 1925, 22). In contrast to what he calls the fallacy of misplaced concreteness (the mistaking of the abstract for the concrete), Whitehead constructs a metaphysics not of abstract objects, things, or substance that rely on delocality, but of events, processes, and relations. On this basis, he claims that "knowledge . . . is an experience of activity (or passage)" and that "the things previously observed" are not things or objects but "events," events that are "chunks in the life of nature" (Whitehead 1920, 186). Whitehead's view of the relational process of knowing and being where knowing is an activity and what is known it not a thing but an event seems a fairly clear expression of an understanding of knowing and being as an originary and continual manifestation through locality.

Deloria recognizes the continuity of locality in Indigenous epistemic practices when he claims that "Indian knowledge . . . has a consistency that far surpasses anything devised by Western civilization" (2001, 2). "Indian metaphysics," he claims, constructs "a unified world, a far cry from the disjointed sterile and emotionless world painted by Western science" (2001, 2). From this perspective of scientific materialism and delocalized knowledge and truth, Western thinkers "frequently suggest," Deloria points out, "that the Indian way of looking at the world lacked precision because it was neither capable of nor interested in creating abstract concepts or using mathematical descriptions of nature" (2001, 2). Deloria's point is that as much as these abstracted and universalizing claims to knowledge and truth appear precise, it is only because these statements are removed from the originary and continual manifestation of their meaning. Thus, the statements are "sterile" and "disjointed," lacking the real context of their meaning and continuity in locality.

When Black Elk states that he does not know if any of what he said is true about White Buffalo Calf Woman bringing the pipe to the Lakota people, he is talking about delocalized truth. He does not know anything about this story or any others where knowing requires a delocalized truth that would speak to the reality of this story apart from locality or through delocality. He does not know what *actually happened*—a common question under Western epistemic practices that requires a delocalized investigation into the abstract, disjointed, and manufactured stratum of continuity described as "truth." This kind of truth, Black Elk states he does not know. He contrasts the truth he does not know with a kind of relational kinship that brings a *seeing* of truth that his listener can have: "but if you think about it, you will see that it is true." This thinking, on Deloria's interpretation, is a never-ending intimate knowing relationship with one's locality (2001, 2). Because knowing is an intimate relationship with locality, thinking is a continual process that produces no anomalies (Deloria 2001, 4). Any completion of the thinking process is necessarily incomplete (which is why there are so many anomalies in Western delocalized epistemology). Just as a kinship relationship can never be completed (in the sense ending or going beyond kinship relationality), neither can the intimate relationship with locality that is knowing be complete. "When we reach a very old age," Deloria writes, "we begin to understand how the intensity of experience, particularly of individuality, and rationality of the cycles of nature relate to each other. This state is maturity" (1999, 14). When one reaches this state of maturity, one is considered wise. But this wisdom is not a container of abstract truths but rather a greater capacity to grasp the moment to moment dynamics of a locality to the point that one can "see" the "truth" that is there. This greater capacity extends one's ability to respond to the dynamic world around, to live in relation to the originary and continual manifestations of meaning in locality in a good way. This greater capacity of wisdom extends one's ability to sustain the intimate knowing relationship that maintains continuity within a locality.

Chickadee Tries to Teach Iktomi Something about Epistemic Locality

Coyote and Thales weren't the only philosophers to fall in holes. Iktomi had fallen in his share of holes too, and today was just one of those falling kind of days. He already had so many bumps and bruises that he figured it was about time to do something about all these holes and all this falling.

He scrambled over to the edge of the hole, and after gathering his breath and cupping his hands over his mouth, he cried out to the opening above him.

"Help! Help!" Iktomi wailed.

"I'm down here in this hole, and I can't get out!"

After yelling at the top of his hole for what seemed like hours, Iktomi finally heard a small rustling near the opening. A little face peered over the edge and down at Iktomi. "Hello?" the little voice said.

"Who is there?" Iktomi responded.

"It is me, Chickadee," said the voice.

"Can you find someone to help me get out of this hole?" Iktomi asked. "I don't think you can help because you are too small."

"Well how did you get in this hole in the first place?" Chickadee asked.

Iktomi thought about it for a while.

"Well I'm always talking, and trying to figure out the propositions of things. You know, what statements are true and false, like that! I want to know *everything*! So, I walk around talking and talking and trying to figure out everything, and before I know it, I'm down in a hole."

"It just seems to be part of the process, part of the ancient history of figuring things out."

"I see," said Chickadee. "I think I can help you."

"Really?" said Iktomi. "Are you going to go find someone bigger to help pull me out?"

"No," said Chickadee.

"You remember that Navajo fair that you and Coyote went to a couple months back? The one where you guys tried to steal all of the frybread and have your own frybread eating contest?"

"Yes!" responded Iktomi. "We had a frybread feast that day! But we were still so hungry and there was still so much frybread that we didn't eat that day."

"What about it?" Iktomi asked.

"Well did you notice how some of those the young Navajo couples were walking around holding hands but not ever speaking to each other?" Chickadee asked.

"Yes I did!" Iktomi retorted. "And I thought it was pretty weird. I mean why wouldn't they be talking to each other? They should be asking each other all sorts of questions! Like, 'What's your favorite video game?'; 'What kind of music do you like'; 'Do you like my new leather jacket with the fringe?'; 'What are you thinking?'; 'Do you like me?'; 'How much?'"

"How are they supposed to know anything about each other without all these questions, by just standing around in silence?"

"See, you would say that Iktomi," Chickadee laughed. "That's why you are in this hole. If you understood silence better then you could learn to keep yourself out of these holes."

"Huh?" said Iktomi.

"See, those young Navajo couples are really getting to know each other in a deeper, more meaningful way than can be gained through asking all those questions and getting all that propositional knowledge."

"You lie a lot Iktomi right?" asked Chickadee.

"Not me!" replied Iktomi. "You must be thinking of Coyote. He does that."

"Well these young couples could say whatever to each other" said Chickadee. "They could just say whatever they thought the other one wanted them to say."

"I would never do that," said Iktomi.

"Well even if they told the truth, do you think some set of true statements about a person can really tell you anything meaningful about them?" asked Chickadee. "Can they tell you how to relate to a person?"

"I mean a person is complex, dynamic, constantly changing."

"Do you really need to keep formulating new propositions about a person each moment that they change in order to really say that you know them?"

"You are giving a headache!" cried Iktomi. "Are you going to help me out of this hole or what?"

"Iktomi! I'm trying to help you," interjected Chickadee.

"When you were a little Iktomi, you studied the traditional ways right?" Chickadee asked.

"I guess," muttered Iktomi.

"Did you read books? Did anyone give you speeches or give you an instruction manual?" asked Chickadee.

"No," grumbled Iktomi. "My uncle wouldn't let me read any books about traditional ways, or even teach me about them."

"He didn't teach you about them?" questioned Chickadee. "You learned a lot about them didn't you?"

"I guess," muttered Iktomi. "But he wouldn't tell me anything. He said I just had to do stuff and go to the ceremonies, and open my eyes and look."

"Did he really think I would be able learn anything without statements and propositions? Did he really think that I would be able to learn anything by just looking, seeing, and knowing?"

"Well just think about it Iktomi, and you will see," advised Chickadee. "In the meantime, I'm going to go try to find someone to help you out of this hole."

Black Elk

You have noticed that everything an Indian does is in a circle, and that is because the Power of World always works in circles, and everything tries to be round. In the old days when we were a strong and happy people, all our power came to us from the sacred hoop of the nations, and so long as the hoop was unbroken, the people flourished. . . . The east gave peace and light, the south gave warmth, the west gave rain, and the north with its cold and mighty wind gave strength and endurance. . . . Everything the Power of the

World does is done in a circle. The sky is round, and . . . the earth · is round like a ball and so are the stars. The wind, in its greatest power, whirls. Birds make their nests in circles, for theirs is the same religion as ours. The sun comes forth and goes down in a circle. . . . Even the seasons form a great circle in their changing, and always come back again to where they were. The life of a man is a circle from childhood to childhood, and so it is in everything where power moves. . . .

But the Wasichus have put us in these square boxes. Our power is gone and we are dying, for the power is not in us anymore. (Neihardt 1932, 194–196)

On Putting Ontological and Epistemic Locality into Practice

Scholars, Native and non-Native both, have a difficult time finding meaning in these kinds of statements. They approach a text like this solely in relation to its authenticity. In this vein, scholars often see these sorts of statements as part of the manufactured Indian mysticism of the narrative of colonial difference. Where scholars take these words seriously, it is then often only as mark of the immature Indian mind, of premodern thinking and out-of-touch mystical metaphysics and epistemology. When Donald Fixico makes similar statements in *The American Indian Mind in a Linear World*, scholars are left with the choice of charging him with reinforcing the manufacturing of Indian mysticism or carrying on the residuals of primitive thinking that were left behind in the rise of modernity. Fixico describes "Indian Thinking" as 'seeing' things from a perspective emphasizing that circles and cycles are central to the world and that all things are related within the universe. For Indian people who are close to their tribal traditions and native values, they think within a native reality consisting of a physical and metaphysical world" (Fixico 2003, 1).

Scott Lyons, not being able to see these sorts of statements outside of the manufacturing of Indian mysticism in the narrative of colonial difference, is quite condescending in his critique of any talk of circles. Of circular time, he writes, "we've all heard the stereotypical line that Indian time is 'circular' rather than 'linear,' a characteristic we apparently share with Disney's *The Lion King*" (Lyons 2010, 9). Lyons rejects the notion of circular time because, he claims, "shape is a characteristic of space, not time" (Lyons 2010, 9).

Iktomi, maintaining the condescending tone of Lyons's original critique, thinks that Lyons has never heard of time-travel since that whole idea pretty much depends on time being marked by characteristics of space.

Condescension aside, Lyon's criticism is rather weak since he does not seem to recognize the fundamental abstraction of spatiality that is at the core of the modernity he wishes to defend. Of Indian space, he writes, "everyone knows what Indian space is like. It is circular, communal, and never near a cosmopolitan center. (Even when it is; it's not). It is always pungent: smoky and sagey in a manner that evokes the past. Things are organized in fours. It is spiritual and stoic" (Lyons 2010, 15).

Lyons's critique is a paradigmatic version of what Deloria envisioned as "Indian scholars merely playing with Indian symbols" (1998, 28).

Lyons seems stuck comprehending circularity as a symbol that is capable of being applied appropriately or not to an Indian world and Indian people. Of course, he concludes, then, that such talk is merely a feature of the narrative of colonial difference in the form of the dark side of traditionalism and the construction of an idealized precolonial past. The problem is that the circle, the division into four, just like the pipe or the Navajo sand painting, is not a symbol, and so Lyons's critique is more a misunderstanding of the nature of symbolism than the lack of a lived relationship to Indian symbols on the part of many current Native scholars. Perhaps it is most clear in the supposed symbolism of a Navajo sand painting, which is after all a kind of painting, and paintings are understood fundamentally as playing with symbols. The easy thought is, then, that the forms created in these sand paintings represent something, and that is how the meaning and the medicine are gathered, but this is not the case. The painting—in particular, the forms or shapes that are created—literally creates something in locality that manifests a medicine or power from the spirit world into the material world, and this power provides healing to the patient. Meaning in locality is an originary manifestation of meaning of a shape or form, as in circularity as it is used by Black Elk, rather than as a symbol as a second order reality that only stands in for something else—an object, a meaning, or the like. In fact, the general idea of a symbol is itself one of delocality, a meaning that floats free from locality both in terms of origination but also in terms of stretching out across all localities in the abstract. The circle in locality has an actual power just as a sand painting does, but without epistemic locality with which to understand its originary and continual manifestation in locality, it appears meaningless or at least significantly less meaningful in a supposedly modern world.

The lack of locality creates a misunderstanding of the nature of words and symbols that often supports the narrative of colonial difference or the premodern primitive perspective of traditionalism versus the advanced and abstract perspective of modernism that Lyons proposes. A delocalized perspective makes us see the word or the symbol as separate from and only laminated onto reality in an ad hoc manner. When confronted with the Indigenous operations of symbols in locality, delocalized thinkers place these ways of thought into the categories of the savage and the primitive. Sigmund Freud, for example, locates the nature of what he calls "savage" philosophy in the overvaluing of psychical processes over physical ones. In this way, he writes, "things become less than the ideas of things" (Freud 1950, 85). James Frazer puts it even more succinctly: "unable to discriminate clearly between words and things, the savage commonly fancies that the link between a name and the person or thing denominated by it is not a mere arbitrary and ideal association but a real and substantial bond which unites the two" (1914, 318). In the context of locality, the bond imagined by the savage mind between words/symbols and things is actually real and palpable. Gary Witherspoon, in his study of Navajo language and philosophy, describes the Navajo understanding of symbols and reality in the following way: a symbol is not "created as a means of representing reality; on the contrary, reality was created or transformed as a manifestation of symbolic form. . . . Language is not a mirror of reality; reality is a mirror of language" (1997, 34). In the context of locality, a symbol does not exist at a level of abstraction. In the context of locality, form literally shapes and creates reality. The *Yeii* (spirit beings) that are formed by the colored sand in the paintings do not represent these *Yeii* as attempted pictures or symbolic representations of them; the material sand shaped into the forms of the *Yeii* become the *Yeii* themselves. The forms of the *Yeii* in the sand painting are the actual *Yeii* rather than mere symbolic representations of them. The *Yeii* are present in the forms that are shaped by the painter in the ceremony, and as the *Yeii* are made present in the painting, they bring their power or medicine to heal the patient who then sits directly on this sand painting. From the perspective of Lyons's, Freud's, and Frazer's delocality, this locality can only be seen as nonsense and from the perspective of the narrative of colonial difference as savagery.

A similar mistake regarding how locality cannot be divided into symbolic and nonsymbolic realms can be seen in Lyons's critique of the slogan "Decolonize Your Diet." Here the mistake is to see the human from a delocalized perspective, such that specific claims about particular humans (the symbols) must match the universal properties of the human species (reality). Lyons describes Alfred and Corntassel's "call to decolonize Native diets" . . . "a bad idea" that is "better handled by nutritionists and health-care professionals." The bad idea is, he writes, "that Natives have a 'genetic predisposition' toward certain traditional foods and many health issues today" arise from losing "our daily connection to those foods and hence [having] our diets 'colonized.'" Lyons calls this "another racialist argument" that is "answered best by a Leech Lake elder named Wally Humphrey who . . . reminded [the Leech Lake people] that our fish—'probably our wild rice too'—was contaminated by mercury and dioxins and thus should *not* be overprivileged as a traditional food." Lyons concludes that "unhealthy diets have nothing to do with 'race' and everything to do with available dietary choices and nutritional education" (2016, 144). The problem with Lyons's critique is that the issue of decolonizing one's diet is not an issue of the delocalized symbol of race in relation to the reality of the human species, but rather the way that the delocalized symbol of the human species obscures the relationship of matter and form to reality (in this case, the health of a particular person) in the context of locality.

Another example might help to clarify this mistake of delocality. I often hear similar claims about scientific knowledge and universal human health in contrast to Indigenous fasting ceremonies. For example, in the preparation for *hanblecheye* (the Lakota term for a prayer fast or vision quest), one can often eat a large amount of buffalo stew just before fasting from food and water for four days. From the perspective of universalized human health, this is particularly problematic—not just going without food or water for four days but in particular the consuming of buffalo meat just before going four days without water. Universal human health science tells us that meat requires a lot of water to digest, and so eating this buffalo meat just before going without water for four days only increases the level of dehydration. In the context of that ceremony though, elders and teachers say that the buffalo will sustain the faster through those four days, but from the perspective of human health science, the buffalo will likely make completing the ceremony impossible. The inability to see how the buffalo could sustain the faster over the four days while not eating or drinking arises from the same delocalized perspective that sees the sand-formed *Yeii* as mere pictures or symbols of something else. Human beings are not generic delocalized phenomena that can be understood through universal ideas of human health any more than sand paintings are just artistic expressions in sand. Human beings are originary and continual manifestations in locality or out of the land.

In the context of the Lakota locality, the buffalo has a material connection to the Lakota people, and so ingesting the material buffalo in preparation for the prayer fast creates a life-sustaining power in just the way the creating the material forms of the *Yeii* in sand in the Navajo sand painting creates the power of the *Yeii*. Little Wound, as recorded by Walker, says that "when anything is food, it is *wakan* because it makes life" (Walker 1980, 69). *Wakan* is often translated as "sacred" or "mystery," but can be thought of more specifically as "life-giving or energy-converting power." The *wakan* in food is its transforming or life-giving power as manifest in its *tun* or *ton*, which is its spirit or potency. Just as in an offering of food to spirits, "the spirits cannot take these things with it (i.e., the actual material food), but the *ton* of the things it takes with it and uses … [*ton*] is that which the spirits get from things which are offered them" (Walker 1980, 108). We can understand the manner in which the buffalo as food gives some of its *ton* to the person who consumes this *wakan* substance (as all food is) in the description that George Sword gives to the use of buffalo chips in any ceremony pertaining to the buffalo: "a Lakota should make incense with buffalo chips in this manner. He should make a fire of anything that will burn easily, and when there are burning coals, he should put dried buffalo chips on them so as to make a smoke. This is because the spirit of a buffalo remains in dried buffalo chips and it is in the smoke from them" (Walker 1980, 77). Just as in the offering of food or the consuming of food as *wakan*, the smoke of "an inanimate thing," says Sword, is its *nagila* or spirit, which "is the same thing as the *ton* of anything" other than *Wakan Tanka* as *Tobtob Kin* (Walker 1980, 98). In the smoke of the buffalo chips as well as the buffalo meat as food, there is a giving of the *nagila* or *ton* of the buffalo, which is why the faster who eats the buffalo meat before prayer fasting carries some of the *ton* of the animal who can face down a forty-below-zero wind in a four-foot snow drift for days without flinching.

Black Elk's talk of circularity is a manifestation of locality in the context of the Four Winds and division of the directions into four. Tate is the wind. The Four Winds are Tate's four sons who create the circle of the four directions as a circle around the world that then bisects the world into fours, visualized as a circle with a cross through it. Tate's four sons, the Four Winds, must endlessly walk this path or the four directions around the world. The journey of each son is measured as a fourth of a year, and so the circle is itself a measure of fours. All measurements of time are then seen through the image of a circle of fours (four parts of the day, the night, the moon, the year). This division of the world into four directions gave it stability. The circle of the four directions reflects the constant movement around the only stability there is according to Lakota thought: the four directions and in general the division into four. While absolutely everything else is constantly moving and changing, the four directions are the one thing that stays the same.

The circle of the four directions (that continue in a spiral out to the Sky and Earth but then back to the Center (the *nagila* of the person), to a spiral of seven directions in total) is then not just about geography. The actual horizons of the sunrise, sunset, and so on are only the first piece of the meaning of this circle. The four directions provide a concrete but dynamically layered framework for the world and seeing ourselves through a lens of kinship and relationality and for placing ourselves in a sacred center that itself is grounded while dynamically moving in relationship to the beings, elements, and energies around us. The circle of the directions as seen in this way is an expression of locality and even human locality itself. The circle of the four directions is an epistemic practice of locality. The circle of the four directions in the epistemic practices of locality are layered circles of the West, North, East, and

South, upon the Heart, Mind, Body, and Spirit, and upon Autumn, Winter, Spring, and Summer, and so much more.

The four directions are not speculative philosophical claims about metaphysical or epistemological divisions in the universe. In the context of epistemic locality, there is no need to either define/defend an articulation of the separation of mind and body or defend the four directions against critiques of Cartesian mind/body dualism. As Black Elk might say, I do not "know" anything about the heart, mind, body, and spirit in that way because that would require "knowing" something delocally. What Black Elk does understand is the function of this circle of fours as a way of manifesting the world and a human relationship to it, through locality. Black Elk does understand this circle of fours in his experience and in relationship to a dynamic and personal human/world interchange. What Black Elk "sees" in coming to know the truth of the circle of fours is not a truth of a delocalized world but of a process of being in kinship with a world of locality.

Thinking through the circle of the four directions is useful for reflecting on the limits of Iktomi's views on propositional knowledge in his story above. Each direction, as Black Elk describes the circle of four, has a color and an animal, often many animals, and many more layers of meaning and metaphor. The West is called *wiyokpiyata*, toward where the sun goes down. The direction, as seen in this rendering of it, is not a place (the West) but a movement, a path or journey. This movement (called the West) is dynamically layered. It is black. It is darkness and death. It is also life in the form of the ocean and life-giving water that is a gift of the *Wakinyan*, the Thunder Beings. The dynamic layering of the movement we call in English the West, the North, the East, and the South can even conceptualize the movement of a person's life. Black Elk puts it like this: "Is the south not the source of life? . . . And does man not advance from there to the setting sun of his life? Then does he not approach the colder North where the white hairs are? And does he not then arrive, if he lives, at the source of light and understanding, which is the east. Then does he not return to where he began . . . to give back his life to all life, and his flesh to the earth whence it came. The more you think about this, the more meaning you will see in it" (Neihardt 1932, 124). Black Elk's final statement is important here because it not only indicates the complex layering process of getting from the personal and phenomenological movement toward the setting sun and so on to the complex layering of meaning for understanding our path in life but also indicates the open-ended horizon of meaning that is possible from what has been layered upon that personal and phenomenological movement toward the setting sun.

In the Navajo locality there is a similar layering upon the movement of the directions. The West is layered through the dusk, the color yellow, Abalone, the San Francisco Peaks, Calling God, Changing Woman, and Holy Girl as well as the Rio Grande that cuts east to west across the Navajo locality. The south is the day or midday, the color blue, turquoise, Mt. Taylor, Behwochidii, Born for Water, and Holy Boy as well as the San Juan River that cuts from north to south across the Navajo locality. This dynamic layer carries on through the different phenomenological movement of the directions. Coming to know all the details of the layered and dynamic meanings of the four directions is not the purpose of this text. What is important is coming to see the dynamic layering process of each direction as it arises out of the personal and phenomenological movement toward each direction. The movement through each direction as a way of conceptualizing the movement of life, as Black Elk conveys it, shows us the dynamic layering and movement that are significant features of the circle of the four directions themselves in addition to the dynamic laying that extends outward in the movement of each direction individually. Both of these layers of movement (around the circle of the four directions and outward through the layer of movement in each direction itself) are instructive of thinking in locality in contrast to delocalized thinking. The simplifying of our epistemologies as directed toward something concrete, even final and simple (often present in Western and even Native academics), constructs our knowledge around only one direction, and that direction is final and simple rather than dynamic and deeply layered with metaphors of different meanings. For example, we often see the coming to know (the light and understanding of the East) as something simple and final, rather than as only one temporary phase of movement in the process of our epistemic journey. What is lost in this more limited epistemology is the sense of process of understanding that is not limited to what can be accomplished with the one simplified direction of the mind—the way that meaning is layered in epistemic locality. Western and Native academics alike often focus on the process of reaching knowledge in a finite sense, reaching delocalized knowledge. Knowledge is understood as a complete process that has a concrete goal, an endpoint in some proposition that is true and can be held in the mind or written in a book—delocalized from any originary manifestation in locality. There is a great simplicity in this thinking. The simplicity has both positive and negative outcomes. On one hand, the simplicity creates something that is graspable and feels complete, finished. This creation is also simple enough to carry with us beyond locality and documentable both in that is supported by other propositions that are thought to be true and in that it can become a shorthand text for something we call "knowledge"—again fundamentally as a form of delocality. Whenever there is a question of knowledge, one need only produce the words from this proposition and feel a resolution of the dissonance the question creates. One can achieve this feeling of resolution across all localities, but this feeling of resolution is false and the unease that feels a need of resolution is the unease, solitude, and immaturity of delocality itself.

The problem is that it is greatly oversimplified both in terms of the process as well as the end of knowledge. This is a common result of Iktomi trying to think and be beyond locality. Iktomi wants the quickest and easiest route to some personal goal or some goal that brings him power and glory. He can often achieve this goal but only at the expense of nearly everything else, including the goal itself in the long run. From the perspective of the circle of the four directions, understanding that comes to the mind as in the dawn in the East is only one part of the circular movement that is the human reflection in locality. This circular movement of the four directions is not only something that happens in human reflection but is a way to understand or see the ground of the movement of the earth, the animals, the heavens, the seasons, the energies, and so on from the perspective of locality. Our attempt to place ourselves in a centering relationship to this dynamic movement of the four directions is an attempt to move with this dynamic movement. In many Native traditions, it is this movement on the grandest scale that English speakers often translate as God and why Native traditions give so much emphasis to harmony and balance.

The attempt to find knowledge for ourselves in our minds—the methodology of epistemic delocality—is both an easy and very hard road. It is very easy to acquire significant propositional knowledge through this method, but the knowledge acquired through this method is never capable of being sustained. This knowledge is too personal and self-centered, and it is too personally goal oriented. The knowledge that comes from looking in one simple direction (without multiple layers of meaning and dynamic movement as grounded in locality) is far too simple to be sustainable beyond the moment and immediate desires of the knower. The great irony of delocalized knowledge is that while trying to be universal, it throws itself back in the farthest reaches of isolation and solitude. This way of knowing cannot possibly align with the complex and dynamic layering and movement in locality. Knowledge as simplified in true statements or propositions can never match the complex and dynamic motion of the world it tries to approach and reach the ends that it seeks.

However, the attempt to do so is itself a result, in part, of the desire for something simple, final, and complete in itself. Thus, the simple ideas of knowledge are themselves a result of the desire for something simple. This is a perfect example of the circling web of Iktomi thinking that arises from a lack of grounding in locality. The thinking of the circle of four directions, on the other hand, sees knowing or understanding as only one momentary part in the dawning of the East that moves (in one version at least) from the West (from the spark of passion and fear in the coming of darkness in the setting sun as well as the joy of the coming of life in the waters, thunders, and ocean) through the cold, quiet stillness and cleansing wind of spirit in the North and on to the bounty of the South and the summer (the body, the physical, the material world, or into action or practice). But the process can start in the South as well, which is why there is often emotional release or emotional sparks (movement toward the Heart/West) when we are working. (This is why many will take a walk when feeling emotionally constricted.)

This process of the four directions is never complete though. A localized process of movement continues along this circular path with the unfolding of each direction growing toward the next and even being intertwined with it in contrary aspects. This can be seen in the way I can witness a spring and a sunrise move toward and blend with a summer and midday and so on. The contrary intertwining is constant as well. The South is sometimes associated with the color white and the North with the color red, but it is the cold snow of the North that is white and the warm blood of bounty of the buffalo hunt in the summer that is red. Thus, there is the oppositional blending of one direction with the other in order to understand the larger circle of the directions itself and its meaning and movement. The human thinking that follows the locally grounded path of the four directions is then a dynamic movement both in terms of flowing from all the aspects of a human experience but also in terms of flowing through that which is beyond human experience in the dynamic movement itself. The circle of fours is beyond human experience as a dynamic movement but is not beyond that locality; it is through locality, there is little room for the self-centered, personal, goal-directed aspect of a search for knowledge as an end for our own needs and wants. Iktomi can only fulfill his own desires through removing himself from his relationship to that larger circle, by removing himself from locality, from kinship.

Black Elk

While recounting his vision, Black Elk speaks the words that were told to him by the fourth Grandfather ("he of the place where you

are always facing [the south], whence comes the power to grow")
regarding the red and black roads. After being "still a little while
to hear the birds sing," the fourth Grandfather speaks to Black Elk
again:

"Behold the earth!" So I looked down and saw it lying yonder
like a hoop of peoples, and in the center bloomed the holy stick that
was a tree, and where it stood there crossed two roads, a red one
and a black. "From where the giant lives (the north) to where you
always face (the south) the red road goes, the road of good," the
Grandfather said, "and on it shall your nation walk. The black road
goes from where the thunder beings live (the west) to where the
sun continually shines (the east), a fearful road, a road of troubles
and of war. On this also you shall walk, and from it you shall have
the power to destroy a people's foes. (Neihardt 1932, 29)

Black Elk and the Philosophical Black Road

The circle of four that marks the four directions and divides the Lakota
world (world as a manifestation of locality rather than of the earth as
a planet) is bisected by two lines or roads in Black Elk's terminology,
carrying forward the vision of the Four Winds traveling only the four
sections of the circle around the world. One of these lines or roads runs
north and south in the image of the circle of four, and the other runs
east and west in the image. When Black Elk speaks of these as roads that
are black (east and west road) and red (north and south road), it is not
completely clear how much of this conception is from his own vision,
from the interpretation of his vision, or from his conception of *Lakol*

wicoun, or Lakota philosophy. Albert White Hat Sr. views the image of the black road and the red road as a reflection of Catholic influence on Lakota philosophy, particularly as it has sometimes been articulated, perhaps even by Black Elk himself, as the black road to hell and the red road to heaven. White Hat says that in the time of Black Elk, the Catholic Church in Lakota reservations commonly had a chart that showed the red road to heaven and the black road to hell, which "in the late 1800s and early 1900s [was] used in training Lakota catechists," including most likely Black Elk himself. White Hat remembers going with his mother to visit Father Buechel, who had hanging on his office wall "a chart showing the red road to heaven and the black road to hell." White Hat says, "I've seen a document that said Black Elk used that chart a lot in his teaching." So "when Neihardt interviewed" Black Elk for *Black Elk Speaks*, White Hat thinks that "Black Elk might have said, 'It's *like* the red road and the black road of the church,'" which Neihardt then turned into "Black Elk saying that if you walk the red road, you believe in one God and go to heaven, and if you walk the black road, you go to hell" (White Hat 2012, 77). While I acknowledge the concern of an influence of Christian ideology onto *Lakol Wicoun*, I am only concerned with such as it regards an influence of Christian ideology in the context of delocality and the coloniality of power. Black Elk's use of the Catholic chart in the context of speaking to Catholics, even Lakota Catholics, about *Lakol Wicoun* seems perfectly aligned with what I describe as a common Indigenous philosophy practice of shaping what is said for the listener rather than on the basis of some abstract sense of truth or authenticity. The concern here seems to be one of authenticity, which in part at least places it in the context of the narrative of colonial difference and delocalized truth. The extent to which the influence of Christian ideology onto *Lakol Wicoun* results in a delocalized sense of truth or a conception of being and value that is based in a binary of abstract good and evil as framed by the coloniality of power is the extent to which the influence of Christian ideology undermines *Lakol Wicoun* as a philosophy of Lakota locality. This, I believe, is Albert White Hat Sr.'s primary concern when he says, "*Black Elk Speaks* gives a feeling of heaven and hell in our philosophy" (White Hat 2012, 77). That White Hat Sr.'s concern is one of delocality and the coloniality of power is also clear in his rejection of the common translations and increasingly common understanding within segments of the Lakota nation that terms like *Sicun, Wakan Tanka, Tobtob Kin,* and *Taku Wakan* reference a supreme being or God rather than a multiplicity of powers and energies within the Lakota locality. In the context of this work, I use Black Elk's conception of the black and red roads only in the context of tools of epistemic locality, which remove White Hat Sr.'s concern of the delocality and coloniality of power within the Catholic doctrines of the binary distinction between good and evil, heaven and hell.

The black road from Black Elk's vision as a tool of epistemic locality corresponds to Iktomi's attempts to reach knowledge through delocality, to reach knowledge for himself and through himself. Using Black Elk's vision, one could see the black road in the great destructive power that comes through propositional knowledge in the history of Western technology as well as the penchant for conflict that comes from following the black road from our own desires and fears to our own ideas about how to understand and act upon our own desires and fears, as the black road is manifestly kinship-less. The red road goes from the body or manifest world to the unmanifest or spirit world and vice versa. Walking on this road, understood as a way of thinking in contrast to the thinking on the black road, focuses on achieving understanding as a function of kinship.

Thinking and processing our desires and fears in the context of the red road, as a tool of epistemic locality, transform our individual desires and fears, which are the basis of shaping action in the context of thinking on the black road, through our kinship as the unmanifest or spirit world of locality itself. The movement to the red North of spirit in the context of the circle of the four directions is a movement through kinship itself or the context of kinship itself in the unmanifest or spirit world of locality itself. Spiritual kinship or the unmanifest connectivity of everything in the context of locality—as seen in the concept of *Mitakuye oyasin* (everything is a relative)—transforms our desires, fears, thoughts, and questions by moving them through the direction of spirit (our unmanifested kinship modality) before completing the cycle into understanding (East) and action (South). The dawning in the East (the understanding) that comes through spiritual kinship in this sense (or what Black Elk calls the red road) is quite different than what comes to understanding along the black road, which instead of moving around the circle of the four directions—going from the fear and desires in the West to the spiritual kinship in the North—attempts to take an Iktomi-style shortcut on the line that bisects the circle west and east.

The Iktomi-style shortcut of the black road is a road of fear and necessary in the context of war, as Black Elk notes, because it is "from it you shall have the power to destroy a people's foes" (Neihardt 1932, 29). In "Theories of Coloniality and Indigenous Liberation through the Land: A Critical Look at *Red Skin, White Masks*," I describe the black road from Black Elk's vision as corresponding to "the Manichean struggle between the colonizer and the colonized, between good and evil," but in the context of the struggle against settler colonial power, which operates through this destructive force, "the black road can be seen as the nuclear option"—an ultimately self-destructive path but seen by Black Elk in his time and more broadly in the face of settler violence and power as necessary for even some of his people to survive (Burkhart 2016, 5). This is the reality of engaging in war—in a literal and metaphorical sense—from the point of view of surviving settler violence and power rather than war as the process by which conquerors achieve power and glory. War from the point of view of the survival of Indigenous people under settler violence and power is the choice to accept murderous violence and the likely death of many of your own people, so that some people or something of your own people will survive the genocidal force of settler violence and power in particular and the violence and destructive force of coloniality in general. As I put it in that article, "from Black Elk's vision, [the black] road was presented as necessary for at least some Indian people to survive, but it was a road where most everyone dies" (Burkhart 2016, 5).

Indigenous philosophy in particular and Native American and Indigenous studies more generally in the context of a settler colonial academy often view the necessity of the black road in the context of the assimilation of Indigenous philosophy into settler institutions and concepts in order for Indigenous philosophy to survive or the assimilation of Indigenous governance into settler institutions and concepts in order to maintain some level of sovereignty within the guardianship framework of a settler state like the United States. However, this is like a nuclear option for the survival of Indigenous philosophy. Philosophy as it happens in the settler colonial academy is already a fundamentally delocalized enterprise. The concepts and methods of philosophy are fundamentally shaped around the practices of epistemic delocality and coloniality. One way that Indigenous philosophers have addressed the possible need to assimilate to the concepts of the settler state and the settler academy while trying to protect the locality of Indigenous philosophies and lifeways is through an attempt to isolate Indigenous philosophy to the red road, keeping it in locality and in the community, while engaging in an externalized and delocalized black road effort that confronts the settler state and the settler academy. Dale Turner, for example, describes "indigenous philosophy proper" as a "kind of activity" that "involves highly specialized forms of thinking; it is a distinctly Indigenous activity. The Anishinaabe have the Midewiwin Lodge (Midé), a society of medicine people who are responsible for preserving Anishinaabe philosophy and ceremonies, . . . and all Anishinaabe people, although most are not privileged to sit in the Midé, learn from these indigenous philosophers" (2006, 99-100). While clearly the Midé is a place of Indigenous philosophy, to make this the only place of philosophy for Anishinaabe people seems to greatly oversimplify the nature of philosophy and possible philosophical practice and reflection. To isolate philosophy in the Midé is to make philosophy a solely institutional practice; in this case, philosophers are like a priest class that do all the philosophical work for the common folks, and the common folks are precluded from philosophy. Of course, the Midé is an important Anishinaabe institution that does significant philosophical work for the Anishinaabe people, but there seems to be a great number of other avenues for Anishinaabe philosophy to operate, including in the most mundane affairs, which if true would not insulate Anishinaabe philosophy from the black road engagement with the settler state and settler academy.

For Turner, the capacity to insulate and isolate Anishinaabe is rather significant because one of the important roles of the academic Indigenous philosopher ("word warriors" who "ought to be intimately familiar with the legal and political discourses of the state") is "to assert, defend, and protect the rights, sovereignty, and nationhood of indigenous communities" (2006, 95). Philosophy so defined, as connected to Indigenous nationhood, is necessarily at least quasi-institutional. Questions about proper philosophy and proper philosophers seem fundamentally politicized on Turner's view. If Indigenous philosophy and philosophers are operating in relationship to rights, sovereignty, and nationhood and so negotiating these with the state, it rightly seems important to keep the traditional Indigenous philosophical institutions out of this negotiation with the state. The Midé creates power through locality and so has little function in a delocalized political sphere of the state. Or worse, by bringing the Midé into this delocalized political sphere, one could be compromising the locality and thereby the power of the Midé. It remains questionable, though, whether the Midé can truly be protected from the political compromise of the black road and the engagement with the settler state in order to negotiate and defend Indigenous rights, sovereignty, and nationhood within the conceptual framework and power structure of the settler state.

The seemingly inherent delocality of both the academic and political sphere gives rise to "a host of serious (some argue insurmountable) epistemological problems in publishing indigenous philosophy," such as *Black Elk Speaks*, according to Turner. Some of these problems, according to Turner, are the oral tradition and Native language of Indigenous knowledge systems as well the "from the inside" perspective of Native philosophy, "which means its content must be situated in an indigenous cultural context" (Turner 2006, 100). The best philosophical project, on Turner's account, is for an "indigenous intellectual [to] engage European ideas" philosophically as well as politically. He writes, "it is not enough to simply engage European thought on its own terms; Indigenous intellectuals need to critically engage European ideas, methodologies, and theories to show how they have marginalized, distorted, and ignored indigenous voices," which centralizes the critique of the "meaning and praxis of colonialism" in the activity of the Indigenous intellectual (word warrior) (Turner 2006, 100–101). The dilemma for the word warrior is still "what it means . . . to claim that they have unique ways of understanding the world, and that the difference matters, both legally and politically; at the same time, they must insist on greater participation in what the dominant culture deems to be exclusively non-indigenous intellectual practices" (Turner 2006, 101). In particular, the dilemma is putting forth this word warrior critique of coloniality in the "language of the dominant culture," and in such a way that it actually impacts the political reality for Indigenous communities. The point is that, as word warriors, Indigenous philosophers must critique political and philosophical coloniality but do so in such a way that the political and philosophical colonizers will actually hear what we are saying (speaking to them in their language and methods) and perhaps even take it seriously, hopefully, to the degree that it has some impact.

Turner uses Donald Fixico's *An Indian Mind in a Linear World* as an example of an Indigenous philosophical text that fails both to critically engage coloniality as well as engage with European philosophy in a meaningful manner. Fixico's use of "Western philosophical concepts—'thinking,' 'seeing,' 'physical world,' 'metaphysical world,'" and so on—is "uncritical," and "doom[s]" his project "right from the first sentence," writes Turner (102). The way Fixico uses these Western philosophical concepts puts his work in the context of Western philosophy, Turner claims, but allows him to "draw conclusions about European philosophical thinking without actually 'doing' Western philosophy." The term "metaphysical" is highly problematic in a Western philosophical context, Turner claims, since "much of twentieth-century philosophy has been obsessed with avoiding metaphysical language." Turner is puzzled, then, as to why Fixico uses "one of the most contentious and some would argue vaguest concepts in the Western tradition to do so much work to explain what he believes is unique indigenous distinction in American Indian philosophy" (102).

While Turner is correct in that Indigenous philosophy and philosophers must critically engage the coloniality of power in any truly meaningful project of Indigenous philosophy, he is not clear, from my perspective, on just why this is necessary and what is necessary to meaningfully engage coloniality. The structure reality of coloniality creates, as shown, the fact of colonial difference—the attempted lamentation of delocalized European locality onto the Indigenous locality. Thus, it is fundamental to the project of reasserting Indigenous locality to mark off the fact of colonial difference—the delocalized European locality. On this account, there is no "inside" versus "outside" for Indigenous philosophy per se because coloniality layers delocality onto locality. The reason that Turner finds Fixico so convoluted is that he does not see that Fixico is engaging with Western philosophical and political discourse in a subtler way than Turner suggests for the word warrior. Fixico's engagement with Western philosophical discourse, using the concepts of "thinking," "seeing," "metaphysical," and the like, is not directed at an equal level (through the black road) with the Western philosophical use of those terms, those terms as created and maintained in epistemic delocality. Fixico is using those terms to mark, in his expression of Indigenous concepts of locality (through the red road), the fact of colonial difference.

This usage disrupts the delocality of those terms, as even Turner would like them to be used, and in that way the delocality and coloniality of Western philosophy as it operates over Indigenous locality. The ambiguity or what Turners describes as "incoherent" terminology and modality of Fixico's work does not render it hopeless. The ambiguity or seeming incoherence by Fixico in the use of a concept like "metaphysical" is what gives the work the capacity to disrupt the coloniality of philosophy through the marking of the fact of colonial difference. What Turner sees as ambiguity or incoherence in Fixico's use of language is simply the perspective of delocality on the expressions of language in locality. Other less ambiguous terminologies or modalities—for example, more directly engaging in the critical Western philosophical discussion on its own terms or expressing the uniqueness of Indigenous thought through Native terminology—are much more likely to fall victim to the narrative of colonial difference and be consumed by coloniality as a constructed alterity and delocality as the most basic framework for epistemological and semantic significance.

In addition, the obsession with avoiding metaphysical language on the part of twentieth-century philosophy is not genuine. Also, it is not correct to say that properly metaphysical philosophy is no longer valued in Western philosophical discourse or that it ever really went away. One need only peruse the significant number of articles and books under the heading of Speculative Realism, a current form of metaphysical realism that explicitly rejects the turn away from metaphysics following Kant. As Deloria clarifies in his work, the attempt to avoid metaphysical language on the part of Western philosophers is merely a feature of the reifying of the assumed metaphysical system that underlies Western philosophy and Western science. The so-called naturalization of philosophical concepts and language is nothing short of normalizing metaphysical systems and structures that can then be "avoided" only insofar as they are now ubiquitous. The "erasure" of metaphysical concepts and language is of the same order as the "erasure" of the structure of coloniality in the Western concepts and praxis of history, subjectivity, polity, nationhood, and so on.

Sometimes an attempt at red road epistemology actual hides black road epistemology, or attempts at presenting locality actually serve to obscure locality through delocality. An example of this can be seen in John H. Moore's "Truth and Tolerance in Native American Epistemology." As an anthropologist, Moore focuses on the structure of knowledge within a culture and how knowledge is produced and maintained, and how new knowledge is created within that context. Anthropologists are also concerned with "who controls knowledge" and "how philosophical knowledge is acted out in ceremonies and in activities of priests, sha-mans, and other intellectuals." In this way, there is a focus on the fact that "the cosmologies and epistemologies maintained by Native North American philosophers are not only different from those of Western philosophy, but radically different among themselves" (Moore 1998, 272). While this way of investigating Indigenous philosophy allows for greater concentration on the "inside" perspective of Indigenous philosophers, who are here too the "priests, shamans," and other individuals culturally sanctioned by tribal institutions, it very often falls victim to the narrative of colonial difference, which limits its capacity to reflect Indigenous epistemology through epistemic locality. The focus on structure of knowledge with a cultural context might seem like a version of epistemic locality, but it is actually a denial of locality and operates through an illusion of locality that masks its fundamental framework of delocality. The claim Moore makes that the "significant scientific advances" of Native societies "in such fields as astronomy, agronomy, art, and architecture" are "consistently couched in religious language, and surrounded by ritual and supernatural belief" seems to take more seriously the epistemologies of these societies on their own terms but actually serves to undermine their power in locality by ignoring the fact of colonial difference—the fact that one kind of language that expressed this power of locality is called "religious" and another that expressed its power through delocality is called "scientific" (Moore, 1998, 272). The focus on difference with a narrative of colonial difference covers over the fact that locality creates a context of sameness through locality that supersedes the superficial differences that are created through epistemic delocality in contrast to the way that delocality creates the illusion of sameness across localities that are actually different in the context of locality. Specificity does not necessarily breed locality. Personalized narratives, specificity, and particularity of the sort often found in Native studies texts can just as likely obscure locality rather than reveal it.

Black Elk

I will say something about heyokas and the heyoka ceremony, which seems to be very foolish, but is not so.

Only those who have had visions of the thunder beings of the west can act as heyokas. They have sacred power and they share some of this with all the people, but they do it through funny actions. When a vision comes from the thunder beings of the west, it comes with terror like a thunder storm; but when the storm of vision has passed, the world is greener and happier; for wherever the truth of vision comes upon the world, it is like a rain. The world, you see, is happier after the terror of the storm.

But in the heyoka ceremony, everything is backwards, and it is planned that the people shall be made to feel jolly and happy first, so that it may be easier for the power to come to them. You have noticed that the truth comes into this world with two faces. One is sad with suffering, and the other laughs; but it is the same face, laughing or weeping. When people are already in despair, maybe the laughing face is better for them; and when they feel too good and are too sure of being safe, maybe the weeping face is better for them to see. And so I think that is what the ceremony is for (Neihardt 1932, 149).

The proposition that contradicts itself would stand like a monument (with a Janus head) over the propositions of logic, facing both true and false.

—Wittgenstein

The truth is what I! do with it.

—Iktomi

On the Two Faces of Truth or Refragmenting as Regrounding in the Land

When Black Elk asks his listener to notice "that the truth comes into this world with two faces," he is not merely speaking of the dualistic intertwining of "laughing and weeping" but the dualistic intertwining of true and false in epistemic locality. The one side of the binary duality between true and false turns into a two-sided face of truth in epistemic locality: true *or* false becomes true *and* false just as life and death are two sides (the visible and invisible) of the same thing in the *Lakol Wicoun* or Lakota locality. Through the backward side of the face of truth—in this case, the humor of the *heyoka* ceremony that is the other side of the face of weeping—Black Elk give us some direction in undoing one of the most basic dualistic binaries that undergirds the power of delocality and coloniality itself: the binary of true and false—considered even by Aristotle as the primary form of opposition. The binary of true and false appears to be one of the most basic assumptions of Western thought and is seen most often in the form of the claim that every statement is either true or false.

In the foundations of Western logic, this aphorism forms the twin foundations of logical laws: the law of excluded middle (LEM) and the law of non-contradiction (LNC). Often Aristotle is credited with the first written expression of this idea in Western thought: (LEM) "Of any one subject, one thing must be either asserted or denied" (*Metaphysics* 1011b24), and (LNC) "It is impossible that the same thing can at the same time both belong and not belong to the same object and in the same respect, and all other specifications that might be made, let them be added to meet local objections" (*Metaphysics* 1005b19–23). Aristotle's expression of the LNC is meant to be very limited because of course there are many ways in which a thing can both belong and not belong to the same object even at the same time in the same respect. Thus, he adds "and all other specifications that might be made, let them be added to meet local objections." Aristotle's limitation requires a complete, abstract delocalization—he even mentions the word "local," which is a clear indication that delocality itself is what divides truth and falsity in this absolute sense. This particular version of the LNC is called ontological, whereas "the opinion that opposite assertions are not simultaneously true is the firmest of all" (*Metaphysics* 1011b13–14) is called logical, and "it is impossible for anyone to believe that the same thing is and is not, as some consider Heraclitus said" (*Metaphysics* 1005b23–25) is called psychological.

Aristotle considers the LNC as a first and therefore indemonstrable principle because "a principle which everyone must have who understands anything that is, is not a hypothesis; and that which everyone must know who knows anything" (*Metaphysics* 1005b18–20). Of those who might ask for a demonstration of the LNC, Aristotle claims they "lack education" because "a demonstration of everything is impossible," as that would require an infinite regress (*Metaphysics* 1006a6–12). We can "demonstrate negatively" the LNC, Aristotle claims, against the "many physicists" who claim that it is possible for the same thing to be and not be "if our opponent will only say something; and if he says nothing, it is absurd to seek to give an account of our views to one who cannot give an account of anything, in so far as he cannot do so. For such a man, as such, is from the start no better than a vegetable." Aristotle's critique of Heraclitus's anti-LNC claim that "everything is and is not" is that such a claim "seems to make everything true," and his critique of Anaxagoras's anti-LEM claim, "that an intermediate exists between two contradictories," is that such a claim "makes everything false" (*Metaphysics* 1012a25–29).

Critics of the LNC have not remained as silent vegetables, however. Heraclitus, although not directly responding to the LNC since his words predate Aristotle's by over a century, makes a variety of statements that conflict with the LNC and/or the LEM in sometimes rather complex ways.

The road up and the road down are the same road. (Robinson 1987, 47)

We step and do not step into the same rivers; we are and we are not. (Robinson 1987, 35)

Although Aristotle's expressions of the LNC and the LEM are directed at Heraclitus, Heraclitus's words go well beyond the issue as articulated by Aristotle. Heraclitus creates a technical meaning for the Greek *logos*, traditionally, a ground, a plea, a word, or an account, which becomes for him something like the idea of originary manifestation of meaning in one's spoken word. Heraclitus writes, "of this *logos's* being forever do men prove to be uncomprehending, both before they hear and once they have heard it. For although all things happen according to *logos*, they are like the unexperienced experiencing words and deeds. . . . Other men are unaware of what they do when they are awake just as they are forgetful of what they do when they are asleep" (Robinson 1987, 1). Aristotle notices the ambiguity in these words. Even in the first sentence, the context of "forever" is unclear, he pointed out. It is not clear if "forever" is referencing "being" or "prove" (*Rhetoric* 1407b11–18). Aristotle regarded this ambiguity as a weakness in Heraclitus's thought, but does not see what seems like Heraclitus's purposeful attempt at layering complex and dynamic meaning in his words—a layering not unlike the layering of the four directions in Black Elk's description. The spoken word is both forever in locality and forever incomprehensible out of locality. Heraclitus, even in the fragmentary nature of what is written and in part because of it—at least in the context of any attempted abstract, delocalized framing of the meaning of his words—displays perhaps the clearest understanding of epistemic locality of any philosopher in the Western canon.

In modern philosophy, Hegel picks up where Heraclitus left off two millennia before (Hegel was born in 1770 and Heraclitus died in 475 BCE). Where Heraclitus sees a world unified through the dynamic strife and resolution of opposites, Hegel and Marx embrace contradictions as a meaningful and important part of reality. Hegel seems to see reality itself as inconsistent: "Something moves, not because at one moment it is here and another there, but because at one and the same moment it is here and not here, because in this 'here,' it at once is and is not" (1977, 440). For Hegel and Marx, it is the resolution of contradictory states that drives the development of the history and subjectivity (or society in the case of Marx) forward. Just before Hegel, Kant argued that some contradictions, as in the statement that "The world must have a beginning in time" are an unavoidable side-effect of trying to comprehend the world as a whole, apart from what can be given to experience (Kant 1997, 386). For Kant, these contradictions are "a natural and unavoidable illusion" as unavoidable as "the sea appear[ing] higher in the middle than at the shores" (Kant 1997, 386). Hegel goes further though, praising Kant's thought that contradictions of reason are "essential and necessary" as "one of the most important and profound advances of the philosophy of modern times," but then criticizing Kant's sense that these contradictions are limited to human reasons attempt to stretch beyond its limits in grasping for an understanding of actual reality beyond experience (1991, 92). Hegel calls Kant's understanding of contradictions, finally, as "trivial" as it is "profound" because it "consists merely in a tenderness for things of this world" rather than seeing that the "stain of contradiction ought to be in the essence of what is in the world" (1991, 92). These contradictory states (the same thing at the same time is and is not) are not really an expression of the multiplicity within locality, as Heraclitus seems to see it, and are the framework for the intertwining of the true and the false in Black Elk's statement and in the context of epistemic locality. These contradictory states are not a true multiplicity in Kant or Hegel—in Kant, because the error is only one of reason, and in Hegel, because the contradictory states, even though they exist in the world beyond errors of reason, are yet only the opposites that drive development through a synthesis or resolution of these opposite in Hegel's philosophical system.

In the stories of teachings of the historical Buddha, the following dialogue takes place regarding the doctrine of rebirth:

> Gotama, where is the monk reborn whose mind is thus freed? Vaccha, it is not true to say that he is reborn. Then, Gotama, he is not reborn. Vaccha, it is not true to say that he is not reborn. Then, Gotama, he is both reborn and not reborn. Vaccha, it is not true to say that he is both reborn and not reborn. Then, Gotama, he is neither reborn nor not reborn. Vaccha, it is not true to say that he is neither reborn nor not reborn. (Robinson 1967, 54)

In East Asian philosophy, there is a more comfortable embracing of contradiction. Contradictions are commonplace in Daoism. Laozi begins the Daodejing with the famous line: "The way that can be followed is not the true way" (Laozi 2002, 1). Zhuangzi say "that which makes things has no boundaries with things, but for things to have boundaries is what we mean by saying 'the boundaries between things'. The boundaryless boundary is the boundary without a boundary" (Zhuangzi 1994, 218). Nāgārjuna, who is often referred to as "the second Buddha" by Tibetan and East Asian Mahayana (Great Vehicle) traditions of Buddhism, states that the teaching of the Buddha is that all four of the possible truths for any claim are true:

Everything is real and not real.

Both real and not real.

Neither real nor not real.

That is Lord Buddha's teaching.

—Mūlamadhyamakakārikā 18:8, quoted in Garfield 1995, 49

Nāgārjuna seems, like Hegel, to view contradiction as a fundamental feature of reality. Nāgārjuna and others in the Mahayan school of Buddhism seem to be espousing the doctrine that "the ultimate truth is that there is no ultimate truth," which is self-contradictory but only from the perspective of the requirement that claim be judged by the semantics of delocality (Siderits 2003, 273).

Many Western philosophical interpreters of Heraclitus, Hegel, Laozi, Zhuangzi, Nāgārjuna, and the Buddha, make tireless efforts to interpret these thinkers in some way that force these interpreters to confront their own locality. If only these thinkers are speaking in mere metaphor, playing on ambiguity, and so on, then we do not have to confront the real contradiction expressed in their thought, that the problem with contradiction is really on a problem of deloclaity. Even Kant realized his own locality, when he realized that contradiction arose from trying to comprehend the world as a whole, but then thought himself out of locality and back into delocality when he limited contradiction to human reason's attempt to stretch beyond itself to actual reality rather than seeing that a delocalized actual reality that floated free from the land was the origin of the problem. The core of what drives Kant away from contradictions and Western philosophers to generally ignore to try to revise Heraclitus, Hegel, Laozi, Zhuangzi, Nāgārjuna, and the Buddha, is not simply worries about contradictions or simply the ideas of LNC and the LEM themselves. What is manifested as worries about contradictions is truly a deeper worry about maintaining the illusion of the capacity of humans, human reason, or human language to float free from the land, to be delocalized. This more fundamental worry that underlies the naturalization of the LNC and the LEM reveals itself in the attempts to undermine the existence of contradictions with the use of expressions of sameness and difference through delocality. Specifically, one might try to undermine a contradiction by claiming that the same thing is being claimed of multiple objects rather than of one single object, or claiming that the localized conditions have changed such that what was one object at one time is now a different object, and so the same thing is being claimed of different objects or perhaps of the same object but at different times. This represents the victory of sameness over difference or the inability to see the possibility of a fundamental multiplicity in being and in thought, which is the same thing as an inability to see locality or to see beyond the illusion of delocality as the framework of the nature of being and of rational thought. This is why Aristotle stops in his version of the LNC to stipulate the complete removal of the possibility of multiplicity in locality by adding to the claim that the impossibility of the same thing both belonging and not belonging to the same object at the same time and in the same respect "all other specifications that might be made" that would be needed "to meet local objections" (*Metaphysics* 1005b19–23). In order to achieve the complete and singular sameness of this "same thing," the thing must become completely removed from locality and so no longer be a thing at all, but an abstracted vacuity, not unlike the notion of identity as the sameness of a thing that is abstractly stipulated as defined by sameness (I am identical to myself). All of these Iktomi-style contortions of thought are to avoid confronting locality which includes the possibility that a thing can be a multiplicity and that a statement can be true and false as well as both true and false and neither true or false.

Although Aristotle's expression of both of these laws begins with the ontological claims about the possibility of being not of truth, which only applies to statements, his defense is directed toward statements and what is true. Aristotle recognizes that this binary opposition is not one of being or even of words because only statements can be true or false (*Categories* 13b3–12). However, from the perspective of epistemic locality, this most basic of binaries is the result of the misapprehension of the nature of multiplicity in locality, for examples as a function of intertwining dualisms in Black Elk. Truth, as Black Elk states, comes into the world as a pair. He says that truth has two faces, the happy and the sad. But these two faces are only one aspect of the multiplicity of the faces of truth or one layer of the dynamic layering of the possibilities of truth in the context of locality. The two faces of truth are also the absolutely serious and important as well as the ridiculously absurd and ludicrous. Just as the serious and the absurd as well as the happy and the sad are each two faces of truth as they appear in locality, the real and the unreal, the true and the false, knowing and not knowing, being and becoming, and so on appear with two faces in locality. In Lakota, this layering of duality is represented, in one way, with the eight-sided star seen on the star quilt that is used to honor or bless individuals during some transforming event: birth, death, marriage, graduation, and so on. In total, the eight-sided star represents the Morning Star, which indicates, at one level, the possibility of a new day, another day of life on the earth. But the star has four directions just like the circle of the four directions that Black Elk speaks of, but in this symbol each direction is split into two, creating an eight-sided star within the circle of the four directions.

Each direction is split to represent the multiplicities of the dualities of the two faces of each direction: the serious/ludicrous, true/false, real/unreal, good/bad, and so on.

In 2013, Lakota of the Oglala Lakota Nation in South Dakota voted on whether to begin selling alcohol on their reservation instead of letting the millions of dollars in revenue go to border towns like White Clay, Nebraska, and ostensibly to raise funds to provide reservation-based treatment programs for alcoholism. Four White Clay stores reported $3 million in gross sales in 2010. The tribe held a special election August 13, 2013, to legalize the sale of alcohol on the reservation. Marty Two Bulls Sr., in an *Indian Country Today* article, describes the tribe's motivations for putting forth this legislation as "seeking to tap the revenue stream to combat the social ills created by liquor. The goal is create treatment centers that would encourage alcohol consumers to stop consuming" (http://indiancountrytodaymedianetwork.com/2013/08/09/pine-ridges-sun-dance-dilemma-sacrifice-or-end-alcohol-prohibition-150805). Oglala tribal president Brewer puts the reasoning thus: "trying to fight firewater with firewater." This provides a kind of prototype for seeing the structure of Iktomi thinking through the black road in action as well as the infectious power of delocalizing coloniality. Two Bulls Sr., in his two-part *Indian Country Today* commentary, brilliantly splits his narrative into two parts that run back to back from paragraph to paragraph. In one paragraph he describes the situation/crisis with alcohol on the reservation, and in the next he describes elements of the Lakota sundance and its meaning. This rhetorical device illustrates nicely the forked path of truth, between good and bad, body and spirit, serious and ridiculous, and so on. This rhetorical device also presents the two faces of good and bad without creating a binary relationship between them. It gives one the possibility of seeing beyond the Iktomi thinking and epistemic delocality without the binaries necessary for Iktomi thinking and delocality itself. It does not try to use "firewater against firewater." It does not try to use Iktomi thinking against Iktomi thinking. It does not try to use delocality against delocality. In the center of the sundance is placed the "flowering tree" as Black Elk calls it, a cottonwood tree with two branches forking out about ten to twenty feet up from the main stalk of the tree. This flowering tree is both life and death. Its life is taken for life to continue, just as the sundancers give of their life blood for life to continue. In the forked tree of the sundancers, as Marty Two Bulls Sr. presents it, we can see both sides of our choices, both sides of ourselves, both sides of reality in relationship to the issue of alcohol on the reservation.

PART 2

Indigenizing Morality through the Land: Decolonizing Environmental Thought and Indigenous Futures

Black Elk

Iktomi was a man in the early days, just like any person. He was the first who attained maturity in this world. He is more cunning than human beings. He names all people and animals, and he was the first to use human speech. Even toward the supernatural monsters, Spider demonstrates this arrogance, establishing himself as the Creator himself: "I made this earth and the sky and the sun and the moon and everything. You are one of the things I made. You were a little grey thing and I threw you away."

—Black Elk

Iktomi

Iktomi is a little one. His body is like a fat bug. His legs are like the spider's, but he had hands and feet like a man. He talks with men and beast and with everything that lives and with trees and stones. He plays tricks on beasts and birds. He can make himself invisible. He is weak, and he must get things by his tricks.

—Old Horse

[Iktomi] can make himself appear like an old man. When an old man comes to a lodge, he should be watched. If he proposes a game, then it is Iktomi. [If you feed him], he will dung in [your] lodge.

—Old Horse

Iktomi is of the oldest. He is full of tricks. He plays his pranks on the Wakan and on the Lakotas. He would go into their lodges and . . . persuade them to scatter about everywhere . . . [and] would laugh at them. . . . So the Lakotas came together in one camp like they were in the middle of the world. . . . [They] made their camp in a circle so that each door would be toward the door of every other lodge, [so] if Iktomi came into a lodge, everyone would know about it.

—Old Horse

Should I think with my stomach or go hungry?

—Iktomi

Iktomi Challenges the Western Thinker to a Trickster Contest

Even Iktomi had noticed that his own stories were circular.

Those who listened to Iktomi's stories often seemed trapped in the same webs that Iktomi spun around himself. But sometimes the listener, in trying to follow Iktomi's journey, can unravel the circle of webs altogether. What seems natural to Iktomi and his followers (the listener) lead, in the stories, to a series of choices that culminate in a forked path, an ultimate either/or. The binary choices as presented in the stories are shaped by deeper and subtler choices that have falsely locked Iktomi and his followers into this binary position. Just as Marty Two Bulls Sr. articulated, a seemingly simple choice between binary oppositions can reveal a deeper choice between paths of delocality and locality. Neither of the choices that Iktomi and his followers are ultimately presented reveal meaningful paths to follow, but it is the naturalness of the choices and the choosing process that begins to reveal to Iktomi and his followers just how deeply the choices and the choosing process are rooted in delocality.

Iktomi's stories are meant to be circular. His stories do not describe his actions or attitudes in the best light but rather present his path and his choices in a natural light to the listener. The listener is then able to see the naturalness of the choice but also the difficulty of following the path of that choice within the context of the choices and the choosing process. This reveals new possibilities of thinking for the listener that go beyond the naturalness of the ultimate forked path that is presented. In what follows, Iktomi tells an Iktomi story about Western notions of value and the land that does not present these ideas in the best light, but rather presents the choices that lead to the ultimate forked path in the most natural light to the listener. Iktomi decided that it was about time that someone else was Iktomi for a while. He had been doing the job for as long as he could remember. Here is part I of Iktomi's version of the story of the Western Thinker/trickster and the Western understanding of land and value.

The Western Thinker Meets the Last Man and Tries to Find Value in the Land

—from the philosophy of Iktomi

The Western Thinker always places the ultimate value upon himself, and upon human beings in general. He never wonders whether anything else has value. He rarely even wonders whether he has any obligations to anything other than human beings. If he did momentarily wonder, he generally ends that moment of wonder with a resounding and final no. Human beings have intrinsic value.

> Iktomi thinks that the Western Thinker would make a better Iktomi than Iktomi, as he is better at only seeing himself and the world as a mirror of himself than any other trickster in history. Iktomi wonders if the Western Thinker was patting himself on the back while he reached for this conclusion.

Intrinsic value is the value of something just for being what it is. It is value in itself. Instrumental value, on the other hand, is the value that something has as a means to an end. For example, corn, presumably, has value as a means for human sustenance. The Western Thinker needs to eat and so finds the corn to have value relative to that end. But the corn has no value in itself. Moral obligation follows directly from intrinsic value in the mind of the Western Thinker. Since the Western Thinker assigns instrumental value to nonhumans (animals, rocks, trees, ecosystems, and the like), any expense to nonhumans that will bring benefit to humans is justified. This is one sense in which the Western Thinker is anthropocentric. Aristotle classically articulates a natural anthropocentric hierarchy in which the less rational and less perfect serves the more rational and more perfect: "nature has made all things specifically for the sake of man" (*Politics* bk.1, ch. 8). According to the Bible, "God created man in his own image . . . [to] replenish the earth, and subdue it: and have dominion over fish of the sea, and over fowl of the air, and over every living thing that moveth upon the earth" (Genesis 1:27–28). Thomas Aquinas also believes humans can use nonhumans in any way they see fit, even unto death, without the possibility of injustice, since all nonhumans are "ordered to man's use" (*Summa Contra Gentiles* bk.3, pt. 2, ch. 112). Following the Western Thinker, one would have trouble finding anything wrong with even the ugliest cruelty to anything nonhuman except insofar as this cruelty has negative effects on human beings. Immanuel Kant, for instance, suggests that cruelty toward a dog might lead to a character that is less sensitive to human cruelty. The wrongness, in this case, of animal cruelty is determined solely by a relation to intrinsically valuable humans (Kant 1967).

> Iktomi wonders why anyone would continue to listen to the Western Thinker after displaying such trickster logic (thinking that presented oneself as both the justification and conclusion of an argument). People have been ignoring Iktomi since time immemorial for just this reason.

In the 1970s, the Western Thinker was presented with an environmental crisis. Rachel Carson's *Silent Spring* (1962) detailed the possible relationship between pesticide use and commercial farming practices (aiming solely at crop yield) and environmental devastation and deteriorating public health. Books like *The Population Bomb* (1968) warned that current growth of human population was set to undermine planetary life support, and *The Limits to Growth* (1972) from MIT affirmed "finally that any deliberate attempt to reach a rational and enduring state of equilibrium by planned measures, rather than by chance or catastrophe, must ultimately be founded on a basic change of values and goals at individual, national and world levels" (Meadows 1972, 112). The Western Thinker began to wonder whether he had been wrong to assume that the nonhuman world did not have intrinsic value or at least some value that approximated the intrinsic value that humans had by definition and default. The Western Thinker was pushed toward a change of values, a reformulation of ethics. John Muir creates "American conservation" and Aldo Leopold creates the "land ethic" and advocated the conservation of things "natural, wild, and free." These values of conservation and preservation arise from both an aesthetic response to nature as well as an ethical response to the purely economic approach to the value of the environment. Leopold's "land ethic," as first articulated in *A Sand County Almanac* (1949), makes the claim that the land is "a community . . . to be loved and respected" (1949, 224). His formulation is as follows: "A thing is right when it tends to preserve the integrity, stability, and beauty of the biotic community. It is wrong when it tends otherwise" (Leopold 1949, 224–225).

> Iktomi thinks it is classic trickster logic to only begin to question one's thinking when one is faced with a life-threatening crisis.

One Western Thinker put forth the "last man" thought experiment, which was an attempt to challenge the Western Thinker's refusal to grant intrinsic value to nonhumans. This Western Thinker imagines a situation where the last person left on earth behaved in such a way as to ensure that nothing would be left after his passing. Since his final destruction of everything would harm no humans, the last man ought to be free from all moral judgment. But the last man would be acting morally wrong with his last act. What is destroyed by the last man's last act has intrinsic value that is independent of its possible human use. The last man is trying to show the Western Thinker that his thinking cannot account for this value.

Iktomi thinks the Western Thinker could care less about what happens in a world where there were no longer any human beings around.

Arne Næss created "deep ecology."

Iktomi thinks Anre Næss appropriated the Sherpa culture of reverence for the Himalayas. Iktomi thinks Næss "transparently sensed" the reverence the Sherpas had for those mountains and extended through delocality this reverence to cover natural objects in general.

Deep ecology endorses "biospheric egalitarianism," the view that all life has a value in its own right (Næss 1973, 99). One ought to take care, according to deep ecology, when even walking through a forest, for example, not to cause unnecessary damage to the plants that live there.

Iktomi thinks this is good advice, particularly when it comes to stepping on spiders.

Næss also develops what he calls the "relational, total-field image" (1973, 99). Organisms are seen as "knots" in the biospheric web. The identity of an individual organism is defined in terms of its relation to the other organisms. One's morality can be transformed by identifying oneself with nature. If I am nature, then respect for nature is just another form of self-respect. The Western Thinker worries that deep ecology is nothing more than an extension of utilitarianism that counted human interests alongside the interests of all living things (trees, flowers, rivers, bears). The Western Thinker also does not think that organisms could have interests of any relevant moral sense at all. Without having interests in a moral sense, the Western Thinker says, nonhumans cannot have moral standing.

Corn doesn't have interests and so has no moral standing, the Western Thinker concludes.

> Iktomi wonders if the Western Thinker reached this conclusion about corn while he was in the process of killing and eating this plant in order to sustain his life.

Some Western Thinker claims that beings that have no language cannot be said to have interests.

> Iktomi says that this Western Thinker has never spoken with Selu, the corn mother, or Inyan, the grandfather stone.

Another Western Thinker claims that beings who do not have mental states cannot have interests. The Western Thinker says that desires are more than instincts. A desire is a "special kind of learning involved in hypothesis formation and testing" (Varner 1998, 29). The "capacity for conscious practical reasoning" grounds desire and provides the capacity for having interests of any kind (Varner 39). This Western Thinker points to neurophysiological evidence that suggests that the capacity for practical reasoning is localized in the prefrontal cortex (Varner 1998, 42).

> Iktomi says that this Western Thinker was not taught how to be a human being by Selu, the corn mother. Selu has no prefrontal cortex but epitomizes practical reason. Iktomi wants to remind the Western

Thinker that Selu deduced that her two sons were going to kill her when she showed them that she could produce corn and beans for them to eat by rubbing her stomach.

The Western Thinker is wont to allow interests and moral standing beyond himself. A few mammals is about as far as he is willing to go. Some Western Thinker also thinks that corn might have "needs" in a way that machines have "biological functions" (Varner 1998, 68). If biological functions can be thought of as creating needs, it seems that mechanical functions could be thought of as creating needs just as well, which means that Western Thinkers would also have to say that not only corn has interests and moral standing but cars might have interests and so moral standing.

Iktomi says that he has met plenty of cars that have moral standing, so wonders why the Western Thinker finds that fact to vitiate this one Western Thinker's view.

Some Western Thinker claims that it is being in something's interests that creates value and moral standing. Corn can have interest in the sense that there are states of affairs that are objectively good for the corn. Inanimate objects, this Western Thinker claims, do not have interests. An object of this sort, such as a stone, "has no good of its own. A stone cannot be benefited or harmed by acting according or contrary to its welfare" (Taylor 1986, 121).

Iktomi says that he hopes no one tells Inyan, the stone grandfather, about this. Inyan would likely have his feelings hurt, and then things could get real messy in the next sweat lodge. Besides, it seems arbitrary or even prejudicial to want to limit the extension of the human realm of value to not include cars and stones. I've seen many actions that do harm to the stone grandfathers, and I have a dozen broken-down cars behind my house, Iktomi says.

The Western Thinker does not want anything other than other humans to have interests and so moral standing. Some will say that only the experience of pain can account for intrinsic value. Feeling pain and pleasure is seen by some as necessary for possessing intrinsic value and extend intrinsic value beyond the realm of humans (Singer 1990, 17–21).

Iktomi thinks this criterion is useless unless the Western Thinker would stop assuming that Selu and Inyan are nonsentient. If Selu did not feel pleasure or pain, then why did she tell her sons that it was acceptable for them to kill her in order for her body to produce the life-sustaining corn for all the generations that followed? If Inyan did not feel pleasure or pain then why did he choose to cut himself open to release his blue blood, the water that became the lifeblood of the earth and was responsible for the generation of human beings in the first place?

Some Western Thinkers see interests as a generalization of the Golden Rule: do unto others as you would have them do unto you. According to one Western Thinker: "if I am my neighbor, I might not want a certain tree cut down because it provides shade for my yard or if I am a squirrel, I might not want this tree cut down because it provides food, but if I am this tree, it can no more matter to me than if I am the bicycle that I knock over" (Hare 1989, 244). The tree and the bicycle have interests in that one can harm them by cutting down the tree or knocking over the bicycle, but neither can have interests of the sort that generate moral obligation since, from the perspective of the tree, I will not care whether I am cut down, and from the perspective of the bicycle, I will not care whether I am knocked down.

> Iktomi thinks that the Western Thinker seems to know as much about trees and bicycles as he does about Selu and Inyan.

The Western Thinker is rejecting the various extensions of interests beyond human beings on the basis of the claim that the value of a tree, a stone, corn, or a bicycle is a value based in what is in something's interest rather than being an interest for that thing. One Western Thinker claims that the only kind of value that creates moral standing is value of a life in terms of "how well it is going for the individual whose life it is" (Sumner 1996, 20). The Western Thinker thinks that interests, intrinsic value, and so moral standing all seem to arise from the perspective of a thing, and if no interests can be found from the perspective of a thing, then no interests, and so no intrinsic value ought to be ascribed.

> Iktomi thinks the Western Thinker has used his own trickster logic to argue himself into oblivion or at least isolation and solitude. Iktomi wonders why the Western Thinker would be proud of his own reason and its conclusion when they seem to both arise from and end in his own narcissism.

The Western Thinker wants to deny the intuition of the last man. He does not want to allow anything but instrumental value for the nonhuman world. The Western Thinker wants to limit the value of the nonhuman world to human-centered, instrumental value. The Western Thinker wants to think about the value of the nonhuman world within a pragmatic anthropocentrism, where the value of nature lies in its relation to the good life or human well-being. One Western Thinker reminds us, "an obscure moth from Latin America saved Australia's pastureland from overgrowth by cactus," and "the rosy periwinkle provided the cure for Hodgkin's disease and childhood lymphocytic leukemia" (Wilson 1999, 38).

> Iktomi wonders whether the Western Thinker has just followed his own trickster logic back to the same place where he started. Isn't he now back standing next to Aristotle facing the original question: Why is value human-centered?

CHAPTER 4

Everything Is Sacred

Iktomi Lessons in Ethics without Value and Value
without Anthropocentrism

I
f we listen very carefully to Iktomi, the choice behind the binary
choice between intrinsic and instrumental value might be revealed.
The naturalness of the process that culminated in a forked path,
an ultimate either/or between intrinsic and instrumental value, can
be seen in the light of constructed naturalness of delocality as the
seemingly common-sense process of abstraction from locality in order
to create a singular sameness over difference that becomes the basis
for what is understood as truth, reason, and the life. If we continue
the story that Iktomi has started, the seemingly simple choice between
the binary oppositions of intrinsic and instrumental value can reveal a
deeper choice between paths of delocality and locality. In this chapter,
I approach the naturalness of the seemingly simple choice between
intrinsic and instrumental value in order to reveal new possibilities of
thinking beyond the ultimate forked path down which this supposed
naturalness leads.

Iktomi's story presents us with the choice only between the two. The delocality of the choices and choosing process opens up the possibility that there is something else, something local that is between or before the two choices. One place that delocality reveals itself before the binary choice between intrinsic and instrumental value is in the notion of value and valuing itself. Iktomi might show us that if morality is going to be localized, it is going to have to be done through something other than value and valuating. The term "value" comes from the Latin *valēre* (to be worth). The choice between intrinsic and instrumental value is not really a choice in the context of locality. Worth is not something that can be separated from human valuation, as John Benson claims as the principal claim that is argued for in his book on environmental ethics (2000, 23). If something is going to have worth, the argument goes, that worth is going to come back, at the end of the day, to worth to me or worth to us as humans in some sense. The choice of intrinsic versus instrumental values is not a real choice, Iktomi would show, because the centering of the importance of human beings is already embedded in the notion of value itself. Either we delocalize our choice, then, in the erasing of the human valuator in the originary manifestation of the intrinsic value found in objects of such worth or confront head-on the prejudice of human-centered value and valuation in the claim that nonhumans have only instrumental value in relation to humans and the foundational value of human beings. In either case, a real confrontation of the actual nature of our choices and the choice-making process seems to limit the creating of a robust environmental ethics in the sense that Western philosophy has so far imagined. Of course, none of this shows that theories depending on mere instrumental value and human-centered value or theories depending on intrinsic value are necessarily unjustifiable, at least in the context of Western delocalized methods of justification. What is significant about the trickster method is that an Iktomi story of intrinsic versus instrumental value can open the listener up to new possibilities of thinking from inside her assumed position. What I intend to do in this chapter is to open that space for thinking through a new approach outside of the bounds of both intrinsic and instrumental value, outside of value. In the following chapter, I articulate the beginnings of a different way of thinking about our moral relationships in the context of locality. What motivates my wanting to understand moral relationships in this way does not depend on internal problems within the Western mode of ethical theorizing as founded, for the most part, on the determination of value and objects of value. I do think that the internal problems within the Western mode of ethical theorizing are a result of theorizing from the perspective of delocality and that reconceptualizing ethical theorizing through locality, from the land, would move thinking beyond these problems, but this chapter hopes to simply open up my readers to the appreciation of a new perspective on ethical theorizing outside the bounds of intrinsic and instrumental value.

In academic philosophy, work is often done from one side or the other of these positional boundaries without much thought to what might lie outside. Truly fresh ground is rarely broken. From the perspective of the story Iktomi has been telling, these sorts of stalemates indicate a greater problem. The issue should not be seen as the choice between intrinsic and instrumental value but as the choices that lead to this forked dead end. The trickster methodology toward epistemic locality is intended to reveal how the moral status of and our moral obligation to nonhumans is constructed through delocality. In this chapter, as we follow Iktomi's story of the Western conceptualization of the relationship between humans and the land, the trickster methodology will draw us closer to that point of the fork in the road that illuminates the delocality of choosing the process and opens a new space for seeing something about Indigenous locality. Iktomi's trickster model allows us to approach locality in the context of delocality, to find a way to speak about locality without speaking about it through delocality, like the fighting of firewater with firewater that Two Bulls Sr. speaks of. The Iktomi trickster model allows the listener to hear something that cannot be meaningfully said directly, at least in a conceptual and semantic context of delocality. When Native thinkers too directly speak from locality in this context, what they say appears as fragmented nonsense.

As a function of the narrative of colonial difference, which serves to create and maintain the coloniality of power, Indigenous people are seen as transparent to the Western mind, which opens an escape route from the trickster methodology for the Western Thinker, who can then claim with supposed scientific validity that he or she truly understands the words of Native thinkers and speakers and that those words are either truly primitive nonsense or can be correctly translated into a comfortable delocalized and so meaningful semantics. As Deloria states, Indigenous people and Indigenous philosophy are transparent to the Western mind: "People can tell just by looking at us what we want, what should be done to help us, how we feel, and what a 'real' Indian is really like. Indian life, as it relates to the real world, is a continuous attempt not to disappoint people who *know* us" (1969, 1). The transparency of Indian-ness is maintained by delocality and the narrative of colonial difference. Thus, in order to create a context of Indigenous locality, the framework of Indigenous transparency must be exposed through the fact of colonial difference. Iktomi, through his contrary modality, allows us to present something of locality even within the framework constructed and maintained by delocality, but the supposed transparency of Indian-ness re-creates the narrative of colonial difference even in the context of Indigenous expressions of locality. The purpose of this exercise is not to justify a localized perspective of the relationship between humans and the land in the context of delocalized Western environmental philosophy but simply to mark the contrast between the narrative of colonial difference and Indigenous locality through Iktomi's illuminating of the fact of colonial difference through the land.

Ecological Saint or Ecological Savage: Nature and the Narrative of Colonial Difference

One reason given for listening closely to and attempting to gain a greater understanding of the Native environmental philosophy lies in the foundational reference to Native moral thought in Western ideas of environmental ethics. This reference and the supposed transparency of Indigenous moral thought within the context Western thought are a creation of the narrative of colonial difference and so can only be countered with epistemic locality and the fact of colonial difference. One way that the narrative of colonial difference shows up in Western environmental thought is in the assumption that in Native environmental thought one finds a classic expression of nonanthropocentric environmental ethics where nonhumans are considered to have intrinsic value. At a deeper level, this assumption is a feature of the narrative of colonial difference in the form of the natural Indian savage and the natural ecological Indian saint.

The challenge is then to circumnavigate through epistemic locality the stereotypical imagery of Native people as pristine creatures living in nature like animals in a Garden of Eden. This framework limits the ways people can understand Native environmental philosophy. This imagery of the Garden of Eden is important for understanding the Western concept of Native environmentalism. After all, Columbus speculated upon meeting the inhabitants of the Americas that he found the Island of the Blessed or perhaps the Garden of Eden itself. In the late sixteenth century, Arthur Barlowe wrote a piece as an advertisement for settlement in which he claims that the Natives were "gentle, loving, and faithful" and "void of all guile and treason," living "after the manner of the Golden Age" (Barlowe 2007, 92). This perspective shapes the understanding of Native people and even the popular conceptions of Native environmental philosophy. The view that Native people are a part of nature in a way that European people are not has to be understood through the fact of colonial difference, which will remove the power of naturalness this view has been given through the narrative of colonial difference. This differentiation through the fact of colonial difference cannot begin through the assumption that humans (at least so-called advanced ones) are not a part of nature. Within the narrative of colonial difference, the story is that some humans are, in fact, outside of nature, and this is what makes them human. Being outside of nature is what makes one human, and the level to which one is outside of nature, natural impulses, or existing in a state of nature is also the level to which one is civilized. The mirrored counterpart of the Indian in the narrative of colonial difference paints Native people as a part of nature and so less than human and more like animals, which means being uncivilized and perhaps incapable of being civilized.

The Native-as-animal aspect of the narrative of colonial difference accounts for both of the traditional stereotypes of Native American people: the noble and pristine as well as the vicious and cannibalistic. If Native people are animals, then, like all animals, on this view, they are either innocent and natural, like a deer, or violent killers by nature, like a bear—I once had a student ask what he thought was a serious question as to whether all Indigenous people killed and ate people. Since this view of Native people was created by the narrative of colonial difference, which itself is a purely mythological construction of Native people from within the Western mind and on the basis of and support of the coloniality of power, there is no actual fact or set of facts that can serve to disrupt these views. Facts and history can hardly touch what is purely mythological and constructed on the basis of the coloniality of power since those are constructed beyond facts and history in the first place, as a function of a delusion world via epistemologies of ignorance. The images of Native people who either still live in the state of nature or have left this state of nature in order to become civilized are so ingrained in the public imagination through the narrative of colonial difference that experiencing the reality of Native people alive today does little to disrupt the seemingly naturalness of these imagined Native people, any more than Winthrop's and Locke's knowledge that the Mohegan people fought legally for their land rights could disrupt Winthrop's and Locke's sense that the Mohegan people were in a fundamental state of nature where there was no conflict over land ownership. It is important to know, then, as the most basic context for thinking beyond these ingrained images, that they—the brutal savage Indian and the noble ecological Indian—were created in Europe before Europeans ever saw an Indigenous person of the Americas, and the image was created in this way just so it could function as a tool of coloniality, to supplant the reality of Indigenous people's rootedness in the land of the Americas with the uprooted European coloniality.

Often well-intentioned discussions of the mythology of the noble ecological Indian are vitiated by their continued insistence on the transparency of Native ways of being within the framework of the narrative of colonial difference without any awareness of the fact of colonial difference, which means that even attempts to deconstruct the mythology of the noble ecological Indian actually serve to reinforce the narrative of colonial difference and retrench the coloniality of power. The most obvious example is Shepard Krech's book *The Ecological Indian: Myth and History* (1999), which is articulated as an attempt to undermine the narrative of colonial difference, specifically the noble ecological Indian, but serves to reinforce it. The book claims to present an unbiased articulation of the Indian relationship to the environment. Krech's attempt to show that the ecological Indian is a myth and that Native people were in many cases closer to ecological savages is based on accounts of contemporaneous Europeans with their crude racial biases, coupled with smatterings of the most controversial archaeological evidence. The evidence Krech uses to construct an image of Native people's destructive relationship to the environment arises directly out of the context of coloniality itself. A major part of the case that Krech makes for his version of Native environmental philosophy and Native environmental destructiveness comes from nineteenth-century Indian hunting practices—a familiar trope and straw man. In the nineteenth century deep into the operation of the delocality of coloniality (separating Native people from their land in both a material and philosophical sense), Indians were a part of the overhunting of deer and beaver. But to use this as evidence for Native environmental practices and philosophies without a deep analysis of the fact of colonial difference that created and maintained the context of these nineteenth-century hunting practices shows a poor understanding of the manner in which the narrative of colonial difference creates the image of the ecological Indian in the first place.

Krech does admit that "ecology … has a distinct disciplinary history," but then goes on to claim that Native cultures might not have conformed to this concept so shaped by Western academics (1999, 22). From the start the ecological Indian is created as a Eurocentric tautology in the inverted mirror of coloniality and through the operations of the narrative of colonial difference. Yet Krech does not seem to see this seemingly obvious aspect of the ecological Indian and so views the question of the ecological Indian as an actual binary choice about whether Native people were really noble ecological Indians rather than a question of how the narrative of colonial difference creates the notion of ecological Indians through delocality and the coloniality of power in the first place. He does say that the question of the ecological Indian is at its heart nothing more than the question of whether Indians are European, which is the question that always provides the inverted mirror that frames the narrative of colonial difference but does not see that if he truly understood what he said, there is no longer any serious factual question to ask about whether Native people actually conform to the idea of the ecological Indian, unless he supposes that Indians could in fact be Europeans. Just as Franciscus De Victoria justifies conquest in the Americas because the people there lack the European God and Winthrop and Locke justify European sovereignty over Indian nations and appropriation of their land without consent simply because of the lack of the exact same European polities and land practices, so the noble ecological Indian is another form of the Indian as animal trope, which itself is nothing more than the inverted mirror of colonizers' view of themselves as the definition of civilized—and so out of nature—humans. Thus, the real question ought to be, not whether Native cultures conformed to this Eurocentric notion of humans in a state of nature, but rather why they come to be associated with this Eurocentric notion at all. If we look at the ecological Indian in this manner, it becomes clear that the notion of the ecological Indian as a version of humans in a state of nature is not constructed Eurocentrically; Eurocentric is the notion itself since the ecological Indian is nothing more than an inverted mirror of the colonizers' view of themselves as the pinnacle of human progress out of nature and into civil society.

One way of looking at Krech's position on the ecological Indian is that he recognizes the fact of colonial difference but sees it as an empty category. Recognizing that the ideals of the Western (delocalized) discipline of ecology are not the ideals of Indigenous locality is the first step in marking off the fact of colonial difference as it regards ecology. However, rather than attempting to actually mark off the fact of colonial difference in this regard, he reverts back to the other side of the narrative of colonial difference: savagery. His work operates on the binary between ecological saint and ecological savage, and so he concludes that the Native people he writes about are primitive savages because he assumes that any amount of waste or destruction is evidence of their not being ecologically minded. If they are not ecologically minded as a function of their natural, animal state, even though he has recognized the fact of colonial difference—that they do not share the ideals of Western delocalized ecology—they must be savages with little sense of their ecological destruction according to the binary possibilities within the narrative of colonial difference.

The power of coloniality in creating and maintaining the narrative of colonial difference creates a limited perspective even for those who are responsible, in part, for creating and maintaining such perspectives. This is because even European and Euro-American thinkers receive much of the background for their thinking about the environment from the same narrative of colonial difference. Nature is Indian and civilization operates through coloniality on both. The narrative of colonial difference then constructs not only the Indian natural savage in relation to the civilized European but also nature in relation to civilization. This should not be surprising given the fact that coloniality operates equally on nature as it does on Indigenous people and land. This is why a fundamental piece of reconfiguring locality is relocalizing the ideas of nature or what is natural, bringing natural and what is natural back to the land. This is why coloniality operates equally over Native identity as well as land and nature, and why the tools of epistemic locality equally disrupt all coloniality as it applies to all three of these equally. The operations of epistemic locality equally free Native identity as well as land and nature from the narrative of colonial difference and the force of the coloniality of power.

Nature is, just as with Indians, under coloniality and the narrative of colonial difference, either pure, innocent, and pristine (noble) or wild, cruel, and without order (savage). Nature is, just as with Indians, conceived of as like a wild angry bear that is ready to devour all life or as an innocent baby deer that is an expression of meekness and purity. It is instructive to see just how these notions play a current role in environmental work, even policy. In the articulation of its position regarding the protection of the San Francisco peaks in northern Arizona, a place that is considered sacred to thirteen local tribes and is central to much of the ceremonial life in that locality, the Sierra Club made the statement that this place must be kept "pristine" in order to remain sacred to the tribes who consider it so. This concept of being kept or remaining "pristine" is not an Indigenous concept, nor is it a concept of environmental philosophy in locality, but it does re-create the intertwining of Indians and nature in the context of coloniality and the narrative of colonial difference. In the context of Native environmental philosophy, the concept of a place as pristine is a function of the narrative of colonial difference and a piece of the view of Native people as existing in a state of nature as seen in the concept of the noble ecological Indian. As ecological Indians, Native people are considered to live *in* nature, whereas civilized people live *outside* of nature by operating or controlling nature to create civilization in the first place. Native people, like their animal counterparts, do no harm to their environment or even modify their environment beyond the manner in which an animal might. A forest where humans have never been is considered pristine, as pristine is another way of describing something existing in a state of nature without human interference. The narrative of colonial difference then constructs Native identity as one where existing in a forest is the same as not existing in a forest; a forest where only Native people have lived is the same as a forest where no one has lived. Such a forest is pristine, without human interference. Thus, the narrative of colonial difference constructs the concept of being pristine both as a matter of fact for people in a state of nature but also an abstract Native philosophical ideal, as expressed by the Sierra Club regarding the protection of a Native sacred place. The irrationality of coloniality appears again in the contradiction that Native people relate to the environment at all given that they are constructed as a part of nature, like a wild animal or a plant. In the context of Krech's study, this can be seen in the unresolved question regarding the ecological Indian in the context of the narrative of colonial difference: if Indians are natural, how could they be to blame (saint or savage are moral terms) for ecological devastation any more than termites that destroy a house? The fact that Krech has no answer to this question or way to avoid this question in the context of his study is evidence that he is completely seated conceptually within the narrative of colonial difference. This oversight is actually necessary in order to even begin Krech's investigation into the truth or falsity of the ecological Indian. In this way, Native people as constructed by the narrative of colonial difference are still and will always be intertwined with the various current environmental agendas as long as land, environment, nature, and Native people are understood through delocality and within the narrative of colonial difference.

Works that attempt to show that Native people did not leave their environment pristine are also used in current environmental agendas to show that the environment is something that must be controlled, much like the savageness of the viscous savage Indian as the opposite to the noble ecological Indian. If nature is not viewed as innocent and loving but rather as savage and hostile, then so are Native people, as the colonial relationship to nature and the colonial relationship to Native people are always identified under the narrative of colonial difference. If Native people are not ecological Indians, then they are savage Indians. If they are savage Indians, then they must be controlled, and as this goes, so goes our relationship to nature and the need to create environmental agendas and policies that maintain that domination and control. Krech's book is used toward this end by political voices as they attempt to carry his work to the exact conclusions just described. Radio talk show host Dennis Prager interviewed Krech on his show in the late 1990s. The conclusion reached in this discussion, by Krech, is that Native people would have been just as destructive as Europeans if they had similar population size and less primitive and religiously based understanding. Rush Limbaugh came to similar conclusions on his talk show earlier in the 1990s even before Krech's book was published. Limbaugh conclusion was this: "The American Indians were meaner to themselves than anybody was ever mean to them. The people were savages. They were out there destroying timber, out there scalping people" (quoted in Barreiro 1995, 1). If Native people are painted as untamed and in need of control, then the closely associated nature is by analogy untamed and in need of control as well, which supports the environmental policies that are the intended conclusions of these arguments. In order to even begin to understand Indigenous environmental philosophy, the questions must move beyond the narrative of colonial difference. A good place to start would be to actually ask Indigenous people—something Krech seems to completely ignore—how they understand their relationship to their environment rather than to simply treat them as animals to be studied in the abstract rather than to be listened to and understood. In order to have these conversations with Native people about their understanding of land, nature, and environment, the non-Native conversant would have to be able to understand the meaning of being and land beyond the delocality under which these concepts function in the present delocal context.

The Semantics of Delocality and Indigenous Moral Terms

The translation problem of Indigenous moral terms into English is then the same problem of speaking about locality within a semantics of delocality—the general academic writing and reading complex. The task is, then, not to find appropriate words for translation, but a context for interpreting words through a semantics of locality. An example on which we can begin to work through this process is the Diné (Navajo) word *hózhó*. Many of the features of *hózhó* are quite common in the context of locality. Terms in locality all resist translation, and for similar and insightful reasons since translation, as we understand it, is often a function of delocalized semantics. *Hózhó* is often thought of as goodness (mostly in terms of function rather than moral correctness), beauty, harmony, prosperity, healthiness, and happiness, but all of these things at once. This word refuses compartmentalization by translation into any subset of these English terms. *Hózhó* is the only sense of goodness. *Hózhó* is the only sense of beauty, the only sense of harmony, the only sense of prosperity. Even happiness is understood solely as *hózhó*. This would be akin to one and only one English word that covered all of these concepts, both in an abstract and ordinary sense. Instead of saying "You are pretty" or "That painting is beautiful," I would say "You are hózhó" and "That painting is *hózhó* (*nizhóní*). Instead of saying "I am happy" or "That makes me happy," I would say "I am hózhó" and "That makes me hózhó (*baa shiłhózhǫ́*)." This would be like using only one word in English that covered all the concepts of goodness, beauty, prosperity, harmony, and happiness in one term and one concept.

In *Diné bizaad* (the *Diné* language), each time that I say that I am happy or that something is beautiful or good I am saying that its being so is due to its being all of these things. As such, happiness, healthiness, beauty, goodness, prosperity, balance, and harmony are all deeply inter-connected as an underlying unity in the context of the *Diné* locality. All of these concepts are not only connected in practice (one cannot achieve one without the other) but are conceptually interconnected as a part of the manifestation of *hózhó* as a multiplicity. What is most important at this point is not getting clear about the idea of *hózhó*, but rather thinking about the deep interconnection between concepts or, what amounts to the same thing, the manifestation of any individual concept as a multiplicity in the context of locality. It is this deep interconnectedness of concepts and the manifestation of individual concepts as a multiplicity in the context of locality that make translating a term like *hózhó* into even a group of English terms extraordinarily difficult. The deep interconnection or multiplicity of the term *hózhó* is not merely some special and exotic feature of the primitive language and thought of Indigenous people; the deep interconnection or multiplicity of this term is rather a feature of meaning in locality. Words like this show us that the difficulty of finding a term or group of terms that capture such a concept is a deeper problem than mere translation because the separation between ideas of happiness, beauty, health, goodness, and so on in English indicates not just ordinary difference in language or worldview but a difference in the very nature of connection and compartmentalization.

This kind of interconnectedness or multiplicity reveals itself through a myriad of Indigenous words and concepts but also in many other ways. Western institutions that are separate are organically interconnected in the context of locality: science, religion, arts, philosophy, and so on. Even metaphysical or scientific understandings of what it means to be a thing (a human, a tree, a spider, or a rock) employ this notion of organic interconnection or manifestation through multiplicity. It is not surprising, then, that interconnectedness and multiplicity show up in ceremonies, moral edicts, and even everyday salutations. In Lakota, as we have heard, one uses the phrase "Mitakuye Oyasin" (everything is related). It is used in ceremonial prayer, articulations of moral responsibilities, as well as everyday salutations. It is said that this phrase reminds people of their kinship with and moral connectedness to the birds, the trees, the rocks, the buffalo, the people, and through this kind of multiplicity to everything there is. There is power in understanding this kind of interconnectedness and multiplicity, for it is the power of being in relation to the land, from being-in-the-land and being-from-the-land. From the perspective of this kind of deep interconnectedness and multiplicity, the smallest parts and the smallest change in their relations can affect the others often more than larger and seemingly more significant parts and changes—something that is borne out by modern systems theory in Western science (Gleick 1987, 18).

One way Native people have conceptualized deep interconnectedness is through a different kind of spider and the image of her web. Kokyangwuti, the Hopi Spider Grandmother—on the opposite end of the spectrum from Iktomi—was told by Sotuknang, the First Power, that while the world as it existed was good, it lacked living beings and that she, Spider Grandmother, had the power to help create them. So, she sang the song of creation and spun living beings into existence. In the Acoma version, the first beings are two females who live underground in darkness. They are nurtured and taught how to live by Spider Grandmother, who gives them a basket of seeds. These seeds become trees that grow only a little in the darkness. One tree finally punches through the ground and begins to grow quickly by the light of the sun. Spider Grandmother gives the two females songs and prayers and instructs them to give thanks to the sun and all things. Spider Grandmother's stories show the deep but precarious interconnection of all things. All things are connected to each other, like the fine threads of her web. A great deal of care is required at each step not to unbalance or undo the delicate interrelations, and it is with great care that one must attempt to rebalance what one has unbalanced or reestablish or make new the interrelations. Interconnectedness is another way of speaking of the kinship modality as the ground of locality, and Spider Grandmother's creative power as manifested through her spinning webs is an image of this kinship modality. Spider Grandmother's web is an image of kinship itself and is instructive of the power of creating new kinship relations as well as the fundamental importance and precariousness of kinship as a foundation of knowing and being that must be maintained and even constantly created anew.

Chief Seattle's Speech: Interconnectedness and Life

The importance of the notion of interconnectedness and multiplicity can be seen in an examination of the concept of life in locality. In the context of locality, one way to understand life is just as the manifestation of interconnectedness and multiplicity. To have life is to be interconnected to be a multiplicity. To have life is to be a multiplicity and so to exist in a context of deep interconnectedness to everything. Life as interconnected also means having a place and impact on everything else. This way of thinking about life means that everything is alive at some level. Being alive is not dependent on any particular property that a thing might have but on having relationality or interconnectedness itself. Life is not the possession of consciousness, the ability to experience pleasure or pain, the power of self-movement, or any biological process inherent in a particular organism, from this perspective of life. Life is fundamentally the capacity for kinship.

To say that life might be understood not as a property of things but as something that exists in the relationship between things belies two standard Western philosophical assumptions. First, the space between things seems to be mostly thought of as a secondary aspect of our understanding because reality is primarily built up out of things in the Western philosophical narrative. The second philosophical assumption is seen in the standard move, which seems to arise, in a way, out of the first, of defining a notion such as "life," "value," or "right" by looking for a feature of a thing that does not merely indicate the presence of that thing but is what "life," "value, "right," and so on truly are. To claim that life is not a property that anything has, because it is not a feature of things, runs directly against some of the most standard Western philosophical assumptions. These assumptions are often described as common sense within the Western paradigm in general but also particularly within the concept of subjectivity discussed in chapter 3, but there is clearly a point in the choice to see the world through the vehicle of things and thing-ness that might reveal a choice to see the world through delocality. At a deeper level, there is a choice to understand things as a metaphysical singularity such that things then come to represent a ubiquitous layer of sameness over a delocalized world. Thus, at this deeper level, the choice to see the world through delocality is not merely a choice to see the world as a world of things rather than relations, but to see things as a static substratum that underlies an abstract and delocalized world rather than to see things themselves as a form of interconnectedness in the context of particular capacities for kinship. Of course, seeing things as a static substratum on which knowledge must depend is only possible or even necessary because the world has been abstracted from locality, which means static things are a delocalized abstraction of localized things in multiplicity. Things can only become concrete enough for grounding knowledge or being that around which value and life can be framed when they are not truly things in their multiplicity in locality, from the land. Knowledge through abstracted and delocalized things seems to create something permanent or static only by being abstracted from locality where things and knowledge float free from the land. The attempt through the perspective of locality to understand life or value without first discovering some feature of things that we might think defines them as having life or value will be discussed in greater detail in chapter 5.

Things from the perspective of locality are a multiplicity, and so things are not understood as separate from their past and future manifestations. The manifestation of a thing is an expression of that thing from its multiplicity. Things display their nature in our experience as an continual unfolding of their being. The manifestations of things as expressions of the multiplicity of things are not something external to the things, not a symbol of things or a representation of things through perception. How things are in our experience of their continual unfolding, in our relationships with them, is how they actually are. The diversity of experiences around a particular thing is an aspect of the continual unfolding of that thing. The manifestation of things in our experience is also a part of us and a part of our unfolding, our unfolding kinship relationships, which are both a part of us and also a part of the world. One way of looking at this is to say that the multiplicity in the showing up of things in experience is part of the world just like a tree or mountain is. In this way, seeing a ghost or a mirage is not different than seeing a tree or a mountain. Any experience is a manifestation of an unfolding world. Experience, as such, is what Deloria claims is "the fundamental premise" behind Deloria's view that "Indians believed that everything that humans experience has value and instruction" (1999b, 45). The "fundamental premise," as Deloria puts it, is that "we cannot 'misexperience' anything; we can only misinterpret what we experience." There is no "such thing as an anomaly in this kind of framework," Deloria claims, since "the world is constantly creating itself" (1999b, 46). Since "everything is alive and making choices that determine the future," on Deloria's account, every experience is a new unfolding of things and the world (1999b, 46). It is not just the unfolding of things that creates the diversity of experience around a thing because an individual human being and the individual human experience are themselves a multiplicity and are themselves a part of the unfolding of the world. My experience is not *of* the world; my experience is a moment in the unfolding of the world.

There are many ways that these metaphors of relationships and the unfolding of being are used in Native narratives of knowledge and morality. One of the reasons to use metaphor and narrative as the modes by which to articulate experience and meaning is that these terms allow for many layers of meaning just as there are many layers of meaning in metaphor and narrative. In the following chapters, I attempt to allow some of these important Native metaphors and layers of meaning within them to unfold. In addition to this unfolding as a trickster story, I hope that this story will lay the groundwork for seeing something of morality in locality or morality as a way of relating from and to the land.

This metaphor of life as a relationship is expressed in the controversial speech of Chief Seattle. Seattle tells us that "every part of the soil is sacred. . . . Every hillside, every valley, every plain and grove has been hallowed by some event. Even the rocks, which seem to be dumb and dead as they swelter in the sun . . . thrill with memories of stirring events." (This is the 1887 version of Seattle's speech. It was printed in the

Sunday *Seattle Star* on October 29 and translated by Dr. Henry A. Smith. The original speech was given many years earlier, in December 1885, in downtown Seattle.) The metaphors I focus on here are that everything is alive and everything is sacred. Now, as many have pointed out there are questions regarding the manner and substance of the translation of Seattle's words. One cannot use the questions regarding the context and translation of Seattle's speech or the questions of its authenticity to show that the metaphor of life as relationship is not an authentic expression of Indigenous locality. In fact, I have chosen this speech particularly for the questions regarding its authenticity. As we have seen, the narrative of colonial difference constructs Native voices as only capable of expressing themselves or their culture authentically or inauthentically. I chose this speech in part because of the controversy regarding its authentically. Because of the focus on the text's authenticity, the deeper meaning of the words themselves have been virtually ignored. Where the meaning has been addressed, it is only in the context of the authenticity or inauthenticity of the words in relationship to the status of the existence of the noble ecological Indian or as a version of Indigenous environmental philosophy that is transparent to the Western mind. As such, the discussions of Seattle's speech have only been analyzed in the context of the narrative of colonial difference, and in fact the speech has only existed in Western thought within the narrative of colonial difference. Only by rejecting the question of authenticity and the question of the existence of the ecological Indian can the power of Seattle's words come into view. Taking his words seriously beyond the forced context of authenticity within the narrative of colonial difference can reveal Seattle's expression of epistemic locality and the fact of the colonial difference.

There is an abundance of similar and similarly misunderstood sentiments expressed by Native thinkers who are speaking from locality. Deloria flatly proclaims that "the universe is alive." He claims that "the old Indians had no problem with this concept because they experienced life in everything, and there was no reason to suppose that the continuum of life was not universal" (Deloria 1999b, 49). In any event, from the perspective of locality, the identity of a tradition is not changed by incorporating or responding to newly encountered narratives and metaphors any more than a river becomes new when it cuts through a new valley. This is seen as a natural course of traditions and ideas as well as rivers. Thus, Western attempts to determine authenticity of Native ideas and texts are misplaced. Even beyond the framing of Native voices as merely authentic or inauthentic, the search for authenticity in the context of locality is an attempt to obscure locality with delocality. In other words, it is not a mere symptom of coloniality in the context of the narrative of colonial difference but a function of coloniality itself as the process by which locality is obscured.

From the perspective of locality, there are an abundance of similar expressions of interconnectedness and from a variety of contexts. From the perspective of locality rather than authenticity, this indicates that Native people found it appropriate to express their interconnectedness and relationality in locality through the metaphor of universal sacredness. I will articulate first what these views are as I understand them and then separate out the actual implications from those only supposed by the many interpreters of the speeches of Seattle and others. Seattle tells us that to be alive is to be connected. The rocks that seem to be dead are actually full of life insofar as they are connected to the overall happening of things. They have "memories" and respond to the events around them. Seattle's expression of the nature of the life of these rocks clarifies the claim that "everything is sacred." Being alive or being in relation (one might say in Seattle's philosophy that being alive is being in relation) is what gives a thing sacredness. But this means that absolutely everything has this property: every rock, every grain of sand, and so forth. The connectedness of all things then results in everything being alive and everything being sacred. Now, clearly these are not the notions of sacred and alive as used in most Western philosophy and discourse. But this is, I believe, an important way to begin to understand the morality in the context of locality.

When these concepts of life, sacredness, interconnectedness, and so on are applied to the intrinsic/instrumental value problem, the possibility of a different understanding arises or at least initially the need for a different understanding is necessitated. When seen through this lens, the response to the problem is clear: neither intrinsic nor instrumental value can be the correct way to account for our moral obligation to nonhumans. Nothing has value in isolation, which means that a thing as static and isolated node of reality would have no value whatever. But a thing on this view is not isolated, since what makes it what it is is its kinship capacity. A thing is alive and sacred additionally insofar as it is in relation to the things around it, insofar as it is in a relationship of reciprocity with the things around it or is in kinship relations. But every single thing there is seems to have this feature, and so everything is alive and sacred. Everything that is alive is sacred and everything that is sacred is alive since both of these propositions reference being in kinship relations. Further, since every single thing, every grain of sand, is sacred, there are no levels of value. *Everything has all the value there is. Everything is sacred.* Something may affect the things around it to a degree that we as Western Thinkers might see as insignificant, but this is to miss the Native point about sacredness. There is no such thing as significance in the sense that something has more value than something else. To focus solely on what we might see as the greater impact is to miss the subtlety of Grandmother Spider's story of things. Impact is much more basic and constant. To try to view impact on a scale of more or less significant is to try to take the things out of their locality in order to create a delocalized structure of what is more or less significant or what is more or less sacred. This subtlety is often reversed on the Western account. There are mighty powers in the universe, things that effect great change. Humans are thought to be one of the primary movers in this category. The scale is then set from the greater powers to effect change down to smaller powers and finally to none. But from the perspective of locality and from Seattle's speech, there is a much more basic sense of power that is constant and underlies all others. The rocks on the ground in Seattle's speech are there together with all the other things moving, responding, and relating to everything that has happened in that spot since time immemorial. What might be thought of as the mighty affect (what comes to be seen as the only impact) of the humans who have inhabited this spot, from the perspective of locality, is only a variation of the much subtler affect that even the rocks and the sun have upon each other as they have reflected upon each other since time immemorial and not something truer or even of its own kind.

There are quite clearly, of course, different ways we should act toward different things. It is not some priority of being or even priority of values that determines this difference of behavior. Our relationships to different things require different behaviors in order to act rightly—to act through our relational reciprocity as the metaphysical and moral expression of kinship—but this does not require different kinds of significance for the things to which we are related. The confusion regarding this leads to the debate between intrinsic and instrumental value. If human beings have intrinsic value and plants and ecosystems do not, then the human relationship to plants and ecosystems is based on the value in-itself of human beings. If plants and ecosystems have intrinsic value, then they have as much value as human beings. If plants and ecosystems only have instrumental value, and humans are the only things that have intrinsic value, then only humans truly have value. The Chief Seattle lesson is that we are not forced into this dichotomy. To make claims regarding the supposed significance of one thing over another is to forget the precarious connection that all things have on Grandmother Spider's web and to forget that only from out of kinship, out of locality, can some things be seen as abstractly more or less significant than other things. The image of Grandmother Spider's web reminds us that just because there is a big initial ripple does not mean that it will have large effect overall or long term, and just because something makes a very small initial ripple does not mean that it will not have large effect overall or long term (these ripples often bring about large impacts overall or long term). This way of understanding the ripples of impact through a web of life is seen from time immemorial in stories like those of Grandmother Spider. This way of understanding also shows that even placing values on our relations in advance (through delocality) is misguided. Because of the subtlety of our relations and because of the interconnectedness of our being-in-relationship, it is really not possible to know in advance how we ought to act toward our relations. To attempt to construct right action in advance or external to our relationship, just as with constructing value in the abstract, is an attempt to construct these from outside of kinship, from delocality.

Intrinsic value requires value in isolation (a thing has value just for being the thing that it is). In the shadow of Spider Grandmother's web, there is no value in isolation (there is no delocalized value). Just being alive makes a thing sacred, and just being connected is enough to bring things to life. Instrumental value requires different levels of value by default since instrumental value is a secondary value. Instrumental value and extrinsic value, for that matter, are parasitic on intrinsic value (the former cannot exist without the latter). Instrumental value seems to require the existence of things that have more a basic and foundational value. One can imagine a structure of value without foundational items, without items that have value only for their own sake. The value of things on this picture can hardly be called instrumental since the idea seems to imply that this value is for something else. The circle of instrumental values would never close, then, without something that has intrinsic value, on pain of infinite regress. Instrumental and intrinsic values, then, both require different levels of value. If *everything* is sacred, everything has the same value. There can be no primary values, and primary values seem required in order to have secondary values. Thus, in a world where everything is sacred, there are no intrinsic or instrumental values.

Instead of a foundational model of value where there are things that have primary value (intrinsic value) and other things that have secondary value (instrumental value), there is a web of value. Things have value only in terms of this web. This is a way of thinking about value in locality. Connectedness or continuity is what gives a thing value. *The amount of value that a thing has is not determined by its place on the web.* In order for this to be the case, there would have to be a center: something that determines, perhaps by distance of connection, the value of the other items on the web. But this centering of things and so of values requires delocality. It might seem quite natural though, as a result of centuries of anthropocentric thinking, to place oneself or humans in general at the center of this value-web, and thus undermine the entire conceptual move and fall back into the intrinsic/instrumental value dichotomy. To place oneself at the center of the value-web, in this way, is to delocalize oneself, to attempt to remove oneself from locality. A true web of value has no primary building blocks, no foundation. No web relations have priority over any other, at least in the abstract. Each item on the web has all the value that there is: it is sacred.

If we accept this proposition combined with a desire to uphold a truly nonanthropocentric ethics, then we must deny much of environmental ethics so far proposed since Genesis and Aristotle. This is because value plays an essential role in these theories. Ethics, after all, is often called value theory. Yet if everything has exactly the same value—everything is sacred—value cannot form the basis of a moral theory. The question becomes can there be an ethics that is not founded in some notion of value, and what would this ethics look like. Another way of looking at this is through the question of how we understand Chief Seattle's claim that everything is sacred in the context of locality.

Nonvalue Ethics: Iktomi Lessons in Nonanthropocentrism

A nonvalue theory of ethics I define as any theory where notions of value do not play a significant role in determining what makes one act right and another wrong or play a role in grounding this determination. More generally, it could be thought of as any mode of thinking about ethics where value does not play a fundamental role in moral reflection. The idea that everything is sacred seems to indicate a form of nonvalue ethics or perhaps even a non-ethics since, as we have seen, it seems rather difficult to operate in terms of traditional moral theories when everything has all the value there is. If everything is sacred, as we are trying to understand, there is no way to use value to determine difference, and so the concept of value cannot play a significant role in moral reflection. As the layers of meaning unfold in this narrative of value and sacredness, it will become clear that this is only one level of the meaning of sacredness in the process of epistemic locality and the fact of colonial difference. Perhaps sacredness is only one kind of important limit and lesson regarding value in the process of epistemic locality. However, for now I want to focus on reflections regarding morality on the implications of universal sacrality where there are no levels of value. These reflections will serve to clarify the fact of colonial difference and help us to reconfigure morality in locality.

A few moments of reflection by anyone familiar with the history of Western ethical theory will raise the worry that such an ethics is not possible or makes no sense. However, let us just suppose that such a theory is a possibility and reflect on what sorts of ways of ethical theorizing are ruled out and what this might teach us about the role of value in ethics and the epistemic locality of morality. As promised, these chapters on sacredness are part of a unfolding process of stripping away the layers of delocality and centuries of misinterpreting Native moral thought through the lens of the narrative of colonial difference. The proposition that everything is sacred and that value is a web is merely an attempt to articulate *in English* aspects of the fact of colonial difference in the process of epistemic locality of morality—unobscuring Indigenous moral locality that has been covered up by the delocality of coloniality.

The main points are simply these: all things (living, in the Western sense, or not) are interconnected as a part of the nature of their being. This interconnectedness of being or being-with-each-other provides no basis for abstract individualization and so for value in isolation. The resulting web of value can be understood to impart a kind of basic and uniform value on everything in this web, which is simply another way of saying that everything has all the value possible, all the value there is for things in isolation. Being-with-each-other is an understanding that already exists at the horizon of locality. It is an understanding of being at the limit of epistemic locality. Universal sacrality is an understanding of value at the limit of morality in locality. The sense by which absolute value is imparted to things in this sense is simply the sense in which values are a web and being-with-each-other is the same as existing in the web of life. These are both concepts that frame locality itself but not as a delocalized thing (locality itself from within locality). The deeper implications of the expressions of being-with-each-other and universal sacrality depend on whether these concepts are being expressed through locality or delocality, on one side or other of the line that marks the fact of colonial difference. Particular individuals on this web seen in the abstract—a delocalized position from outside of the web—are all just as valuable as any of the other individuals, but to state this is simply to mark the fact of colonial difference through delocality. Further reflection is required to bring this point into clear relief in relationship to the delocalized nature of value in ethics and in order to move closer to the possibility of morality in locality.

The Western Thinker Chooses Between Nonanthropocentric, Nonvalue Ethics and Just Loving Himself

—from the philosophy of Iktomi

The Western Thinker often constructs moral theories teleologically. There is some higher good or some higher state of affairs toward which individual acts or kinds of acts aim, and it is in virtue of aiming at or reaching this higher good or higher state of affairs that individual acts or kinds of acts have a good of their own. Teleological moral theory then requires different levels of value.

> Iktomi thinks he sees the seeds of the Western Thinker's trickster logic here. Isn't what shapes the focus on some higher end the supreme value of human beings in contrast to other things, like corn, stones, and spiders?

The Western Thinker in thinking teleologically is also thinking anthropocentrically. Consequentialist theories, for example, hold that the goodness or badness of the consequences of a particular action determine the rightness or wrongness of that action. In order to conceptualize the consequences of a particular action, the Western Thinker must always ask, "Good consequences for whom?" The Western Thinker must choose some select group of beings for which these consequences are good in order for this theory to be action-guiding for the Western Thinker. If the Western Thinker were to see the consequences for everything there is, if everything were given equal moral weight in the abstract, then consequences would have no function as a foundation for moral reflection.

Put in positive terms, consequentialism is the view that actions are right insofar as they maximize the good. Consequentialist theories are then divided by how they define this good. Utilitarianism, which claims in particular that an action is right if and only if it produces the most good for the most people affected by such action, holds pleasure or happiness to be the ultimate good (what is intrinsically valuable or good in itself). Utilitarianism is incompatible with universal sacrality. Utilitarianism requires moral foundationalism: a two-tiered structure where, on one level, there are foundational values that are valuable in themselves and require no other value whatsoever, and, on a second level, nonfoundational values, values that are such insofar as they ultimately derive from the foundational values. The Utilitarian Western Thinker sees the unquestionable good of pleasure or happiness as the foundation of all value, and it is the most amount of this for the most people that makes an action right. Universal sacrality stands in contrast to any kind of moral foundationalism. In practice, this means that a fundamental value like pleasure or happiness must be related to some unequal value of beings. If everything or even just every being were equal in capacity for pleasure, then the theory cannot differentiate one action from another in moral deliberation. One Utilitarian Western Thinker's work on the treatment of animals underlines this point. This Western Thinker extends value very slightly beyond the mere human realm to consider the pain and pleasure of those animals that seem to have any significant levels of such. The resulting Utilitarian calculation concludes that animals should not be eaten by humans (Singer 1975).

Iktomi wants to point out that the Western Thinker finds this conclusion distasteful and counterintuitive, that he sometimes even

concludes that this Singer person has accidentally created a reductio argument against Utilitarianism as a plausible moral theory.
Iktomi is happy that humans don't eat spiders very often but can't
understand why what one eats has a negative relation to value.
He knows of people who both eat the buffalo and hold them in the
highest regard as relatives.

Virtue ethics are also based in moral foundationalism. Aristotelian virtue
ethics are based in Aristotle's foundational claim that actions aim at the
primary good of happiness or *eudaimonia*. *Eudaimonia* plays a foundational role in hedonistic ethics such as Epicureanism (where happiness
is pleasure and morality is concerned with the pursuit of pleasure).

Iktomi disputes the Greek origins of hedonism. Iktomi is almost
certain that he invented hedonistic ethics all by himself.

In modern virtue ethics, it is just assumed that people aim at the good
life, and the work of the theory is to lay out the tools (virtues) to attain
this life. The good life is founded, though, in what is good for human
beings. It is nonsensical within the context of virtue ethics to imagine
that the well-being toward which one directly aims could be of others
(nonhuman or not) since this well-being can only figure into the picture
insofar as it relates to the good life of the Western Thinker who is doing
the aiming. The well-being of others can only function in relationship
to an increase or decrease of MY well-being.

Iktomi likes the idea of aiming at the good life of the aimer but
doesn't like the fact that the Western Thinker doesn't think that

spiders are good aimers. Iktomi thinks he is one of the best aimers
at his own good life that there ever has been. But Iktomi does
recognize the trickster logic at work here. The idea that aiming at
the good life as the good life for the aimer is a form of the same
self-congratulatory reasoning that Iktomi is the master of. Perhaps,
Iktomi wonders, thinking about universal sacrality can show us that
one of forks of the trickster logic is the one that leads to aiming in
the first place.

Kantian ethics do not focus on particular goods, intrinsic or otherwise,
but rather on right action proper. However, Kant gets to this focus by
asking the question "What is unconditionally good?" and answering that
it is the good will. Good will is a will that acts out of duty and for duty's
sake only. Right action is then acting according to the good will and doing
one's duty for duty's sake. Universal sacred implies that nothing is good
in itself since everything is good in itself, insofar as its self is a function
of the web of life. Thus, without moral foundationalism, doing one's duty
for duty's sake cannot carry the moral weight necessary to define right
action. One Western Thinker attempted to extend deontological ethics by
claiming that animals that meet the criterion of being a "subject of life"
have intrinsic value and thus have rights (Regan 1983). Another Western
Thinker rejects this extension by saying, "Animals cannot be the bearers
of rights because the concept of rights is essentially human" (Cohen and
Regan 2001, 30). The view is that this extension is an undermining of the
very notion of intrinsic value and the concept of rights.

Iktomi points out that once again the Western Thinker sees the
conclusion that even some animals have intrinsic value as a reductio

either on duty-based ethics or on the argument that morality can be extended beyond the human realm. Perhaps the fork in the trickster logic is the choice to start with intrinsic value since that is what causes both the self-congratulatory focus on human value and the denial of universal sacrality.

In 1972, one Western Thinker proposed that trees and other natural objects had rights and so should have the same legal standing as corporations. He reasoned that if trees, mountains, and the like were given standing in the law, then they could be represented in courts. They could also become beneficiaries of compensation if in court it could be shown that these natural objects suffer injury at the hands of humans (Stone 1972). Of course, the Western Thinker as well as the Western courts responded by saying that only those things with interests can have rights and legal or moral standing, and so there can be none of these for trees, stones, corn, or spiders.

Iktomi thinks one should contrast the ridicule of Stone's position on the rights of nonhumans in the United States' legal system with Bolivia's law 071 Ley de Derechos de la Madre Tierra (Law of the Rights of Mother Earth) passed in 2010. This law, created by the Bolivian Indigenous and campesino organizations along with Indigenous Bolivian president Evo Morales, gives the earth the kind of legal standing that Stone suggested. The law grants seven specific rights to Mother Earth—defined as a "dynamic living system" that includes all "living systems and living beings, . . . shar[ing] a common destiny"—and creates the office of the Defensoría de la Madre Tierra, a counterpart to the human rights office of the Defensoría del Pueblo.

In 1975, one Western Thinker argued there was a moral obligation to protect species (Ralston 1975). He argued that it would be wrong, for example, to destroy the last living butterfly of a certain species simply to increase the value of specimens already held in collections. This Western Thinker claims that species are intrinsically valuable and went even further to claim that species are more valuable than humans since species carry with them genetic possibility. Destroying a species is disrespecting the very biological process that makes individual living things possible. All nonanthropocentric ethical theories, including Deep Ecology, face the difficulty both of supporting the claim that nonhumans have intrinsic value and the charge of misanthropy.

> Iktomi thinks that this is just turning the problem around: the biotic community has intrinsic value, and the individual members, including individual human beings, only have instrumental value. The Western Thinker views the conclusion that individual human beings only have instrumental value as a reductio argument against the view, claiming that the disregard for individual rights is "environmental fascism" (Regan 1983, 362). Iktomi thinks this is a distinction without a difference for the Western Thinker. His trickster logic teaches him to see the claim that nonhumans have the same value as human as necessarily misanthropic.

Nonanthropocentric Value in Locality

When viewed from the Chief Seattle perspective, nonanthropocentric value without the charge of misanthropy seems possible. Value theory in the context of locality, so far uncovered, can allow for a nonpolarizing, nonanthropocentric moral point of view. The problem with traditional theories of value as articulated above is that even when they attempt to assign intrinsic value to nonhumans, they must assign instrumental value to something else on pain of destroying the meaning of intrinsic value since they operate in terms of the intrinsic/instrumental dichotomy as a result of the delocality and anthropocentric framework of moral theory. In some cases, it is individuals, including human beings, who are given mere instrumental value, which gives rise to the charge of misanthropy. In others, ecosystems and species are given this higher-level value, which also leads to the charge of misanthropy. If everything has the same value in the abstract, then the charge of misanthropy is eliminated. If everything has the same value, then nothing is left out of the picture, including species and ecosystems, and the possibility of a nonanthropocentric environmental ethics that cannot be called misanthropic arises.

I claim that beginning with Chief Seattle's words and moving through the epistemic locality of Grandmother Spider's web, we can perceive of morality without different levels of value for individual things or kinds of things. In fact, having different levels of values seems to be part of what creates anthropocentric ethics in the first place, and not having different levels of value seems to be one way of the intrinsic/instrumental value forked-path that ends in itself or endlessly repeats itself in an Iktomi loop of the search for meaning or value in oneself or in isolation, from delocality or floating free from the land. If there are not particular values within a reflective moral framework, in the sense that value cannot ground a given theory because there are only relational values, there can be no anthropocentric moral theory, and maybe this is also the place to begin to mark the fact of colonial difference through morality in locality. A moral theory is most often classified as anthropocentric when it assigns greater value to humans (usually in the form of intrinsic value) than nonhumans (usually in the form of mere instrumental value), but if everything is sacred and so everything has all the value that there is, there is no hierarchy and thus no anthropocentrism. Someone might question, though, how there can be a differentiation of things that might be deemed necessary in order to say that everything is sacred in the first place. In other words, if there is no differentiation of values because everything is sacred as a result of the web of life or the deep intercon-nectedness of the nature of things, then what sense does it make to say that every*thing* is sacred? After all, is saying that everything is sacred not the same as saying that every individual thing is sacred? If it cannot be reasonably said that there are different levels of values, then, for the same reason that leads to this conclusion, should it not be reasonably said that there are different things? The first response to this question is, yes. From the perspective of Iktomi's story that is supposed to lead the listener back to the forked-path of her choice between locality and delocality, the story could start with the claim that there are no things in isolation as well as the claim that there is no value in isolation. Iktomi uses "everything is sacred" because it is the best version of the story that presents this fundamental choice to the listener. From the perspective of locality, on the other side of this choice and after the fact of colonial difference is marked, the claim that everything is sacred can be seen as an expression of morality in locality but an expression of such from within locality itself.

Moving through deeper layers of epistemic locality, this issue might be explained more in this way. If value is relational, then in the abstract, all values are equal. Value is a limit that things are only limited by when we understand them in particular relations or from particular perspectives. Before that, and even as our particular relations with particular things are articulated, all things have this background universal sacredness that each thing carries from the web relation of all things. This is one way to understand Chief Seattle's claim that "everything is sacred." If the term "value" is used in the abstract philosophical sense, as it most often is, as in "*the* (as in delocalized) value of something," then everything is sacred, that is, everything has equal value. If value is purely relational, then there can be no center in which to place anything, human or otherwise. There is a more pedestrian way of thinking of value beyond the more technical concept used by philosophers and economists. One might say, for example, that value is not merely the value of something in the abstract but value is more intimately connected to action, that value is, in fact, betrayed by action. Thus, the thought continues, if harm is caused to one thing and not another, then the one is valued over the other regardless of the perspective one has about what one is doing. Thus, what arises in relation and not through abstraction might be understood as value in a certain sense, but unless this value goes beyond the actions themselves, then it is hard to think of them as values in themselves. After all, I could act in all sorts of inconstant ways (harming and then not harming the same thing on different days), which would mean that my values as mere actions are in flux and so would be irrelevant perhaps from the perspective of morality that seeks to find something action-guiding. If values are simply determined by actions, they are merely descriptive, which means by definitions they cannot be action-guiding. Perhaps the first place on the path of choices back to locality is the choice between morality and value. Perhaps there is a choice between morality and value as some distinct and foundational aspect of morality.

Morality arises from my reflection regarding what are the 'right things for me to do. It is, of course, then, from my perspective as a human being in locality that I must decide what to do, to figure out what is right and what is wrong. As Deloria describes it, the question is "what is the right road for me as a human to walk" (1999a, 38). Simply being required to figure out what is the right path for me to follow in relation to my reciprocal relationships cannot be what is meant by anthropocentrism. In other words, one cannot be charged with anthropocentrism when one is simply as oneself in locality reflecting on what is right to do—what is my right road to walk through life. If it is not from my place in the universe that I determine what to do, one is hard-pressed to imagine what place it would be. Even the Golden Rule, which Hare references in his attempt to criticize extending intrinsic value to nonconscious nonhumans, does not imply otherwise. The Golden Rule is a tool that I might use to help me figure out what is right to do by extending my reflections to what someone else in my shoes might experience and desire. It does not imply an attempt to figure out what is right as another since to do that seems to make little sense.

A second issue revolves around the question of just what makes something anthropocentric in the vitiating sense, the sense that gives rise to the repugnancy one feels in response to human destruction of the environment for human gain alone—repugnancy at strip-mining the top off a mountain and destroying the entire ecosystem of that mountain and mountain region for the profits of a coal company and its human investors. If this does not feel like a repugnant form of anthropocentrism, imagine a scenario that captures the sense of anthropocentrism that causes so many thinkers to vehemently oppose theories that espouse it. Moral theories that place significantly more value on humans than on nonhumans are one way that theories are said to be anthropocentric in a vitiating way. But the controversy with this sort of view in particular is not simply an issue of abstract value. It seems to be that it is really an issue not only of value in the isolated sense but rather an issue of equal consideration. Since humans are thought to have intrinsic value almost necessarily and, as we have seen, it is nearly impossible to justify assigning such value to anything but the smallest class of nonhumans, the discussions of equal consideration have centered on intrinsic value. But regardless if intrinsic value is even mentioned, the great gap between the value of humans and nonhumans in moral theorizing leads to charges of vitiating anthropocentrism. The thought goes like this: first, the seeming platitude that equal consideration is for equals. Humans have much greater value than nonhumans, and so equal consideration is not required for nonhumans. In this light, the charge of anthropocentricism is lodged at a theory when it assigns significantly greater value to humans. Under this sense of anthropocentrism, all moral theorizing seems to be necessarily anthropocentric—even nonanthropocentric theories appear indefensible in this light since any kind of human moralizing will, it seems, give more consideration to humans than to nonhumans, on pain of being described as misanthropic. In the end, the situation is nicely described by Brenda Almond when she writes, "a language of value may meet environmentalist needs," but we cannot "formulate the notion of objects of value outside the experience of human beings" (1986, 301). This language of value holds promise for a plausible environmental ethic but only insofar as that ethic is inherently anthropocentric.

What I believe the reflections on moral theorizing in the light of the words of Chief Seattle and being on Grandmother Spider's web of life have shown is that a main stumbling block in the way of thinking nonanthropocentrically and through locality is the thought that we must begin our reflections from the determination of the levels of value that things have. What I believe reflecting on Chief Seattle's words has shown is that as long as we attempt to force what I might call relational value—the value that things might have in particular relationships to other particular things—into an absolute value—the value things may or may not have just as they are or in themselves—our theories will either be anthropocentric or misanthropic. This is the binary of delocality. If we operate with abstract, absolute (delocalized) value, then our morality cannot be localized, which means that localized issues or relational contexts cannot be accommodated for or even truly conceptualized from this imagined place of delocality. Value is set upon things by the abstract (delocalized) things that they are. There is no changing or accommodating at all. Since things in the abstract do not change, their value does not change. Either humans have greater value than nonhumans (anthropocentrism) or nonhumans have greater value than humans (misanthropocentrism). The web of value universal sacredness as a background to all particular relations that exists, and as a background for my reflection on what to do regarding my particular relations, creates a context for a defensible nonanthropocentric and localized approach. If I begin my reflection not with the question of what sorts of things out there have what sort of value in the abstract, but with the thought that all things because of their connectedness begin with sacredness, then I remove myself in my reflections, it seems, from the core of anthropocentrism.

Morality in locality as way of conceptualizing environmental ethics is nonanthropocentric in the sense that it does not place different values on different things or kinds of things in the abstract or through delocality. However important this first and important step toward locality and away from anthropocentric ethics is, it might appear that the claim to nonanthropocentrism achieved by this sort of ethics comes rather cheap. One might wonder whether this simple change in the nature of the beginning of human moral reflection regarding our relationship to the nonhuman world really makes any substantial difference in our actual moral relationships. My view is that it does make a significant difference in actual moral decision making. At another level, I do not think that morality in locality makes radical changes of the kind that could bring to such reflections a charge of misanthropy. After all, the charge of misanthropy seems to carry the most weight in the rejection of an environmental ethics based on intrinsic value. The worry here is if we take the idea that the environment has intrinsic value to what seems like its natural end, we might be required to not eat animals and even plants, to not walk on the earth, or to not scrub the bacteria off our bodies in the shower. The morality in locality as I am seeing it unfold does not require—or even set up the possibility of—these radical actions. The radical change in the view I am proposing is in our understanding, attitudes, and positioning (in locality) of our moral actions themselves.

Another way anthropocentrism is criticized is in the centering of considerations of right and wrong behavior on the harm or benefit to humans alone. Those who defend anthropocentric views respond that most nonhumans do not have a defensible sense of interests and the associated sense of harm and benefit that we speak of when articulating right or wrong behavior. But this assumes that our way of speaking about right or wrong behavior is not itself open to criticism. If we assume that interests and related notions of harm and benefit are in fact the correct ways to speak of right and wrong behavior and that relevant notions of interests and the like cannot be extended to nonhumans, then notions of right and wrong behavior cannot be extended to behavior in relation to nonhumans as well. However, if we do not allow the beginning of our moral reflection to be on the determination of the abstract value of objects, then the claim that only interests and related notions of harm and benefit determine right and wrong behavior is false. After all, what might be described as the interest criterion and the harm and benefit criterion are just those things that have been proposed as criteria for determining the abstract value of things and kinds of things, and so are further layers of choosing that must be uncovered in the journey of Iktomi's story and the process of epistemic locality.

As was promised from the beginning of this work, I offer levels of engagement with locality along the way to uncovering morality in locality in the land. The reason was to offer delocalized thinkers a place to get off along the way if the entire journey through Iktomi's story of the choices of delocality and the process of epistemic locality is overwhelming—at least there would a place for philosophers to start to begin to inject some locality into their thinking. At this level, what is offered is an environmental ethic that is nonanthropocentric from the start, but does not succumb to all the problems raised with nonanthropocentric theories that are founded in intrinsic value. But an environmental ethic might, regardless of its being nonanthropocentric just by default in the sense of not assigning widely disparate values to humans and nonhumans, end up anthropocentric in a deeper sense, in still focusing the deliberations regarding right and wrong on the value of humans. From the perspective of a web view of value, where there are neither intrinsic nor instrumental values, a nonanthropocentric moral theory might be understood as a theory where relational values—values that are determined by the particular relationships between particular things—ground deliberations of right and wrong. This kind of theory would be nonanthropocentric, but it would be so from the start rather than simply trying to extend an anthropocentric theory beyond its initial limits. This new kind of theory satisfies the requirement laid out as one possible manner of engagement with locality at this level of not requiring us to accept the view that nonhumans have intrinsic value and is nonanthropocentric from the start but also not misanthropic. Its nonanthropocentrism arises out of the attitude of relationally—that all our relations are sacred.

CHAPTER 5

The Metaphysics of Morality in Locality

The Always Already Being in Motion of Kinship

There are spiders, and then there are trickster spiders, and then there are Grandmother Spiders who hold the world together with the webs they weave. I brought my weaving loom, my dog hair thread and cactus needles.

—Iktomi

T he next chapter in Iktomi's story of our choosing delocality and the next level to undercover in the process of epistemic locality arises from the question of whether there can be moral theory or even moral reflection without objects of value. If there is not value by which to determine right action, then there would be, the line of thinking goes, no way to determine, even in the loosest sense, which actions were right and which were wrong. Suppose, for example, that we replaced the notions of intrinsic and instrumental value with absolute equal value while maintaining the idea that what kind of behavior is morally required in a given situation is, in some way, a function of the value of the individuals the behavior is in relation to. The result would be that everything in the universe demands the same exact moral response. This surely cannot be a plausible ethical theory. Even what seems to be clearly innocuous behavior would turn out to be morally wrong. For example, it seems that cutting down a handful of trees in order to build a house would be just as morally wrong as slaughtering a handful of humans to eat dinner. This is surely a misunderstanding of Chief Seattle's claim and the direction that morality in locality is going to lead us. This common manner in which Native moral philosophy is interpreted (as primitive nonsense) is a function of the narrative of colonial difference through delocality and a lack of clarity on fact of colonial difference. This means that many thinkers—even Native thinkers—who see their work as critiquing the narrative of colonial difference fall into this interpretive framework where the words of Chief Seattle and the like can only be seen as nonsense in the context of delocality. But just as with Lyons's mocking of the concepts of circular time and circular thinking, the problem is not with the words of Chief Seattle or the idea that everything is sacred; it is with the delocalized interpretation of the meaning of such words. The claim that everything is sacred is understood as leading to a ridiculous moral situation where no being can perform any nonmorally repugnant action whatsoever. In turn, this interpretation leads scholars and non-scholars both to suppose that Native people are portraying themselves as noble savages, at one with nature, or that Native people have borrowed from the environmentalists the idea of intrinsic value and pushed it to its farther extremes, in turn showing us the ridiculous outcomes of such a view. This construction of Indigenous moral thought is framed by the narrative of colonial difference where the Indigenous reality can only be savage in either the noble or ignoble sense or at the least a primitive stage that must reach for the final advanced stage of delocalized constructions of Western theory. Going beyond this framework of the narrative of colonial difference requires the marking off of the fact of colonial difference or where the narrative of colonial difference is laminated upon Indigenous locality through the delocalized constructions and operations of European identity that float free from the land.

Against the Primitivism and Hypocrisy of Indigenous Morality

There are a number of statements made by Native people—in addition to the words of Chief Seattle—that are similarly framed through delocality and the narrative of colonial difference and similarly misunderstood. A Wintu medicine women once claimed that "white people never cared for land or deer or bear," and that in contrast, "we [Indians] don't ruin things. . . . We shake down acorns and pinenuts. We don't chop down trees. We only use dead wood." Her diatribe continues thus:

> But the White people plow up the ground, pull down the trees, kill everything. The tree says, "Don't. I am sore. Don't hurt me." But they chop it down and cut it up. The spirit of the land hates them. They blast out trees and stir it up to its depths. They saw up the trees. That hurts them. The Indians never hurt anything, but the White people destroy all. They blast rocks and scatter them on the ground. The rock says, "Don't! You are hurting me." But the White people pay no attention. When the

Indians use rocks, they take little round ones for their cooking.... How can the spirit of the earth like the White man? ... Everywhere the White man has touched it, it is sore. (McLuhan 1972, 23)

With historical, anthropological, and archaeological evidence that Native people torched forests in order to chase out animals to hunt and chased buffalo off of cliffs for food, Western Thinkers scoff at what they see as hypocritical, romanticized, or nonsensical primitive morality. In the context of nonsensical primitive morality, the delocalized interpretation that everything is sacred makes Western Thinkers scoff. If everything is sacred, they reason, then everything—rocks and trees in this case—should be treated with the same respect one would treat a human being. This conclusion is seen as a reductio argument against the claim that everything is sacred and reveals once again the lack of reason on the part of primitive Indigenous "thinkers," or so the Western Thinker might conclude. The claim that everything is sacred is seen as hypocritical and romanticized in the sense that the delocalized interpretation above does not match what is thought to be documented evidence of contrary action. These views of the claim that everything is sacred only arise in the context of a delocalized interpretation of the claim. The delocalized interpretation results in the most radical version of environmental egalitarianism (everything is sacred) coupled with the Western assumption that treatment of things is determined by the value of things (equal treatment for equals). The charge of nonsense only arises if (1) we assume that only different levels of value can determine what kinds of actions are right and what kinds are wrong, and (2) we assume that equal value (or even equal status) requires equal treatment. We are already operating under the assumption, from the preceding chapter, even at this fairly superficial level of locality that (1) is possibly false—that there is a possibility of a nonanthropocentric moral theory that does not require different levels. What (2) means and the manner in which it is a perspective of delocality is the next level of epistemic locality that we will engage. The truth of (2) depends on the basic Western moral sense that equal value requires equal treatment or equal treatment requires equal value. The truth of (2) also depends on the primacy of individuals rather than relationships in moral reflection. A way to begin to peel away the layers of delocality at this level is through the following thoughts: if value is shared equally by all (everything is sacred) but moral action is determined by relational context, then equal things in different relations might not in fact require equal treatment since it is the relationship that is primary and not the individuals or the value of those individuals—human or nonhuman. The value of universal sacrality is important because it provides an extra sense of care—a way to contextualize my moral deliberations in locality—that we must carry with us in our moral deliberations. The charge of hypocrisy—that Native people propose this equal treatment of all things because of their sacrality but did not act accordingly as history seems to show—is rooted in the same misapprehension of locality. Only if the Wintu medicine woman is claiming that everything is sacred and deserves equal treatment according to assumptions (1) and (2) above can the charge be made that such claims are necessarily contradicted by the possible behavior toward forests and buffalo suggested above. In this chapter, I attempt to articulate a deeper layer of locality in the relationship between morality and the land. Locality, as a reminder, is the originary and continuing manifestation of being, knowing, and morality through the land. Locality then requires that we understand how morality is manifested in an originary and continual way through and out of the land and not floating free from it. One of the results of epistemic locality, then, is a greater capacity to operate with semantics of locality, which allows for a deeper understanding of many of the Native environmental texts and other aspects of Native culture that have been so systematically misunderstood. We must also remind ourselves that the delocalized understanding of Indigenous morality in locality is not an innocent mistake; the delocalized framework for understanding the Indigenous locality through delocality and the narrative of colonial difference are operations of coloniality and always serve the political gain for coloniality and settler colonialism in the United States. The de-localized framework for understanding Indigenous locality supports the settler coloniality of power in the context of everything from Indigenous property rights and land claims to Indigenous religious freedom, the creation of the National Park system, and the protection of sacred places.

Spider Grandmother often has a powerful creative power in Native traditions. Because of her power to weave together the basic threads of life and understanding, she is, as we have seen, often the foundation of human goodness, knowledge, and creativity. As a child growing up in the Diné and Hopi locality, I heard stories of how she taught the people how to weave, how to create beauty, but also how to live beautifully. This chapter extends the teachings of Spider Grandmother's web regarding the continuity, completeness, and bottom-unity of being, knowing, and morality in locality. In a deeper unfolding of epistemic locality (building an intimate knowing relationship to locality), the next chapters will extend our reflections on Vine Deloria Jr.'s philosophy of locality. One of the reasons that Deloria was so insistent that I complete a Ph.D. in philosophy, and his constant encouragement of Native students to do the same, was his sense of the need to underscore Native American philosophy with a deeper sense of its metaphysical and epistemological base. His belief was that Native American philosophy will always be seen as merely "represent[ing] the stage of human development in which superstition and ignorance reigned supreme" unless philosophers are given a bigger picture of the deeper unity and completeness of Indigenous philosophy through locality (Deloria 1999a, 3). In fact, it was this unity and completeness in Native philosophy that recommended it, to his mind, as a foundation for current and future reflections on knowledge, goodness, and the like—unity and completeness both in the philosophical manner by which Native philosophy comes together and to its ends as well as the desire for unity and completeness as important philosophical ideals. Even in the positive sense of the recent "awaking to the fact that Indian tribes possessed considerable knowledge of the natural world," Deloria viewed the Western understanding of Indigenous philosophy as framed by the narrative of colonial difference and understanding of this knowledge through delocality (Deloria and Wildcat 2001, 1). The manner in which Indigenous philosophy was framed, even in the positive sense of some "recognition of Indians' practical knowledge" or the "outright admiration for their sense of the religious," is "unsettling," Deloria claims, as "it does not attribute to Indians any consistency" (Deloria and Wildcat 2001, 1–2). It was on this basis that Deloria suggested that as Indigenous philosophers we should "focus our attention on the metaphysics possessed by most American Indian tribes and derived from this central perspective the information and beliefs that naturally flowed from them," instead of speaking of "Indian 'science' or even Indian 'religion'" (Deloria and Wildcat 2001, 2).

Deloria understood the term "metaphysics" as an expression of the locality of Indigenous philosophy that undergirds its operations and ways of speaking. Articulating the "metaphysics" of Indigenous philosophy was clearly, for Deloria, an operation of epistemic locality. This fact is made clear by some of the quotes he borrows from Alfred North Whitehead to articulate what he thinks an expression of the underlying Indigenous metaphysics amounts to. Deloria speaks of the difficulty of finding "intellectual respectability" for the manner in which metaphysics has been done in "Western circles." "Its conclusions," he claims, "were greatly abused by generations of Europeans who committed what Alfred North Whitehead called the 'fallacy of misplaced concreteness,' which is to say that, after they reached the conclusions to which their premises had led them, they came to believe they had accurately described ultimate reality" (Deloria and Wildcat 2001, 2). In Whitehead, like with his review of Feyerabend, Deloria finds a proto-locality philosopher (Deloria 1999b). Whitehead (1861-1947) was a famous English mathematician and philosopher who in the 1910s took a radical turn against Western philosophy by arguing that reality consists of processes rather than material objects. Paul Feyerabend (1927–1994) was an Austrian-born philosopher of science who was at the University of California, Berkeley for three decades and famous for his anarchistic view of science and rejection of universal methodological rules for science. In Deloria's review of Feyerabend's philosophy of science, "Perceptions and Maturity: Reflections on Feyerabend's Point of View," Deloria uses Whitehead's proto-locality to frame his understanding of Feyerabend's critique of delocalized thinking. Where Whitehead identifies the belief within the Western philosophical tradition that the "principles of philosophy were 'clear, obvious, and irreformable," Feyerabend "speaks directly to . . . the barriers that cultures raise against foreign critical ideas to protect their central integrity" (1999b, 4). The attempt to define the world through "certain rigid categories" produces a sense of the world that "seems clear, orderly, obvious, and without the possibility of reform," Deloria writes. "The product of this clarity," he continues, "is a certain kind of insanity that can survive only by renewed efforts to refine the definitions and that, ultimately, becomes totally self-destructive." To support this idea that an understanding of the world that is divorced from locality produces clarity and order only through an imagined being and reality that is homeless, floating free from the land upon which reality and our being depends, Deloria again quotes Whitehead: "a system will be the product of intelligence. But when the adequate routine is established, intelligence vanishes, and the system is maintained by a coordination of conditioned responses" (1999b, 4). In the concept of intelligence, from Whitehead, Deloria finds an expression of being in locality, while, in the need to maintain a system that has been delocalized, an "adequate routine is established" and "intelligence vanishes" through a "coordination of conditioned responses," Deloria sees the common results of thinking that has been removed from locality, that floats free from the land and so can only be maintained by operations of "routine" or "conditioned responses" (1999b, 4).

To articulate the metaphysics of Native philosophy is not to engage in the abstract operations of thinking divorced from the land, but to articulate the groundedness of Native philosophy in the land or from out of the land itself. It is in this context that the claims that Native philosophy lacks reason, sense, coherence, truth, and the like are a function—just as with Lyons and circle and Chief Seattle and sacrality—of delocality, and an articulation of the land or locality of Native philosophy removes it from the delocalized interpretive framework that opens up the possibility of it being seen as irrational, senseless, incoherent, and the like. It is through

conceptualizing the "metaphysics" of Indigenous philosophy through
epistemic locality that the layers of delocality can be removed enough to
see Native philosophy beyond these supposed limitations. Deloria puts
the situation in this way:

> Non-Western knowledge is believed to originate from primitive efforts
> to explain a mysterious universe. In this view, the alleged failure of
> primitive/tribal man to control nature mechanically is evidence of his
> ignorance and his inability to conceive of abstract general principles
> and concepts.
>
> Tribal methodologies for gathering information are believed to be
> "prescientific" in the sense that they are precausal and incapable of objective
> symbolic thought. This belief is a dreadful stereotypical reading of the
> knowledge of non-Western peoples and wholly incorrect. (1999b, 41)

It requires more than simply pointing to and criticizing these stereotypes
and culturally centric biases if the goal is truly clearing the way for viewing Native philosophy on its own footing as reflective method through
locality, because, as it should be clear from what Deloria says above,
Native philosophy is criticized by Western philosophy exactly because
it operates through locality and seems incapable of operating through
delocality. One way I have been performing this task of confronting delocality on its own terms is in the manner of Iktomi's story that presents
delocality to itself. Another way of confronting delocality in the context
of the narrative of colonial difference that constructs Native philosophy
as irrational and primitive nonsense is to articulate some of the ways
in which Native philosophy is systematic, ways in which very specific
views arise not out of primitive mistakes but rather out of what Deloria

describes as Indian metaphysics or locality. In doing so, it is very likely that one can peel back some of the layers of delocality that empowers Western Thinkers with a kind of Iktomi-like hubris that allows them to see their philosophical traditions in relationship to Native philosophy with the same kind of exaggerated scale by which they see themselves as humans in relation to nonhumans.

Deloria's Philosophy of Locality: Bottom-Up Unity and Regulative Completeness

Vine Deloria Jr.'s proposed place of departure for this task was with the concepts of bottom-up unity and completeness. A philosophy or approach to knowledge is complete, from one way that Deloria talks about it, when it weaves together all of the important aspects of our lives into one understandable and usable system or approach. According to this notion, Deloria views the Western worldview as markedly incomplete since, for one example as articulated by Daniel Wildcat in his book with Deloria, "the most vexing issue confronting" it is "the irreconcilable duality between facts and values, most often discussed as the science-versus-religion conflict" (Deloria and Wildcat 2001, 47). The idea is that Western systems of knowledge, as exemplified in the form of Western science, can only articulate facts but not values. If our systems of knowledge—what we consider our ultimate learning tools—can tell us nothing of meaning and value, then, according to Deloria, they are markedly incomplete forms of knowledge. The fact that science purposely ignores meaning and value as a part of its mission to only seek out the facts is not as simple of an operation as it seems. Part of what underlies the claim that meaning and value are not real is, in fact, that science cannot reach them. The circular manner in which science eliminates meaning and value from its operations and from what is considered real is a part of the same delocalized conceptualization that limits Western science and Western philosophy, on Deloria's account, from greater unity and completeness. In this process of Iktomi's story of our choices between locality and delocality, a new and important choice can become clear. In the context of locality, when faced with the reality that a science cannot speak to issues of meaning and value, the choice would not be that meaning and value are not real or understandable in terms of scientific knowledge but rather the choice would be that something must be done to help that science find a deeper unity and completeness. The completeness of knowledge is more than just its ability to bring together the reflection from all the various aspects of our lives. Completeness is also a regulative ideal. This emphasis on completeness is a function of locality because completeness is a function of kinship.

One way that we can understand completeness in the context of kinship and locality is to look at Indigenous expressions of a generalized world in a scientific or even spiritual sense. The expressions of the world in this sense and articulations of a human kinship (intimate knowing relationship) to this world do not provide abstract codifications of the world as such and the proper modes of humans relating to this generic construction of the world, but rather provide background for expressions of being-in-locality where the human kinship relationship to a world is always already in motion. This always already in motion framework for being-in-locality and a human kinship relationship to a world are what create the impetus toward and the value of completeness as a necessary feature of a way of knowing but also as a regulative ideal for kinship relationships themselves within this always already in motion framework of being-in-locality or being-from-the-land, which from the edge of locality can be described as the world. The world and human kinship relationships that are always already in motion within it are living and growing expressions within locality. The world is dynamic and never complete, and human kinship relationships within that world are dynamic and never complete.

There is a purposeful ambiguity here regarding the concept of completeness. Within the context of locality, there is constant motion because kinship relationships are always already in motion. This always already being in motion is one way that Native people conceptualize life at its most basic level, similar to Spider Grandmother's web that has no abstract structure or hierarchy of relationships or levels of being. Alternatively, the lack of motion is one way of conceptualizing death, or as Native philosopher Gregory Cajete puts it in his work on Native science, "when something becomes static, whether it be human, animal, or the ecological processes of an environment, atrophy and death usually follow" (2000, 184). It is only after a death, stasis, a lack of motion, or the like, that a certain kind of completeness takes place. It is only through this sort of completeness that a search for a complete understanding is possible or meaningful. There is a certain kind of death, then, that is sought as the ground for knowledge in delocality. But this death can also be understood just as delocality itself, for the death that Cajete speaks of is not a delocalized death; it is not a thing but a delocalized abstraction of the idea of an end in itself. It is not death in locality; it is death as a delocalized conception of what is beyond locality, or particularly here the end of motion or a completely still or frozen image of the world. The idea of death in relationship to this frozen world of delocality also clearly carries moral weight, which in this sense is not only death per se but even killing. Talk of death and even bringing out such death (killing) in the context of a lack motion is metaphorical and pejorative in the main. Death, in the context of a world in locality, is not an end in itself.

In the context of the locality of *He Sapa* and *Lakol wicoun*, life is understood as a visible side of death, and death the invisible side of life. The visible and invisible sides of being in the Lakota locality are not two sides of reality: locality and delocality. The visible and invisible sides of life and death are the visible and invisible sides of life and death in locality. The invisible vital and nonvital parts of life (*woniya, sicun, nagi, nagila*) and the visible parts of life (the body, the physical manifestations of [*woniya*] breath in smoke or steam, the physical manifestations of [*sicun*] influence) are two sides of the same being in locality. The invisible parts of life (the *wanagi*, for example) that are included in what we call death are not separated from life itself in a fundamental way, nor are they separated from locality or from the always already in motion reality of kinship relationships (or being-in-locality). Death is an invisible part of life and a transformation through the same *tun* (power or energy) that allows anything to transform what is visible to what is invisible and vice versa. Death and life, then, are transformations of the same thing, in some sense. Death, then, in the *Lakol wicoun*, is not a transformation of a life as motion into stasis. Death is not truly an end of motion or a freezing of the always already being in motion of life. The vibrancy of motion that is life increasing slows down as it reaches the point of the transformation into death, but there is also a vibrancy of *tun* (power or energy) that is used in the transformation of life into death, visible into invisible, just as there is a vibrancy of *tun* that is used in the transformation of death into life (being born), invisible into visible. Death is not an ultimate end, a transformation into nothingness, but yet it is something we try to avoid in our life, and for our family, our people, or even the ecosystems in which we are embedded. Avoiding death and working to increasing life (life-continuing actions) are not delocalized goals. In the context of locality, there is no desire to rid the world of death itself. There is no meaning to the concept of eternal life, such as there is no meaning to the concept of eternal truth upon which the ideas of delocalized epistemology depend. Within the locality framework of an understanding of the inevitability of death as part of the nature and meaning of any and all things that have life, death is avoided, and insofar as human communities can, they do the things they can to increase and extend life, which includes sustaining the life-maintaining power or life-vibrancy of being-in-motion. Death as the end of motion is an expression of a delocalized end or perhaps an expression of delocality itself. In the context of locality there is always motion, and whatever stasis that happens is only momentary and in the process of transformation. Given this kind of expression of dynamic complexity in locality where there is always already motion, there can be no complete articulations since the idea of completeness involved here is articulated from delocality and so requires an absolute end in order to be achieved.

The always already being in motion reality of being-in-locality and human kinship relationships make the abstract configurations of sameness impossible or meaningless. Without such delocalized grounds for the creation of continuity and unity, a dynamic process for the creating and maintaining of continuity and unity is required. One broad way that unity or continuity is approached in the context of always already being in motion is through a bottom-up method. The same kind of considerations regarding completeness in the context of the dynamic nature of always already being in motion of being-in-locality lead to these particular conceptions of an approach to continuity or unity. Bottom-up continuity or unity refers to the manner in which these things are woven together that matches the dynamic nature of the always already being in motion of being-in-locality and reflects how relationships can be built and sustained within this dynamic space of being and kinship. Loosely, I would define bottom-up continuity or unity as a weaving together that builds up from very basic elements while always accounting for the individual variety of the basic elements in this process of continually bringing together. This conceptualization of continuity or unity as continually bringing together seems quite common in Native philosophy and culture. In political philosophy, it is often seen as a process for creating a just and sustainable polity. Here the idea is that all political and social unity must continually arise from the individual variation in human personalities, desires, experiences, and the like, which is just like knowledge in relation to multiplicity or diversity in manifestation of things in locality more generally. In the context of the creating of a just and sustainable polity, part of the idea seems to be that there can be no top-down structure of governance, for example, since this would be to determine what is right for a community not on the basis of this individual variation, the always already being in motion of the community, but by something much narrower and in the end exclusionary regarding the individuals. The exclusionary and delocalized nature of this kind of coming together creates a fundamental tension that seeks to break apart this unity, both in the sense of the tension placed upon individuals but also the fundamental tension between abstract ideal and the reality in locality, which includes the reality of the exclusion of individuals but also the struggle to be included by those individuals.

The political unity of a community in locality must arise out of what is present at each step in the individual's heart and mind as expressions of the multiplicity of being-in-locality. Contrast this, on a very simple level, with the idea of a nation-state where a people are held together by a common government and territory. There is a deep contradiction at the heart of such unity. All the people are included in this unity, and yet this inclusion necessarily implies the exclusion of individuals and groups that are not of the delocalized concept of the group (not citizens, not landowners, not the dominant ethnicity, not the dominant sexual orientation), which are excluded necessarily by the process and nature of the delocalized conception itself. This kind of unity continues to seek itself through conformity. This drive toward conformity that maintains this kind of unity further removes those who do not fit into this preset notion of culture and identity that serves to construct this unity, thus further polarizing conformity and nonconformity, which serves to remove more individuals and further remove others, creating a constant and seemingly vicious cycle of exclusion and polarization. These opposed and bounded identities further codify and gain strength in responsive opposition to the mainstream identity, which continues to expand its exclusionary core. This kind of unity is inherently unstable. It is very easy to create but very hard to maintain since any opposing identities that arise must be repressed, an act that causes increased force and response from those identities being repressed.

I've heard in Cherokee and Pueblo traditions the people conceived of as an ear of corn. The symbolizing of the people as an ear of corn is a way of seeing the community as like a single organism made up of the people who are mere pieces of that organism. The people are not parts that can function on their own, but are pieces of the whole (the community) and need it to live. Vine Deloria Jr. describes this notion of people in a community this way: "Tribal man is hardly a personal 'self' in our modern sense of the word. He does not so much live in a tribe; the tribe lives in him. He is the tribe's subjective expression" (1973, 201). This notion of a kind of radical unity of people within a community is not, however, an abstract and delocalized conception of community because the singularity of community in the sense of the people as an ear of corn functions through a multiplicity of individuals and individual variation within the always already being in motion of being in locality. In the Cherokee locality, the people are also like an ear of corn, as conceptualized by Selu, the Corn Mother. In the oral tradition of Cherokee story and history, there are stories that indicate the complexity of this conception of community. I have heard Cherokee family stories about members of families living in Cherokee towns (autonomous communities) who left their family while the village was being attacked and the town was at war to protect itself. These individuals would go and stay with relatives in another town some distance away while their own community and family were under attack. After the time of bloodshed had passed, these individuals would return to their community and family to joyous welcomes from their friends and relatives. In these stories there seemed to be no sense that these individuals, in making this choice to leave at this crucial time, were doing anything inappropriate, doing anything that was out of conformity with the notion of being a central community member. Perhaps better put would be to say that there seemed to be no context for describing their behavior as either appropriate or inappropriate: it just was what those individuals who left had in their hearts to do.

It inevitably appears to many after hearing these ideas and stories that there is a serious contradiction at work. Radical community identity and radical individualism are in contradiction. Many cannot imagine that upon returning to their communities after leaving during an attack, the Cherokee in question would not be ostracized by their relatives. Many see the actions of the Cherokee in question as a clear example of neglecting duties and responsibilities. From the perspective of unity from the top-down or from the concept of unity from delocality, these seem like reasonable conclusions or questions. From a bottom-up perspective of unity, these questions are less clear and the conclusions less reasonable. The seeming contradiction between individual and community (as seen in chapter 3) is a function of delocality. From the bottom-up perspective, however, there are not communities except at every moment as they are made from the hearts and minds of the individuals. Individuals and communities are two sides of the same intertwining duality of the always already being in motion of kinship as a manifestation of being-in-locality. In this way, neither individuals nor communities become realities unto themselves, and neither do the desires or values of each. Even obligations and duties are not things in themselves in the context of locality; they are not reified beyond the dynamic and ever-changing flow of the already always being in motion of being-in-locality. Thus, there are not abstract values, duties, or obligations to which one must conform or to which the community must conform. In the context of locality, values, duties, and obligations are being constantly remade through the always already being in motion reality of kinship as the substance of locality. This constant remaking of values, duties, and obligations includes the variations in the hearts and minds of the individuals who are always coming together as the community. In Cherokee, the idea of the community as that which is always coming together is seen in the very concept of Cherokee or Cherokee identity itself. The true and original name for the *Jalagi*, as we came to be called by others and then codified in English as Cherokee, is *Anigaduwagi* (the people who come together as one). In this context, the Cherokee community and Cherokee identity are not the conceptualizations of an abstract unity or of abstract individual identity as a process through which the always already being in motion of the kinship substance of locality can manifest into an always coming together of the Cherokee people as *gaduwagi* (always coming together as one). The Cherokee value of *dejadaligenvdisgesdi* (responsibility for one another) is not an abstract value that becomes a duty or obligation but a way of conceptualizing the process of maintaining the bottom-up unity of community as the always coming together in the context of the always already being in motion of locality.

As seen in chapter 3, these two seemingly contradictory ideas of the radical community and the radical individual actually depend upon each other. The deep sense of community is only realizable and sustainable on the foundation of always coming together of exactly what is in the hearts and minds of all the individuals without any exceptions. There is a sustaining strength in this sense of community that is not found in top-down unity communities that are based on abstract values, ideologies, laws, and so forth. In the context of the always already being in motion of locality, that kind of abstractly structured community is just like, as Deloria puts it, the science that tries to control nature rather than figuring out how to relate to it. This sort of science, according to Deloria, and this sort of community produce constant remainders and constant anomalies. Knowing in locality and the weaving of unity in locality leave nothing as a remainder and nothing that needs to be weeded out—no exceptions to account for, nothing to assimilate, or nothing to destroy. The community is a reality that is made of the dynamic and constant movement of individuals, but individuals are taught values in locality that make them capable of functioning in relational reciprocity to a dynamic *We* of community. I am, therefore we are, and we are, therefore I am, both.

This bottom-up approach functions the same in the acquisition of knowledge. There are no theories by which to test the world, no theories for which the data of experience can conform or not conform. All experiences, no matter how strange or hard to fit into preconceived views of the nature of the world, are accepted at face value. There is no context for questioning the validity of experience in the way that there is no context for questioning the conformity of an individual to the preconceived notions of duty and obligation. This is just the nature of bottom-up unity. Only if one allows the sense of reality that develops in understanding to become a thing in itself over and against the continually developing and transforming of that reality and the experience of it can the perspective develop whereby this kind of questioning of the validity of experience is realizable, just as community relationships and ideals must become a reified reality in order to question the actions that arise from the variation of individual hearts and minds. Just as this kind of variation is not only accepted but its coming together is seen as integral to the sustainability and movement toward completeness of a community, the variation of experience and manifestations of reality are seen as integral to sustainability and movement toward completeness regarding knowledge.

Singular Manifestation and the Facticity
of Experience: The Metaphysics of Locality

From the perspective of locality, the political and epistemological boundaries that seem so important from the outside (delocally) are absent. The
world and all that is in it, as seen from the perspective of locality, are in
a state of constant motion and transformation, which is not an abstract
picture of a world in motion and transformation, but a world of motion
and transformation in the context of the always already being in motion
of being-in-locality. Motion and transformation are then the originary
and continual manifestation of things in the context of locality. Reality
as a function of being-in-locality is not static, nor is it only becoming in
a positive, linear direction, but also circularly as in becoming and rebe-
coming. Even space, most often understood as a static and simple void, is
a qualitative process, from the perspective of locality. In Diné philosophy,
for example, "all *entities*, *objects*, or similar units of action and perception
must be considered as units that are engaged in continuous processes.
In the same way, spatial units and spatial relationships are 'qualitative'
in this same sense and cannot be considered to be clearly defined,
readily quantifiable and static in essence" (Pinxten et al. 1983, 168). In this
dynamic context of locality, space and time are intertwined in the flux
of already always being in motion of experience. From the perspective
of locality, one might understand reality as a singular manifestation.
In Diné philosophy, for example, reality is understood "as a continuous
manifestation . . . [or] a series of events, rather than states or situational
persistences through time" (Pinxten et al. 1983, 20–21). The future is
seen as more expansive and filled with much greater possibility than in
Western views of what is predictable within a delocalized conception

of causality. In Diné philosophy, the future is a range of "incompletely realized events . . . [that] are still most of all 'becoming' and involved in a process of 'manifesting' themselves" (Pinxten et al. 1983, 36).

In the context of already always becoming of reality in locality, then, there is no supposition in advance that one experience will be like the next or that my experience will be like yours. If the universe is conceptualized as a process of one singular manifestation, it seems rather odd to attempt to describe one part of it as a negation of another part of it. The truth of all the individual experiences are taken as given in the already always in motion dynamic of reality. There is no need, then, to judge these experiences against some static truth. The idea is simply that all the different experiences are of the world as it is presenting itself, and the different experiences are simply regarded as a part of that process of the continual manifestation of reality or the always already being in motion of the becoming of things. Understanding the world is not, then, achieved by reducing it to delocalized abstractions (determining which experiences to count in order to normalize and erase the movement) but rather by finding a way to understand what it is as it is presented. Instead of trying to erase the movement or delocalize the already always being in motion dynamic of experience so as to judge some experiences as veridical and others not, all experiences, however disparate, are considered a part of what just is, or put another way I might say that every experience is not only of a world always already being in motion but every experience is itself a manifestation of this world of always becoming. Instead of trimming off the excess and reformulating in reaction to anomalies, Native epistemology tries to understand the shape as it is presented and is being presented.

Many Native American philosophers see Indigenous knowledge

systems as relating to such a sense of world that is always becoming. Gregory Cajete, again, in his book *Native Science: Natural Laws of Interdependence*, describes Native scientific methodology as rooted in a kind of responsivity to the dynamic interrelationship between humans and the world. He says of truth that "[it] is not a fixed point, but rather an ever-evolving point of balance, perpetually created and perpetually new" (Cajete 2000,19). Truth, then, is not a function of statements in the ordinary Western sense since statements as representations of fact are not thought to be responsive to dynamic changes in the world they are meant to represent. Truth in the context of a world that is always becoming might be thought of as a function of relationships rather than of static representations of relationships or things in the form of statements or even of things themselves. The concept of truth has no context, then, as it relates to individual experiences. Truth comes to bear only upon our understanding of the relationships between and in our experiences. Our understanding must be dynamically related to the relationships between and in our experiences since these are never static in themselves.

Individual experiences are not questionable in a context of locality. They are just as much a feature of the world as anything that Western thought has described as "in" the world. Our experiences are not of the world since they are just as much in the world as anything else. Returning to Deloria's discussion, recall that he describes a "fundamental premise" of Native philosophy as the view that "we cannot 'misexperience,' we can only misinterpret what we experience" (1999b, 46). Deloria is articulating the facticity of experience in locality. Every individual experience is a feature of the always becoming or unfolding of the world in locality, or a world that is always already in motion. The question is not does some experience actually map onto a world that is external from that experience, but how do I understand or continually remake my kinship relationship to an ever-unfolding world, a world that now includes this particular experience as a feature of it. The meaning of "misinterpret" in this context comes out of the manner in which experiences, like stories, ceremonies, and so on, give us "interpretations" of our lives and our path in the world. What Deloria means by "misinterpret" is merely to misunderstand the meaning of this experience for our lives. We misinterpret experience when we misunderstand what this experience might be telling us about how to continually re-create our kinship relationship within world that is always becoming. Deloria describes the way that experience can instruct in this way in an interview in the *In the Light of Reverence*. He put it like this: "all that this revelation [of the experience] is telling you is how you and your community at this time in life can adjust to the rest of the world" (Deloria 2001). It is this revelation of the experience (what it is telling us about how we can adjust to the rest of the world) that we can misinterpret. The revelation of experience, Deloria continues, does not, however, form the basis for an abstract belief that anyone should have or even any claim about the world. The mistake is not one about the nature of the world or about the relationship of that experience to a world beyond it. The mistake has nothing to do with the experience itself but with its meaning for my life, its relationship to me or to us, or to how I or we ought to respond to this experience and what it reveals about the moment of the always unfolding kinship of locality. To interpret experience in the Western context of delocality implies a representation, a gap between me and the world or words as symbols, and what those symbols represent that does not exist in the epistemic and semantic context of locality. What we can misunderstand is what our experience is saying to us—how it is calling out to us—but not the so-called representational content of experience.

Seeing the dynamic nature of the world and the dynamic human interrelation with that world as well as the sense that sustainable and completeness-directed understanding only comes about from bottom-up epistemic structure provides independent reasons for viewing individual experience as given, but together these views create a framework where judging individual experiences for veracity has limited merit. In fact, there is a deep-seated contradiction in the methodology by which one acquires knowledge through experience (Western science) only to turn back around—once theories are created out of that experiential relation—and judge the individual veracity of the very individual experience those theories were founded upon—a contradiction that seems to threaten the validity of the very methodology itself. The suppression of this perhaps natural tendency to question experience was countered by what Deloria calls the philosopher's training in "suspended judgment." "The hallmark of the true Indian philosopher," he writes, "was the ability to hold in suspended judgment the experience he or she had enjoyed or was told" (Deloria 2001, 6). For the Native philosopher, this experience was added to further experiences enjoyed or conveyed. All the various manifestations of being-in-locality, experienced or conveyed, were added together not to show the Native philosopher what is or is not, what to believe or not to believe, but to give her better understanding of what is becoming, of the continuing transformation or unfolding of being in locality so as to continue to adjust and remake kinship within this always already being in motion of the world in locality. Knowing is, then, a never-ending process. Knowledge is never complete. Completeness is always regulative. Knowing is also always already being in motion, which means that it also never really begins in the sense of ever being outside of itself, being out of kinship, being delocalized. It is an understanding of the regulative nature of the completeness of knowledge and the always already being in motion of the knowing relationship—knowledge as an intimate knowing relationship—that allows knowledge to interact with a world of locality that itself is always already being in motion. It is in this context that Deloria describes the regulative completeness in Native epistemology as "philosophical" and the Western scientific epistemology as "dogmatic." Native philosophy is, in this setting, more philosophical and less dogmatic, Deloria claims, because "Indians did not discard any experience" and have no place for dogmatism in epistemology since knowing is always ongoing and understanding is never complete (1999b, 44). Western scientific epistemology operates—in epistemic delocality—he claims, "through a refining process whereby we throw away the 'anomalies'—the facts that do not fit into our definitional schemata" (1999b, 4). He writes:

> [Indians] obtained their knowledge by accepting everything they experienced as grist for the mill, [while] Western science has drawn its conclusions by excluding the kinds of data that the [Indians] cherished. Western science holds that ideas, concepts, and experiences must be clearly stated, and be capable of replication in an experimental setting by an objective observer. Any bit of data or body of knowledge that does not meet this standard is suspect or rejected out of hand. (Deloria 1999b, 44)

Instead of finding which experiences or claims to knowledge to exclude, the Native philosopher or scientist considers all data in an operation of bottom-up unity and regulative completeness.

What one attempts to find through these epistemic practices are the connections between all the data, between all the variety of manifestations of being. "The task," Deloria writes, "is to find the proper pattern of interpretation for the great variety of ordinary and extraordinary experiences we have. Ordinary and extraordinary must come together in one coherent comprehensive story line" (1999b, 46). Native knowledge, Cajete claims, "is the collective heritage of human experience with the natural world; in its most essential form, it is a map of natural reality" (2000, 3). Native epistemology does not weed out the true from the false but rather attempts to grapple with the relationships in an ever-transforming world as manifested through the variety of experiences of generation after generation of Indian people. Deloria believes that focusing on weeding out the true from the false limits the ability to understand the natural world, which in this context is to be able to sustain kinship relationships within a world that is always already in motion. "Imposing certain restricted patterns on the natural world," he writes, "[limits] its potential for response" (Deloria 1999b, 12). This openness denies the possibility of dogmatism since to claim that things are and will always be a certain way (the dogmatic claim), on this view, is to claim that there will be no more experience and no more unfolding of being. In the completed world of dogmatism, there is also no possibility for kinship, since kinship requires a response. Kinship is sustained by adjusting to the response. This openness to the potential response rather than imposing restricted patterns on the world allows my knowledge to be, itself, responsive to a world always already in motion, while the dogmatic knowledge cannot relate to such a world but must maintain a delocalized and static world or be forced to revise any claims to knowledge. This openness is necessary for epistemic locality since it seems that only through delocality are limits imposed upon the world in such a way to undermine this demand for openness that knowledge as an intimate knowing relationship demands.

In addition to being understood as an intimate knowing relationship, knowledge is a kind of story, in Deloria's articulation. In knowledge we weave together all experiences, even ones only conveyed to us in the stories of others, into our own stories. But knowledge is a story filled with layers and dimensions of meaning through metaphor. Knowledge is synthetic, relational, and moral. Knowledge is the synthetic story of variation and individual experience of the manifestation of a world that is always becoming. Knowledge brings together, through the bottom-up creation of unity, all of this variation into narratives that incorporate this variation through layers and dimensions of meaning and both continued and possible kinship. Knowledge is an account of kinship as an individual's relational balance within a situation where kinship is always already in motion. In this space, terms such as "harmony," "kinship," "balance," and so on are appropriate. Knowledge is also then moral because knowledge is an always ongoing kinship relationship. Knowledge is also a story, but it is my story, and so it is the story of my life as I am conceiving it and continually reconceiving it in the context of the always already in motion framework of kinship in locality.

The Metaphysics and Epistemology of Morality in Locality

This moral dimension of knowledge is reflected in the goal of completeness. Sakan'ku Skonk (Rising Sun) of the Turtle Mountain Dakotas pronounced to Harry Boise, who in 1919 spent eight months teaching science to his people, that "the scientific view was inadequate. Not bad or untrue, but inadequate to explain, among many other things, how man is to find a road along which he wishes and chooses to make ... progress" (quoted in Deloria 1999b, 43). As Deloria expresses it, Native knowledge is about "finding the proper moral and ethical road upon which human beings should walk. All knowledge . . . was directed toward that goal" (1999b, 43). In order for knowledge to be complete, it cannot merely convey "the abstract structure of physical reality," but must be capable of supporting our search for "the proper road along which, for the duration of a person's life, individuals were supposed to walk" (Deloria 1999b, 46). Knowledge of mere physical reality (physical reality as delocality) is markedly less complete than "a knowledge of the physical universe arranged or understood in such a manner as to call forth some form of moral response" (*physical reality and morality in locality*) (Deloria 1999b, 47). The fear that results from this possibility Deloria describes thusly:

> This conclusion is anathema to most scientists, whose fear (well justified considering the history of warfare between sacred and secular forces in Western civilization) is that if such ethical dimensions are admitted, it would once again allow ecclesiastical authorities to gain control of social and political institutions and so prevent or inhibit investigative scientific activities. (1999b, 49).

This worry, however well-founded in the history of Western civilization and particularly in the context of Western civilization's experience with coloniality, is not a worry about knowledge in locality and epistemic locality as a counteragent to coloniality. This worry is a worry about the power that arises from delocality and the destructive force of that power as it operates through coloniality to manifest itself upon others. This is not a universal worry but only a worry that the kind of dominating or kinless power of coloniality will be turned back upon those who have been wielding it on others. Delocalized knowledge, when combined with a delocalized morality—which both are constructed apart from the land and apart from kinship—has the capacity to bring about these feared results. In the context of locality, we have no reason to suppose that knowledge that calls for a moral response would result in an authoritarian moral order that limits the possibility of further knowledge and kinship reciprocity. In fact, it is only through delocalized epistemology and moral contexts that knowledge and morality, truth and value, are separated such that this kind of worry can arise in the first place. Thus, the worry is not truly a worry regarding knowledge or morality but about the delocality and so coloniality of these.

In the context of Indigenous locality, knowledge and morality do not operate with the power of coloniality. Indigenous epistemology and morality operate with the power of locality that is in the land and moves across land and locality without delocality. Let us return to the case study of the difference between delocalized and localized knowledge and morality from the early 1800s debate between Reverend Cram and Red Jacket. Reverend Cram, a representative of the Boston Missionary Society, came to the Seneca in order to convert them. The Indian agent who introduced him stated that this missionary has "not come to get your lands or your money, but to enlighten your minds" with Christianity, the "one true religion." Cram tells the Seneca stories from the Bible, including the story of Adam and Eve. Cram tells the Indians, "if you do not embrace the right way, you cannot be happy hereafter" (Densmore 1999, 136). Upon completing his telling of the story of Adam and Eve, the

Seneca insisted on telling a story of their creation as well, which did not please Cram. As Deloria puts it in his discussion of this exchange, "Cram was livid, arguing that he had told the Seneca the truth while they had recited a mere fable to him" (Deloria 2004, 9). The Seneca found this perplexing and wondered why he had been so rude when they had sat quietly and listened to his story. There was surely truth in what Reverend Cram had said, but the Indians wondered why that meant their story had to be false. Red Jacket, in his famous speech to Reverend Cram, puzzles over just these issues:

> Friend and Brother! ... Our eyes are opened that we see clearly. Our ears are unstopped that we have been able to hear distinctly the word you have spoken.... Brother! Continue to listen. You say that you are sent to instruct us how to worship the Great Spirit agreeably to his mind; and if we do not take hold of the religion which you white people teach, we shall be unhappy. You say that you are right and that we are lost. How do we know this to be true? ... Brother! You say there is but one way to worship and serve the Great Spirit. If there is but one religion, why do you white people differ so much about it? Why do not all agree, as you can all read the book? Brother! We do not understand these things.... We never quarrel about religion. (quoted in Drake, 283–87)

The delocalized perspective on what I should know and how I should live my life (knowledge and morality) is represented by Reverend Cram. From his perspective, a story tells simple and straightforward facts that are real or not and represent the whole of reality or do not. There is some story that captures all of reality so that if we come to understand that story for what it is, we can know what is true in total and if we follow what that story, do what it tells us directly or indicates examples for us to follow, we will have happiness, a good life or we will live right and be moral. Cram tells the story that he believes captures all of reality as a delocalized abstraction. When the Seneca respond to this story by reciprocating with their own story, he was angered, in part, simply by their lack of a delocalized understanding of the nature of things. Red Jacket describes an understanding of what I should know and how I should live my life through locality, through the land. From his perspective, a story, while it is real and true in the sense of being an expression of reality, can never express all of reality on its own. Reality on its own does not exist, for one, except as a delocalized abstraction of reality in locality. A story is true insofar as it is an expression of a person's or a people's experience in locality. A story like this is just as true and just as real as the experience is—an experience is an unfolding of the always already becoming of reality itself. A true story in this sense does not, however, guide action, at least by itself or apart from locality. A true story does not contain a delocalized kernel of truth that can be then carried across localities to create generic guides for action. The sense of the possibility of truth for a true story is the truth from Black Elk: if you think about it, you will see that it true. What is true in a true story, what can guide action, is something that might show itself to the listening of this story if I listen carefully to this story in the context of building and maintaining kinship relations. I can only come to know the truth of this story (and the story can only become an acting guiding) when I come to know the story in the context of Deloria's knowledge as an intimate knowing relationship.

The truth of all stories that are meant to be true does not guide action, just as universal sacrality does not guide action. Everything is sacred, and every story is true. There are stories that are meant to be lies, of course. These stories, however, are also true in the localized sense that stories that are meant to be true are true. Thus, every story is true in a very similar sense that one might say that everything is sacred is true. Every story is true and everything is sacred until one tries to use stories and sacrality against their purposes, to lie or to create hierarchies of value. The sacredness of something, in this sense, or the truth of some story is not what determines my moral relationship to that thing or brings the possible moral layers of that story to life. It is my relationship to that something and my relationship to that story. But my relationship to that something and my relationship to that story are just my knowledge of them as an intimate knowing relationship. But what is necessary for guiding action is understanding the meaning in locality of that story. I must understand how to relate to it, how it presents a relational context for me to follow, or how it presents a path of kinship, in order for this story to guide my action.

In addition, Red Jacket provides a reductio argument on the perspective of delocality in his speech. He shows that delocality is coloniality, that delocality and coloniality are failures. Coloniality cannot through delocality destroy locality, and neither can delocality actually remain delocalized. It is a ruse that always and only obscures even its own locality. If a book can tell you how to live, if a book can tell you what is true, Red Jacket argues against Cram, then all who read it should understand how to live and what is true. Since all of Reverend Cram's people have read this book, they all should know how to live and what is true. Red Jacket, using the fact that one of the main arguments Cram's people have is about how to live and what is true, presents a reductio argument against Cram's position. Clearly, just as delocalizing coloniality leaves the remainder of Indigenous locality, the delocalizing epistemology of Reverend Cram hides the locality of its own European Christian position that is attempting, through delocality, to be abstracted and forced onto foreign localities.

Morality in Locality: Beyond the Real and the Fictional

These articulations provide a very different context for reflection on the nature of realism and fictionalism. In Native philosophy, there seems to be little room for questions regarding what is real and what is not. The history of Western thought and culture manifests something rather different. A commonplace concern, even among nonphilosophers, is whether certain entities that we speak of actually exist (God, ghosts, angels, demons, and so on). There is a sense in which their existence must be established in order for people's talk of experiencing such things to carry any weight. If God is going to be said to exist, it must be on the basis of some manner of establishing the existence of such a being. This is the reason many give for saying that God or ghosts or whatever do not exist: their existence cannot be verified. Even those who say that God exists, for example, often give some verification procedure as evidence for the existence of such a being, proof by reason, indirect cosmological evidence, and so on. Both sides of this way of speaking assume that talk about something (such as God, ghosts, or whatever) can be about nothing or can actually be about something. Verification of some sort establishes that the talk is of the latter kind. In what follows, I articulate some of the issues behind the debate between moral realism and moral fictionalism, and then I address these issues as a feature of epistemic locality and reconfiguring morality in locality, in the land.

The Western Thinker Asks an Open Question about Moral Realism and Moral Naturalism

—from the philosophy of Iktomi

The Western Thinker tries to capture the nature of moral realism as a feature of moral statements. To say that I have an obligation to help my less than fortunate neighbor is the same as saying that is just rained 1.2 inches in Malibu or that the tree outside my window is 9.23 feet tall. These are all supposed to be simple matters of fact. Moral statements purport to report facts and are true if they get these facts right. Moral realism holds that at least some moral statements are true. Moral fictionalism, then, can take at least two possible forms. One can reject the idea that moral statements purport to report facts. Moral statements are neither true nor false. One can instead reject that any moral statements are in fact true but concede that moral statements do mean to report facts and would be true if such facts held. This rejection of moral realism is like an atheistic view of statements about the existence of God. The statement "God exists" is meant be true, but, as it turns out, there is no such thing, according to the atheist, and so this statement or any statement about such a being is false.

Iktomi thinks that this is just more trickster logic leading to more nonsense. Iktomi knows that Wakan Tanka exists because Wakan Tanka is just life. Since life exists, so does Wakan Tanka. What more needs to be answered? Isn't the existence of life and the energy for life that is seen every time a baby is born or when the sun rises enough? Does life not exist? Iktomi thinks that perhaps the thinking that leads to the question about whether something beyond life and the power that continues to generate life is perhaps a fork that leads to trickster logic in the first place.

Moral realism is difficult to reconcile with naturalism. Naturalism is the view that facts must be derived from or at least be compatible with the results of natural science. Naturalism limits the kinds of experiences that can be added as data for reflection.

Iktomi doesn't think experience should be limited from the start since that would mean that certain things would be necessarily unexperienceable. Iktomi thinks this is classic trickster thinking, telling someone what they can experience before they have even experienced it or not.

The Western Thinker often denies moral realism in an attempt to defend moral naturalism, which is the claim that ethical properties are natural properties. Reductive moral naturalism claims that moral properties are reducible to natural ones. Weak ethical naturalism claims that moral properties are natural but denies that there are particular natural properties to be determined and in some cases that ethical properties are natural but irreducible (Boyd 1988).

One Western Thinker created the Open Question argument in 1903. It was meant to refute strong moral naturalism and presents the traditional position used to refute moral realism. The argument states that if good is just pleasure, then "pleasure is good" should mean the same as "good is good," and be equally informative. However, the question is always open as to whether pleasure is in fact good. The statement that "pleasure is good" cannot mean the same thing as "good is good" in a logical sense. But if good is pleasure is not discovered logically (in the meaning of the words "pleasure" and "good") but discovered empirically, the question is not open in the same sense. If good is pleasure means something like water is H_2O, then whether water is actually H_2O or whether pleasure is good would be discovered empirically and not discovered merely as a function of the meanings of the words.

> Iktomi doesn't think anyone should try to reduce one language or story to another. There is no reason, Iktomi thinks, to suppose that there is just one kind of language or story that can express reality and that all others must coincide or be reducible to it. Iktomi thinks there is no reason to suppose that one kind of language or story can be reduced to a simpler language or story that reflects more directly an expression of reality than other stories. Articulations of reality ought to take on some of the characteristics of what they are attempting to articulate, which Iktomi thinks means that language and story should reflect the dynamic and ever-changing character of reality. This is why Iktomi likes stories so much, he says. Metaphor and narrative are expressions of a dynamic world and a synthetic method of unifying our understanding of the complexity through, rather than against, its variation.

The Open Question shows that strong moral naturalism involves identifying moral properties with something else (Shafer-Landau 2003) or perhaps does away with moral properties altogether (McNaughten 1988).

One Western Thinker tells this story to explain this problem: suppose a friend claims that God is love, and she believes in God because she believes in love. If she is a strong moral naturalist, it would be reasonable to conclude that she is an atheist (Schroeder 2005). By analogy, strong moral naturalists are "atheists" about moral properties. If moral properties are like water, then strong naturalists might not be "atheists" about moral properties. The Western Thinker responds that if water were like God, then I could not be said to believe in water if I merely believe in H_2O. The empirical reduction of moral and religious concepts to natural properties undermines the nature of these concepts itself, worries the Western Thinker. If I say God is nothing more than a collection of natural forces, like gravity and so on, then the Western Thinker might say that I do not believe in God. However, when I say that water is nothing more than H_2O, there seems to be no such worry for the Western Thinker. The Western Thinker must decide whether moral concepts are like the concept of water or the concept of God before he can decide whether they can be reducible to natural properties without ceasing to believe in moral concepts in the first place.

> Indications are to Iktomi that morality is more like the concept God for Western people. When Western people believe that morality is nothing more than a set of survival skills inherited from our evolutionary ancestors, they tend to believe, at least from Iktomi's experience with these people, that morality does not exist. Iktomi views the ideas about naturalism and realism expressed in these criticisms as greatly confused. The question of whether moral claims can be reduced (a priori or a posteriori) to natural properties already assumes that only properties countenanced by science are

natural. On the question of whether God is natural or not, Iktomi has already expressed the nature of the trickster logic that founds that question from the start. Iktomi knows that all experiences are natural, whether of God or of some other phenomena approved by science. He knows there is no procedure for determining which experiences fall under the category of natural experiences or of natural phenomena. Iktomi knows that the world is manifest in the variety of experiences of the world, and so it is not appropriate to determine in advance what sorts of experiences can be brought to bear in moral reflection.

The Western Thinker criticizes moral realism just as belief in the existence of God on the basis of the nature and extent of disagreement. The disagreements about morality and the existence of God moral disagreement are no ordinary disagreements about facts. Emotions, attitudes, interests, and the like seem to motivate moral disagreement, and so it seems that moral claims serve only to express such emotions, attitudes, interests, and the like. This leads many to see these claims as statements of fact despite appearances. Moral and religious disagreements seem to arise in the absence of facts, and so perhaps even though moral and religious claims are meant to state facts, the necessary facts are absent and so these sorts of claims fail to do what they intend. To defend a Western version of moral realism, one must claim that the nature of moral disagreement does not undermine the assertive aspect of moral claims or claim that at least some moral claims are true.

Iktomi doesn't think there is any reason to worry about moral disagreement in the first place. Iktomi wants to remind the Western

Thinker of Red Jacket's words. Iktomi knows that reality is dynamic. The universe is in the process of constant transformation. In this light, it is difficult to imagine what real disagreements would regard. Simple disagreement in the sense of one experience not being the same as another or even one story not being the same as another (Red Jacket and Reverend Cram) are not a context for worry. Knowledge is supposed to bring together, to incorporate, all these various experiences and stories into a comprehensive narrative. From the perspective of Indigenous morality in locality and epistemic locality in relation to a radically dynamic world, disagreement seems to be expected and commonplace and provides no worry for claims of knowledge or truth. The issues that arise regarding moral disagreement that lend support to fictionalism indicate, to Iktomi, a place where simplification regarding the nature of some reality is exposed in a way it ordinarily remains covered.

Just as the Western Thinker has created division between intrinsic and instrumental value in environmental ethics, the oversimplified dichotomy between reality and fiction creates problems that call out to be solved. Just as with the division between intrinsic and instrumental value, these are problems that arise on the basis of the division in the first place. For the Western Thinker, disagreement is seen as a flaw in the epistemological program rather than as a sign of progress.

Iktomi thinks that individual experiences are part of that singular and continuing manifestation of being and reality in the context of locality, and so there is no reason to be surprised or worried about disagreement. What the Western Thinker views as vitiating disagreement can often be normal and expected variation that is, in fact, integral to the bottom-up unity of knowledge. The Western Thinker supposes, Iktomi suggests, that there is just one way that the world manifests itself and this ought to be identically experienced across all localities in order to be objective or real. Iktomi reminds the Western Thinker of Red Jacket's words to Reverend Cram. The worry about moral disagreement, as described by Leksi Deloria, only comes to be after the attempt to streamline understanding, to push aside the messy parts of experience and concentrate on certain aspects that are amenable to abstract formulation and replication or coincide with preconceived notions. Iktomi thinks this displays the deeply embedded delocalized coloniality in Western moral epistemology. The worry about disagreement shows the false delocality in Western moral epistemology. Iktomi thinks that instead of returning to locality, however, the Western Thinker uses disagreement to maintain the delocalized moral epistemology.

To the Western Thinker, the experience of something unusual or unverified is usually enough to call the experience into question and destroy the possibility of knowledge on the basis of that experience.

Iktomi thinks that if someone experiences a spider talking to them while another person has never spoken with a spider is not grounds for the falsification of the experience of talking to a spider. This variety of experiences, Iktomi knows, calls out to a context for greater understanding of the complexity of the manifestation of being and knowing in locality and how it shows up through plurality and becoming. The Western Thinker is worried about the possibility of variety because he assumes that the world is singular, static, and so shows up just one way. For there to be true knowledge of a singular and static world, that knowledge must also be unchangeable and absolute. Iktomi thinks that if we are attempting to account for a complex world and with a bottom-up approach to knowledge, then our descriptions, our metaphor-filled narratives, must be responsive to the transforming world and the variety of experiences of it. Our knowledge, moral or not, must be in an ever-changing relational balance. Iktomi thinks that it is only through the trickster logic that constructs a false power of delocality that the Western Thinker thinks he can force agreement across locality.

To the Western Thinker, moral realism also undermines important aspects of moral psychology. A number of Western Thinkers think that moral properties or moral judgments are connected to motivation. The idea is as old as the Western Thinker and widely held, as evidenced in phenomenology of morality. The Western Thinker Socrates claimed that no one does wrong voluntarily. The idea is that understanding something as wrong is motivation enough to not do it and is required by what it means to be rational. If I truly believe that murder is wrong and I am rational, I ought to be motivated in some part at least against committing murder. The Western Thinker has argued against moral naturalism by claiming that natural properties cannot motivate and so cannot be moral properties if they cannot motivate (Mackie 1977). Some Western Thinkers have attempted to claim natural properties can in some cases motivate (Smith 1994).

Iktomi thinks the Western Thinker is struggling with the same trickster logic again. Just as with the questions about whether there is something beyond life and whether the energy that generates life exists, these questions are looking for something beyond the question of what to do, Iktomi thinks. The Western Thinker is trying to figure out what the world is really like and is not satisfied with trying to figure out in relation to the world I have experienced. Leksi Deloria thinks humans should seek "knowledge of the physical universe arranged or understood in such a manner as to call forth some form of moral response" (1999a, 47). Iktomi thinks the trickster logic has pushed the Western Thinker to externalize physical knowledge in such a way that he cannot hear the moral call of an ordinary understanding of the physical world. In locality, Iktomi says, the connection between the physical and the moral is quite natural and seamless (locality is the originary and continual manifestation—in a physical as well as conceptual sense—of knowing and being). Iktomi thinks that it is only from the delocalized perspective and its internal self-generating trickster logic that these localized manifestations are perceived as strange, unnatural, awkward, and senseless.

Conclusion

In this chapter, we have moved beyond the layers of delocality through universal sacredness as the foundational moral attitude with the layers of bottom-up unity and regulative completeness. These metaphors function also as aspects of a critical framework for locality since when they are applied to ways of seeking knowledge, both moral and otherwise, insights can be gained regarding just where these ways of seeking fall short. Bottom-up unity carries with it the value of sustainability—an all-important concept in environmental philosophy. While many are speaking of sustainable development, sustainable agriculture, sustainable ecosystem management, and so on, the metaphor of bottom-up unity, and its emphasis on sustainability as a feature of the way things are brought together at the most basic level, indicates that sustainability is more a function of how things come together in a foundational and originary manner (communities, economies, knowledge, agriculture, ecosystems, relationships, and so on). Attempts at sustainable unity are inherently unstable when they attempt to create this unity from the top-down. There is much than can be gained in reflecting on as well as operating with bottom-up unity in sustainability rather than the instability of top-down unity. In Seneca stories of distant time, the three sisters—corn, beans, and squash—came to the people and expressed a desire to make a relationship with them, to establish kinship. They told the people that if they did certain ceremonies and planted the sisters all together in a certain pattern that the sisters would sustain the people. Western scientists came along centuries later and discovered that this planting relationship created a perfect nitrogen balance, something they had been looking for to fix their problems of sustainability that had already begun to appear in the approach to create methods for agriculture, relationships, and so on in accordance with already conceived ideas and then attempt to fix problems or patch the holes in these already set-down ideas as they appeared. In this case, the hole was nitrogen imbalance, which was caused by depleting the soil by the overplanting of single crops, and so on. The Indian knowledge that began with sustainability as it attempted to bring together what was there into an appropriate relationship did not have this sort of problem to solve. The relationship created with the three sisters also carries with it the metaphor of search for completeness. This knowledge was moral from the start. It was not merely about what plants would grow best but about the right relationship of support between humans, these plants, and their environment.

The lessons regarding morality in locality are also extended in this chapter. The worry about what kind of value nonhumans should have creates a kind of entrenched anthropocentrism in our moral reflections. If we begin our moral reflections with the determination of the objects of value and their kind and amount, we are severely limiting our circle of moral relationships. We cannot expect to discover right relationships with the nonhuman world if we do not include reflection on the nature of those relationships from the beginning. If we simply determine their value, we will have little in the way of a relationship with them at all—no matter how much work we put into the effort to patch the holes from the top-down approach. The lesson seems to be that in order to open the possibility of right relationships with the nonhuman world, we need not rework our moral theories; we must rework the notion of a theory as a delocal moral abstraction. This lesson extends to debates regarding moral realism and moral fictionalism as well. The problem seems to have little to do with moral metaphysics and epistemology, but has much more to do with the attempt to streamline all knowledge. Supposing that all knowledge will and ought to be just like Western scientific knowledge is a top-down and delocalized approach that ends up with the attempt to deal with a reminder, in this case, moral knowledge. The problem arises also from the inherent incompleteness of Western scientific knowledge since the assumption from the start is that the best knowledge cannot give us more guidance or help us see the moral response called for by the physical world. It is no wonder, then, that they are puzzled about the nature of moral knowledge after starting from this acceptance of incompleteness.

CHAPTER 6

The Naturalness of Morality in Locality

Relationships, Reciprocity, and Respect

As described in chapter 5, the concept of sacredness is a kind of limit: it does not tell us how we actually ought to act. The claim that "everything is sacred" only tells us how we cannot understand morality in locality, that is, with different levels of abstract value. Universal sacrality does give us a starting point for ethical reflection in a positive sense as well. It requires that we take each thing we relate to with the seriousness that sacredness requires. There are none of our relations that we can take for granted in the search for our moral path. In this chapter, I take another step away from the choice to walk the path of delocality and another toward the path of epistemic locality. I try to express some ideas in the context of locality about the relationship between human beings and the land through a detailed look at actual moral claims that Native people make about human moral relations to the nonhuman world. Here the metaphor-filled and multilayered story of morality in locality extends from talk of life and sacredness to kinship, respect, relationships, person, and naturalness.

I begin with a general moral claim espoused by Native and non-Native thinkers alike, a claim that might have a different meaning in locality than in delocality: there is a connection between what is moral and what is natural. Assiniboine elder Walking Buffalo once said that in nature and the connection with nature, one will find the book of the Great Spirit. "If you take all of your (Western people's) books, lay them out under the sun, and let the snow and rain and insects work on them for a while, there will be nothing left" (McLuhan 1972, 23). The import is that in nature and in a connection to nature, and not in abstracted or delocalized text, one will find the instructions for a proper path to follow as human beings. It is implicit in these words that there is an unnaturalness to the Western way of knowledge and a naturalness to the Native approach. Oglala Lakota writer Luther Standing Bear expresses something similar about nature and being moral. He claims that the Lakota were "true naturalist[s]" and that they "loved the earth and all things of the earth." This love was something that grew with age to the point that the old ones "literally loved the soil and sat or reclined on the ground with a feeling of being close to a mother power." This "natural" relationship imparts moral understanding so that "kinship with all creatures of the earth, sky, and water," he claims, "was a real and active principle" derived from actually being in nature and having this "natural" contact (McLuhan 1972, 6). Apart from nature, this love and kinship are lost. As he writes, "the old Lakota was wise. He knew that man's heart away from nature becomes hard." In another place, Standing Bear claims the elder who sat on the ground and came to accept the kinship of all things "was infusing into his being the true essence of civilization" (McLuhan 1972, 6).

Western Moral Naturalism and the Binary between Natural and Unnatural

Western people have made similar claims and are often thought to be inspired to make these claims from these old Indians, whom they consider the first Western ecologists in the context of the narrative of colonial difference. In this context, saying that what is right is natural means living in accordance with the earth in some manner. Specific reference is often made to the words of the Native sages as quoted above. In this context of what is natural, Western people recommend eating organic foods, using earthly-produced products, and using what is called "natural medicine" (nonsynthetic medicine made from plants, animals, or minerals). In this context, there are several possible meanings to the Western claim that something is good or right because it is natural. Most reasonably, the claim is simply that using products made from organic materials or engaging in certain "natural" activities eases the human impact on the earth: such products are more likely recyclable, cause less pollution, and the like. Some of these "natural" activities are recycling, growing one's own food organically, bike riding, riding the train instead of driving, and the like. These "natural" activities are meant to have a similar result as the "natural" products. The idea is that these products and activities lead to a greater good: the mitigation of negative impacts on the environment and its ecosystems, particularly in the face of an environmental crisis.

There is more behind the claim that what is natural is good than the simple sense of being "good to do," but it is difficult to articulate just what is supposed to be natural about these "good to do" activities or what exactly is the good in what is natural in these activities. Simply because such activities lessen the human impact on the earth does not seem enough to define an activity as natural. There are plenty of natural acts, albeit not always acts by human beings, that have a devastating impact on the earth: floods, earthquakes, lightning fires, glaciations, and so on. Imagine a certain animal (a keystone species) was to die out in a certain ecosystem because of lack of rain. The result might be the natural devastation of much of the other animal and plant life in this ecosystem. Imagine a new predator naturally wandering into an ecosystem unaccustomed to such a hunter. This animal might wipe out entire species of creatures who are unable to defend against this new hunter.

When pressed, the point seems to be that the idea of naturalness expressed in these slogans only applies to human beings. In the narrative of colonial difference there is supposition that humans through a civilizing process have literally come out of nature. These "unnatural" human colonizers operate through a process of separating the European locality from nature, land, and Indigenous people. Human beings in the context of coloniality, unlike animals or Indians as noble savages in the narrative of colonial difference, can be "in" nature or "out." This is the conversation with naturalness that this book is trying to initiate, to subvert the delocalized power of European coloniality that operates on Indigenous people and land. Perhaps there is some sense of locality in these general proclamations about the need for more naturalness in human activity, but there is little epistemic locality in these proclamations. In other words, there is little understanding of what might be the force of locality that underlies these proclamations, even on the part of those Western people who are making them.

There is also clearly more to the common use of the term "naturalness" than lessening the negative human impact upon the earth, and some of the deeper sense of naturalness here arises from delocality and coloniality rather than from an attempted move away from these. A friend of mine has been taking lithium for many years to ease the most severe symptoms of a bipolar disorder. She made the claim that it was fine to be taking lithium because it was natural. Her argument was not that it was good to ingest lithium because it was better for the earth. Her argument for naturalness as goodness was constructed in terms of a human good rather than an environmental good. Her argument that lithium was good because it was natural was a function of the idea that natural products and perhaps natural activities are better for the functioning of human organisms. Ingesting some manufactured product, some humanly created product meant to alleviate the symptoms of some illness, is not as good for the long-term and perhaps even immediate functioning of the human organism. However, even the impact of the interruption of natural function alone does not account for the full force of the claim that naturalness is good. Again, it is difficult to characterize the exact idea of what more is involved in the claim that naturalness is good though. Perhaps what is best for me as a human defines what is natural, but this seems to be so contingently. If some unnatural product were shown to be better in the long run for humans than some natural product, then the unnatural product would have to be better, leaving us again looking for the force of the claim that a product is good because it is natural. To say that the natural product is nevertheless better is to simply equate goodness and naturalness by definition, which undercuts the idea of natural in the contingent sense of being better for humans. In other words, if it turns out that some unnatural product is much better for humans than lithium, in the long and short term, then to keep saying that lithium is better because it is natural cannot be understood as supporting the view of naturalness where "natural" means better for human beings.

These lines of support for the claim that what is good is natural are indirect. Engaging in certain activities that are natural or using products that are natural brings about a greater good: the good in this case is a decrease in possible harm to the environment, a betterment of human beings, or perhaps some combination of the two. Whatever the case, there seems to be no particular good that emanates directly from what is natural. Put another way, naturalness as a concept need not play a constitutive role in the goodness of the activity. It just so happens that certain activities result in a lighter human impact on the earth or are better for human beings and that these activities or products are called "natural." The questions remain: what is it about these activities that make them natural, and what is it about this naturalness that leads to a lightened impact or make products or activities better for human beings, or is there something about naturalness that makes it good in itself? Attempting answers to these questions leads us to a more direct form of moral naturalism that is more deeply entrenched in the conflict between locality and delocality. The gist of the more direct form of moral naturalism seems to be that there is some way that the earth can be called natural or in its natural state or natural processes. It is thought to be a good to be in accord rather than in discord with this natural state of things. As it regards the amount of harm one causes things, in this case the environment or the world itself, the idea seems to be that it is better for a thing to be in accord with its natural functioning than not. Imagine that I attempted to use my car not for driving but as a giant wrecking ball. The result, insofar as it affects the functioning of my car as a driving machine, would be disastrous. It is highly likely that my car would no longer be able to perform its intended function. This idea of natural function is only one of the ways in which direct moral naturalism is defined. I attempt to articulate some of the different ways one might define direct moral naturalism below.

Direct moral naturalism is simply put: any unnatural action or object is bad or wrong. Depakote (as opposed to lithium) is an unnatural object. Therefore, Depakote is bad. Unnatural actions can include, it seems, the consuming of unnatural objects. Taking Depakote is then wrong because it implies an unnatural act. The various forms that the unnatural/natural dichotomy might take include:

1. What is natural is what conforms to the laws of nature, while what is unnatural is what defies these laws.
2. What is natural is not human made or nonartificial, while what is unnatural is human made or artificial.
3. What is natural is what is common or normal, while what is unnatural is uncommon or abnormal.
4. What is natural is what is in accordance with the function of a thing, while what is unnatural is what is contrary to that function.

The first form is relatively useless, as least for the purposes of articulating moral naturalism. The only kinds of actions or objects that could be unnatural in this sense would be of the supernatural sort. Only supernatural beings can perform supernatural acts, and so there would be no sense in which human action would be unnatural and so morally bad. All human actions are then not wrong by definition under this view, since humans are incapable of supernatural acts. Further, supernatural acts are thought to be performed by the most perfect of moral agents: God. Miracles too are supernatural events by definition and also not thought to have any particular moral turpitude. Miracles are not something we are obligated not to do, but on this view, they might well be morally condemned.

The second form seems the most likely basis for the claim that Depakote is bad while lithium is not. Depakote is bad because it is artificial or humanly created, while lithium is not because it occurs in the world without human action or is nonartificial. The second form is no better off for articulating a sense of moral naturalism. While the first form implied that no human actions were morally wrong, this form implies the opposite: that all human actions are wrong. This is the case at least if we understand human actions as producing themselves. The thought is that one of the things that humans produce are their actions. Human actions are then human products and so artificial and therefore wrong. Even if we don't suppose that human actions are human products, everything that humans do produce is morally bad. It is hard, then, to imagine what a human could do that was not morally bad. One could perhaps attempt to be a passive observer of the world, trying hard not to produce anything. Even this seems absurd, however, since even something like eating and defecating—which are required to live at all—seem to leave a human product.

The third form does not have the flaw of the first two: it does not make all human action impervious to wrong or make nearly all human action, in effect, wrong. It makes little sense, though, to speak plainly of what is uncommon. In terms of things in the universe, blonde hair and blue eyes are relatively uncommon. The commonness or uncommonness of something is always relative to a set of objects. From the perspective of the history of the universe, human products such as Depakote are uncommon, but lithium does not seem to be much more common. Further, highly common organisms, like harmful bacteria, seem to carry no particular goodness, but a relatively uncommon product like efavirenz, used to treat AIDS in Africa, seems to carry particular goodness. It seems quite a mistake to say that something is wrong just because it is uncommon. After all, many acts that are thought to elevate one to sainthood are certainly uncommon. Take the example of taking a bullet to save another person: this is certainly a highly uncommon act but also certainly morally praiseworthy. There seems to be nothing wrong in particular with an uncommon act, and in some cases the uncommonness of an act is a exactly what recommends that act for goodness. It also seems wrong that a thing be called good just for being common. Murder is becoming increasingly common in many parts of the world. It does not follow that murder is good where it is common.

The Western Thinker and the Forked Road of Natural and the Unnatural Functions

—from the philosophy of Iktomi

The Western Thinker thinks that all things have a natural function and that this function indicates what we ought to do or what is good. According to Aristotle, nature is an inner principle of change and being at rest (*Physics* 2.1, 192b20–23). The nature of a thing is sufficient to account for its change or being at rest. The final cause always resides within a thing and does not come from anything outside. Everything has a natural end or telos that is in its nature. Aristotle thinks there is an ergon (function) of everything that is directed toward this natural end or telos that each thing has in its nature. For human beings, this ergon is the rational activity of the soul in accordance with virtue (*Physics* 1097b22–1098a20). Aristotle, unsurprisingly, thinks that rational activity is unique to humans, which is why it can be seen as the function of human beings. Since what is good for a thing is to strive for its own ultimate end and that ultimate end is derived from the unique natural function of a thing, it follows that if the unique natural function of a human being is rational activity, then doing this is a human being's ultimate end and what is good for him.

> Iktomi can't help but think about that time that he farted himself into space when he hears the Western Thinker talk about "natural functions." His stomach has never recovered, but he will never forget the lesson his relative timpsila (wild turnip) taught him on that day (http://nagualli.blogspot.com/2012/02/iktomi-farts-himself-into-space-rosebud.html).

The Christian Western Thinker adds to Aristotle by claiming that nature as a whole is also teleological and created by God, and so when one is pursuing one's natural end, individual interests and overall order are in harmony. Christianity adds to the idea that rationality is the distinctive human function by defining rationality as a capacity to follow God's orders, a capacity that is given to us for our own good. This is the "Divine Corporation" model of ethics, where individuals are part of a cooperative endeavor that is aimed at a supremely valuable good (Schneewind 1984). Each kind of creature has a role to play in realizing this good. Some creatures simply strive in their functioning toward their ends and this goal unaware through divine instinct or whatever, but human beings, who are the rational ones, are aware of their function by directives from on high, where God infallibly allocates tasks that rational beings can understand as coming from God and as being infallible.

> Iktomi thinks his natural functions are infallible, or was it inflatable? Iktomi also thinks is pretty rude to say that spiders only do what they do because of divine instinct. Iktomi says he has always been as capable as anyone of making bad choices of his own accord without the help of anything divine or natural. Well, except that one time that he farted himself into space. But maybe that was not his fault at all and totally something natural.

The Western Thinker created modern mechanistic science, which denied the notion of natural function. From the perspective of mechanistic science, the idea of natural function is seen as a vestige of primitive and prescientific thinking (http://www.bu.edu/wcp/Papers/Scie/ScieSpas. htm). The Western Thinker thinks that the teleological biology of Aristotelian ethics makes little sense in the contemporary Western scientific context (Hull and Ruse 1998). Discovering natural facts about human biology that could indicate what is good for humans seems hopeless from the perspective of post-Darwinian biology, which has no capacity, as a feature of its construction, to say anything positive about morality whatsoever. Some Western Thinkers have defended a neo-Aristotelian naturalism in support of modern versions of virtue ethics. One Western Thinker sees moral evaluation as continuous with the evaluation of the excellence of a thing as a thing of its kind. To evaluate something like a plant, this Western Thinker evaluates how it functions toward the ends of survival and reproduction. To evaluate certain types of animals, she adds freedom from pain and the enjoyment of certain pleasure indicative of the species. In evaluating social animals, like humans, the function of the group is also considered (Hursthouse 1999). All of these evaluations of excellence are thought to be based on facts about how well a thing is functioning toward its own end.

> Iktomi thinks the idea that evaluation of the excellence of a thing as a thing rather than the evaluation of how things are going for me from my perspective was rejected as carrying no moral weight by the Western Thinker in the debate on the possibility of nonhuman intrinsic value. Iktomi thinks the Western Thinker is back in the same spot of trying to defend nonanthropocentric value in a context where all value is foundationally and self-congratulatorily human.

A dancing bee who finds nectar and does not dance to alert the other bees can be seen as defective (Foot 1995), but the Western Thinker does not see this defect as a moral one.

> Iktomi wonders why human beings don't evaluate themselves as morally defective in the same way they evaluate bees and spiders.

One Western Thinker uses the example of male cheetahs and male polar bears who do not help their pregnant and vulnerable mates hunt for food. If these male animals did help their mates in these circumstances, they would be seen as defective.

> Iktomi wonders whether the Western Thinker will stop calling human males who leave their pregnant mates "deadbeat dads" since

most would think this action is just as natural as the action of the male cheetah or polar bear. Or given that animals naturally engage in same-sex mating, will the Western Thinker stop saying that homosexuality is wrong because it is unnatural. Iktomi thinks that the Western Thinker does not really view the evaluation of natural function on a continuum with human moral evaluation. The Western Thinker's moral evaluation has more impact on the evaluation of natural function than the other way around, Iktomi thinks. The Western Thinker seems to make special consideration for human evaluation that he doesn't extend to nonhumans. Slipping between different kinds of value in the nonhuman to human realms indicates, Iktomi thinks, a continuation of the trickster logic that transforms the individual Western Thinker into the entire world.

Indigenous Moral Naturalism through Locality

The second sense of naturalness (the artificial/inartificial form) has had the clearest role in the coloniality of power as it operates through delocality over Indigenous people and Indigenous land. Western ecologists use this form of the natural/unnatural dichotomy in determining the stability and functioning of a particular ecosystem. The idea is that if I am trying to understand human impact on ecosystems, then it might benefit me to attempt a separation between human impact as artificial and other nonhuman impacts as inartificial. If this is meant to be a distinction in the nature of things rather than a more pragmatic distinction, it is much more problematic. Unless it is shown that human impact on the environment is somehow unnatural or that humans are somehow unnatural and not part of their environment, it will not do to simply rename human actions and products as unnatural. But to conceptualize humans as separate from their environments is a function of delocality, and to see Native people as embedded in their environment as savages or animals and so not fully human is a function of coloniality and the narrative of colonial difference. The manner in which the labels of natural and unnatural can be arbitrarily applied to Native people depending on the particular wishes of the colonial powers reveals the delocality and coloniality of this framework from the start. Before the creation of national parks in the United States, for example, the land upon which Native people lived was seen as wilderness because of the fact that Native people inhabited it, but when the United States decided it wanted to set aside these areas for the undisturbed enjoyment of American tourists, a new concept of wilderness was born where Native people were no longer a natural part of these places, and so must be removed (Spence 2000). This is why Black Elk in 1929 laments that in creating the Badlands National Park, the United States is making separate "little islands" for Native people far removed from the "other little islands for the four-leggeds" (Neihardt 1932, 9). When the land of Black Elk's people was put into protective status so as to preserve its natural state, the Native people who had until recently been seen as part of what made these lands savage and wild were banished from the land in order to protect its wilderness state. The arbitrary assignment of natural and then unnatural to Native people as a function of the process of coloniality reveals a remainder of locality that is always left over no matter how hard the colonizer tried to inject the abstracted European delocality onto the Indigenous land. In this case, the anomaly is humans are both natural animals from the delocalized science of biology and unnatural from the delocalized science of ecology. This attempted contradiction through delocality reveals the fact of colonial difference in the land, which is merely the ill-fittedness of coloniality through delocality onto the Indigenous locality, land. The fact of colonial difference is marked through the absorption of this seeming contradiction (being both natural and unnatural) in the context of locality. From Black Elk's perspective of his people and their land (his locality), the people and the land are both natural and unnatural: His people "were happy . . . and seldom hungry" when "the two-leggeds and the four-leggeds lived together like relatives, and there was plenty for them and for us" (Neihardt 1932, 9).

he fact of colonial difference articulates the difference in locality between the nature of Native moral naturalism and the Western concepts discussed above. An interesting place to start to clarify the nature of Native moral naturalism is with uranium. Uranium, like lithium, is a natural substance in the sense that it is not produced by humans. It is well known, of course, that uranium is dangerous to human beings and the environment and has had a sordid and tragic and toxic legacy in the settler colonial history of the United States (Eichstaedt 1994). It is also interesting that the poignant descriptions of the problems of mining uranium from the perspective of Native people focus on ideas of moral naturalness. In the Southwest, Native people have known for a very long time that mountains in the area had special rocks that were part of what imparted them with their power. Western people discovered that these rocks were uranium and decided to mine the mountains. Native elders say that they warned the Westerners not to remove the rocks from the sacred mountains, that doing so was wrong and dangerous. Westerners mined the mountains on Indian land anyway, and even still do to this day. The result has, of course, been devastating. There are water sources in the

Southwest that are toxically contaminated by uranium (water I spent the better part of my childhood drinking). Thomas Banyacya Sr., Hopi elder and interpreter for the Kikmongwis (Hopi spiritual leaders), reports that the Hopi prophecy warns of this future from time immemorial. The Hopi prophecy warns that people will come and take these rocks and build a gourd full of ash, which he interprets as the atomic bomb (Hopi Tribe 2014). In the Native discussions of such, it is seen that doing wrong things will of course bring harm. But the focus of the discussion is always on the manner in which the action is performed that determines if it is a good thing. Native people often talk about doing things "in a good way" or not doing things "in a good way." As we shall soon see, this is where naturalness and right action connect in Native thought.

It is clearly not wrong to mine and use uranium because it is artificial like Depokate is. Uranium is more like lithium in this regard. It might be thought that the problem with uranium is the unnatural removal of it from the sacred mountains where it belongs: its being there is a part of its natural function. This too does not quite account for the Native moral approach to uranium. What Banyacya and other Native elders stress is the treatment of the mountains and the rocks (uranium) that are in them. They say removing the rock is not treating the mountain or the rock respectfully, not respecting the relationship between humans and the mountains. This manner of speaking is the norm regarding many natural objects that are thought to be quite harmful. Tobacco, for instance, is believed to be quite harmful to humans. Tobacco is of course quite natural in the sense of being inartificial and so ought to be a good in that sense. One might say that smoking or ingesting tobacco is not in line with natural human functioning and so bad in that sense. Native elders do not speak in any of these ways. The sense is that smoking or ingesting tobacco is not harmful. What is bad is not respecting tobacco. Not acting with respect can of course bring harm as not respecting tobacco can cause harm, but it is not the harm that causes these actions to be bad. Relating to tobacco improperly is wrong because it is improper. In the context of locality, the question is not what makes such action wrong in general—in delocality—but what are the conditions of my proper relationship to tobacco in particular.

From a Native perspective, the business of actually figuring out what path I ought to walk through life is wrapped up in talk of relationships, respect, reciprocity, kinship, and the like. An understanding of who you are and who I am in the broadest sense of story and metaphor helps determine the context of our relationship. An understanding of who I am in the context of my particular place helps determine what sorts of actions are respectful and what sorts are not, which makes it difficult to create universal statements of moral relationship and leads to many of the ridiculous interpretations of Native moral claims. It is the locality of morality. Reciprocity is the nature of relationality in the context of locality. Relationality is always between an I and a Thou in locality. The dual agency of reciprocity is the very context, then, of relationality itself. Relationships are never one-sided. You are a Thou to me, and I am a Thou to you. I have my place (my extended relationships in the ecosystem or community that we share), and you have your place. The agency required by relationships is not determined by the kind of facilities a thing has—in particular, the delocalized facilities that only humans seem to possess. Agency is something much more basic.

Morality, just like subjectivity in Buber's Thou, cannot be brought under a universal in locality. Morality is then not theoretical, at least in the Western sense of that term. Creating abstract moral theories that conceal concrete relationships is a primary function of morality in delocality. From the layers of the fact of colonial difference, moral theorizing in the Western sense also conflicts with always already being in motion of relationality itself. One cannot speak of what is right to do through delocality since relationships, respect, and reciprocity are only manifested through locality. Trying to make rules for all human relations and then stretching these same rules, or even making new ones to cover all animal or environmental relations, is only possible under the philosophy of delocality. This sort of morality cannot account for morality in locality since in that sense morality is in the land—it is an originary and continual manifestation in the land. The argument often lodged against morality in locality—that the development of massive and complex societies necessitated the creation of laws and related delocalized concepts of morality—is a function of coloniality in the sense that, at root, it is simply a defense of the delocality necessary to create and maintain the power and structure necessary for the coloniality of power that shapes this very world system that the argument defends. Also, the argument defends an abstraction of locality—a delocalized locality—of the Euro-Christian perspective that rationality is the capacity to follow laws issued by God and then the state as the form of natural law. The "Divine Corporation" model of ethics delocalizes itself in the assumption that rule-following is a necessary feature of all human moral psychology. Within Indigenous locality, this is not an inherent feature of morality itself or of moral relations. The fractionalization of societies, arising from coloniality and delocality, to the point that moral relations between individuals appear more like relations between warring states so that delocalized following of rules through human rationality is necessary to maintain order, is not seen as a necessary outcome of morality in locality. From a perspective of

Native locality, the social unit is structurally unified through bottom-up unity. Even beyond the problems with massive societies with complex internal social relations, the original sin myth that paints humans as inherently evil and not to be trusted, so that laws that tell them what to do are necessary in order to maintain order and control this inherent evil of the state of nature, is a function of coloniality and the narrative of colonial difference. It is not simply a different morality in locality because the ideas are abstracted into delocality as a power necessary for coloniality itself. Within Indigenous locality, there is no reason to suspect that my relations are malicious. This perspective of trust within locality is one of the reasons why Native people kept talking peace and making treaties with the United States even though the United States broke every treaty it made with them. Native morality had no context for the kind of continual and willful maliciousness that is created and maintained by coloniality because such continual and willful maliciousness requires a delocalized view of relationality that is self-defeating and so irrational. Morality that is delocalized and based in abstracted laws must necessarily deny trust in my relations because relationality has been delocalized, which means that relationality as such is destroyed and in its place a manufactured and illusional concept of mere relationality is imagined. Relationality that is based in Thou-based agency and reciprocity cannot and need not function under abstract and universalized moral laws. Human morality that is based in mere relationality, alternatively, becomes focused on capitulating to laws—rules to follow that determine my moral choices for me in advance.

Law, in the Indigenous locality, is about values. In Cherokee, the word for law is ᏗᎧᏃᏩᏛᏍᏗ (*dikanowadvsdi*), but this word has little to do with rule-following and the determinations of moral choices in advance.

Dikanowadvsdi are values or teachings, and one of these teachings, *duyugtv iditlv datsadesehesdesdi*, SGAᏫ TᎫP SGᏝ4ᏢᏬᎠᏚᏬᎠᎫ, instructs the Cherokee locality to direct one another in the right way, which is without confinement or coercion. This teaching specifically guides me to not push people in one direction or another—that the choice of understanding, doing right, and so on, must be up to you. There is no coercion, then, in Cherokee law and morality, and the people are taught SGᏝCB4ᏬᎠᎫ, *detsadatliyvsesdi*, "to struggle to hold on to one another or cling to one another" and ᏫᏢᏬᎥᎫ SGᏝᏰ14ᏬᎠᎫ, *ulisgedi detsadayelvsesdi*, "to treat each other's existence as being sacred."

In Navajo, the phrase "it's up to her" is also fundamental to the legal and moral fabric of Navajo locality and is violated by the "punishment or correction of a person" (Yazzie 2005, 2743 of 8358). Navajo morality is expressed by the form "Do things in a good way," but this is not an abstraction into delocality but a reference to morality in locality itself. Chief Justice Robert Yazzie writes, "as Indians, we know what it means to do things in a good way." It is "the people's shared values" in Navajo locality "that fill in the broad term of law" (2623 of 8358). In the Navajo locality, these values are centered around *k'e* (solidarity, respect, reciprocity, and more). This centers morality in relationships, relatives, and relationality. In Navajo locality, as Yazzie points out, I introduce myself by clan, which is an extended family network of relationships, which contextualizes my current relationality within the traditional Navajo legal system. This extends to the Navajo teaching to "treat strangers like they were a relative" (2638) and the notion of an offender, which is what is said of a person who "acts as if he has no relatives." The example of the operations that Yazzie gives of Navajo morality in locality subverts morality in delocality in the strongest way: "a [Navajo] man stole a woman's blanket and jewelry at a dance so he could sell them and buy wine. The woman suspected the man and confronted him the next day. He immediately admitted what he had done and gave the woman enough sheep to make up for the loss." This exemplifies morality in locality where what is right is to "act in a good way," without any instructions on how this would necessarily function across localities or in broad circumstances.

Part of this trust in locality is the result of the sense of "it's up to her" as it appears in locality. The point is that only from the perspective of delocality can simply following some rules that are laid down for me be considered being moral. If there is nothing particularly moral about my actual choosing, then there is nothing particularly moral about my actions. Only from a delocalized perspective can one view the operations of acting according to moral rules within a locality as having any moral import. From within locality, it is through the morality of my choosing and action that creates the context of being moral. Just like the sort of radical empiricism that permeates Native languages and epistemology, what is right to do really is best specified in the very particular context wherein the relationships that determine such are actualized, and not through a delocalized general formula that both limits my understanding of relationships in locality but also limits the actual morality of my choosing and acting.

As claimed in the previous chapter, from a Native perspective value is only such in relation so that in the abstract everything has all the value there is (everything is sacred). But things, human or otherwise, are not abstract and so are always in a deep I/Thou relation from the start. I can never be out of relation with that to which I am related. (This is why I have argued elsewhere that Native science and philosophy are internal: there can be no separation between simply coming to know and then doing something good or bad with that knowledge. I am always in relation, and so everything I do, even my search for knowledge and the manner in which it is carried out, holds moral weight [see Burkhart 2004].) Figuring out what to do is based on understanding one's relations, which is also what and who one is, since, like value, individuals are not what they are in isolation. Native science is the tool for understanding this deep relationality, which is the connectedness and relatedness of and between things. Native science is very different than Western science, however, in large part because of the sense that one can never be out of relation—that knowledge is always kept in locality. The manner in which one goes about finding knowledge is in relation. Knowledge is then always internal in locality. I figure out what to do while I am doing it. Just like a jazz musician playing a solo who cannot stop the song to figure out what the right note is to play next, I cannot stop my life, my relations, to figure out what the right act is to do next. Knowledge is always knowledge-in-relation, and so attempting to abstract it out of relation, to delocalize knowledge, is an attempt to obscure the actual foundation of knowledge in locality. Native natural science, then, as the science of deep relationality, founds morality in locality. This creates a kind of moral naturalism for Indigenous morality since part of the definition of moral naturalism was the founding of morality in natural science.

Another way to look at this is through the perspective that all my relations are sacred; they all carry the same weight, and none can be ignored. But an understanding of how I am related to things gives a shape to the web. Things have a place on the web, as my relations. I cannot forget the metaphor of the web of life and its power to imbue all things with a sacredness, and so I must make my reflections of how to act properly with my relatives against this background. I must see myself as an agent, but not an active agent in relation to passive things but an agent among agents. This is part of coming to terms with what I am in concrete locality. What I am is a thing-in-relation and not an isolated thing that can come into relations or not. Part of the point of Native elders using the concepts of the "natural" is to point to this relational agency as the basic, "natural" context of all things. Just as I do not think of myself as an agent among passive things when I attempt to understand my relations with the humans around me, I ought to understand all of my relations as agent-relations. Think about the context of my relationships with other humans: I understand my friend is having a bad day and that when I am around her I cheer her up. I do not simply grab her and drag her by my side even though it might in some sense be thought to be in her best interest. I talk to her, and perhaps I find out that today it might be better for her to simply lie down and take a nap. Suppose she knew that my being around would cheer her up, she could not on pains of destroying the very relational context that provided the cheering grab me and drag me to her side to cheer her up. I have to choose to come to her freely in order for the benefit of my coming to be realized. I ought to think of and operate in in terms of all my moral relations in locality with this same framework in mind and practice.

Two basic ideas of Native moral naturalism, then, are these: (1) Native science founds Native morality, and (2) all relations are relations between agents. Let us first examine premise (2). The idea that all relations are relations between agents is founded on the metaphysics of chapter 5. Our experiential relations to things are as agents. This is not based on a theory about what people are or even what agents are in delocality but arises from an experiential relationship with the things around us. Charles Eastman relates an experience from his boyhood among his Lakota people in the late nineteenth century. He and his uncle were hunting a deer when they encountered a coyote. After his uncle had killed the deer and hung it on a tree, there came all manner of yelps and yips from the forest, as if an entire pack of coyotes had surrounded them. With a bit of investigation, they found it to be a lone coyote who had been running in circles around them kicking up dirt and making the various noises to imitate an entire pack (Eastman 1971). Eastman's experience and his retelling of this experience to us give us the context for understanding coyote. These intelligent actions must not be denied to coyote because we do not have a place for them to fit into an already existing theory of animals or the coyote species. Deloria comments on this story in comparison to Western models of thought:

> We are taught to believe from the very beginning that animals have no feelings, emotions, or intellect. We assume that they function by "instinct," but this word only covers up our ignorance of the capabilities of animals. This incident is very rare, it could possibly be observed only once in a lifetime by a very small percentage of people.... Empirically, it is possible as reported by an observer meeting all the requirements of the coyote world. (2004, 7)

There are many stories and continual experience of relational agency to nonhumans in Indigenous locality. In the *inipi*, the Lakota sweat ceremony, the rocks are the first people in Lakota stories and the first items brought into the lodge. The hot rocks are then doused with water, which are the second people in these stories of distant time. The sweat then pores from the people's bodies back down to *Unci Maka* (Grandmother Earth), the third being in creation. The humans, rocks, *Unci Maka*, and water come into, once again, a very ancient relationship—not as a reenactment but as a coming together again of the exact same thing from earliest times. The humans are sitting pitifully before the oldest beings on the planet, offering their water back to these most basic of life-giving and healing beings. These relationships and the power or agency of these beings are not something that comes through Western-style scientific investigation but are experienced in the relationships one has with these beings, here, in the locality of ceremony but also in the stories of all these beings since time immemorial. This is all the evidence one needs to come to know these beings as agents, as people.

The context for understanding moral relationships, of any kind, is, then, kinship. All beings around us are our relatives, not simply in some metaphorical sense where we understand inanimate, lifeless objects as somehow related to us, but in the fullest sense of moral relationships between agents, between people. Kinship is, I would argue, the primary mode for understanding all behavior, concepts, powers (even to heal), and the like in a Native philosophical worldview. For example, concepts like virginity or two-spirited when used by Native people express issues of relationality and kinship. Virginity, it would seem, has very little to do with sexual relations but more to do with kinship relations. When the young girls are shamed for losing their virginity in Ella Deloria's novel about nineteenth-century life among the Dakota, *Waterlily*, the shame is not from a sexual act but from the entering into a frivolous kinship relation. Being a two-spirit, in the same manner, has little to do with sexuality but to do with the gender roles one takes on in relation to one's kin. Two-spirits in traditional Navajo culture were considered very rich because they had the ability to enter into a variety of kinship relations. Healing is also always about kinship. In Navajo medicine ways, the person being prayed for or, more literally, "sung over" is instructed to sit directly on a sand painting that is made of one or some of the holy people or healing powers of the universe. The idea is that by doing so and in the right way, with the right songs, prayers, and so forth, one will reestablish a kinship relation with these healing powers and so create the possibility for healing. It should not come as a surprise that morality would be understood also in terms of kinship.

The founding of Native morality in Native science connects Native naturalism to current trends in Western naturalism. Western philosophical moral naturalism is rather different from any of the popular concepts of moral naturalism I have attempted to describe. It is a metaethical view meant to cohere with current trends of naturalism in metaphysics and epistemology more generally. Naturalism in philosophy as a current trend takes Western science as a foundation. Daniel Dennett, for example, argues that natural selection is a universal acid that can eat through any dogma. He points out that the idea of natural selection had been born as an answer to questions in biology, but it leaked out to questions in cosmology and psychology (1996, 63).

Native moral naturalism has little connection to these Western technical issues. It is true, however, that Native moral naturalism is deeply connected to Native science. Native science, as was clear in the case of coyote's attempt to steal the deer and with rocks in the ceremony, does not limit the kinds of things that can be justifiably used in reflecting about morality in the way that Western moral naturalism does. Native science is in part a first-personal and ongoing reflection with deference to the past and all that has been experienced (by oneself, shared by others, or passed down in story) while leaving the future open (there is no future experience that is ruled out) regarding the right path to walk through life. Native science is a part, then, of Native morality. One of the things that I come to understand when reflecting in this way is that I am related to all the beings (including rocks and trees) around me, and that they are alive in this relation. The question regarding what is alive or what is an agency in isolation, a question that is often raised by philosophers, does not arise since the metaphor under the metaphor of life and agency is relationship or kinship. When Luther Standing Bear describes the kinship that arises from being in a natural relation to things in the beginning of this chapter, what he is referencing are the actions that arise out of this understanding of our relationships to things based on Native science. I am being unnatural, primarily, when I am not acting with awareness of and respect for my kinship with the things around me.

This way of understanding naturalness paints a very different picture than those given in the beginning of this chapter. There is nothing about uranium or lithium that makes them natural in this sense. Naturalness, like so many concepts I have described, is based on kinship; it is a relation, not a property of something. Tobacco is not natural, but it is how I act toward this relation, with respect toward our kinship, that makes my relations natural or unnatural. When I act unnaturally toward tobacco (when I do not treat it with respect) it is rather harmful to me, but it is not the harmfulness that makes the action bad. I am acting disrespectfully and so behaving badly. It does not matter to the wrongness of this action that there is a consequence to such bad behaving in this case, but it is only possible to receive the benefit of kinship by acting respectfully, as in the case of my sad friend to whom I can bring cheer. When we apply this notion of naturalness back to notions that lithium, willow bark, or whatever is natural and so better, we find little support for this notion. It is not that one is using something that occurs in nature without human interference that makes something natural. It is the relation of respect toward the kinship we have with something, be it natural in this other sense or not, that makes our actions natural. It is not puzzling, then, when elders said to me as a child that I was treating my blanket or my toys unnaturally. I did not treat them with the respect that toys and blankets are to have as the kinds of kin they are to me, and so I was not treating them naturally—that is, I did not understand how they were related to me and how that relationship called out to me for a moral response. What is referred to as "natural medicine" in Western culture is also not natural in the Native sense. When one takes a plant and grinds it up into particular compounds that are believed to have effects that we desire, and places these compounds in bottles on a shelf for people to consume, there is nothing natural about this from a Native perspective. Where is the relationship to the plant as one's kin? The healing power of the plant is akin to the healing power of my being able to cheer up my sad friend. In order to receive the healing power from my relationship, I must ask it what it wants to give to me and not simply take what I think I should have from it if I am to act naturally, to act out of respect for our kinship. Giving, as intertwined with receiving in the metaphor of reciprocity as the form of relationships between agency, provides the material form of agency. I show my respect and understanding of our relationship as mutual agents by giving or giving back, through reciprocity. When I take leaves from a plant for medicine, I might, as a Chumash medicine woman instructed me in the Indigenous locality here in California, give back to the plant some of my hair as I am taking its. This is the material expression of our moral relationship as agents.

In order to figure out what is right for me in my path, I must start with an attitude of respect. This attitude first arises from the background context of universal sacrality. I am fully aware in my reflections on my particular relationships that all things near me now or at a far distance removed are connected together on this web of life and are each one imbued with the sacredness and seriousness that this provides. Moral reflection and even moral action all arise from this attitude of respect. Universal sacrality provides the foundation of the initial attitude. In my search for the right path to walk for me as a human or for the right relations between a human community and its broader nonhuman relatives, I must extend my reflections beyond the mere sacredness of all my relations to the particularity of those relationships. This particularity is kinship. When the Cree bands of James Bay drafted a petition to the Canadian government to ask for an end to the plans to build a massive hydroelectric power plant, they rested their case on the following proposition: "We ... oppose ... these projects because we believe that only the beavers [have] a right to build dams in our territory" (Quoted in Desbiens, 43-44). The moral claim was not meant to express some abstract relationship between all people and animals or even all people and all beavers, but to say something about the particular kinship morality of the humans of James Bay and those beavers in that locality. The understanding of this kinship relationship required a lot of knowledge to build up over a long time in the story of those people and those animals. The people had to understand the history and meaning of the place, the plants, the animals, and themselves as far back as time immemorial. The people had to understand the meaning of the Native science story of these relationships, which is often expressed with the metaphor of older (animals and plants) to younger (humans) siblings. As our older brothers and sisters, the animals and plants provide us with guidance and nourishment. We humans, the story continues, are very young and naive in relation even to our closest relatives. This natural knowledge story provides moral guidance for humans in their search for the right path to walk in life. The James Bay Cree understood this kinship relationship with their neighbors, the beavers, and they understood the beaver's place in that ecosystem they shared. This relationship the beavers had with that place developed over millions of years, even millions of years before humans arrived at that place to establish kinship. This is what forms the foundation of the claim made by the Cree that those rivers were only supposed to be dammed by the beavers. The particularity of these kinship relations provides a context for better understanding the often misunderstood and misappropriated words from Indian people. When the Wintu women speaks of her and her people's relationship to their place such that chopping down trees is inappropriate, and when Smohalla of the Paiute people refuses to plow as to not "take a knife and tear my mother's bosom" or to harvest as to not "cut my mother's hair and sell it," one should not understand their statements as universal ethical claims. They express particular kinship relations that those people have to that place, their community in that locality. When the Seneca establish the kinship with the three sisters (corn, beans, and squash), they have accepted a different relational role between their people and their place—its plants, soil, and so on. In their kinship relations, these plants, their sisters, provide for them by allowing their "hair" or their "children" (the corn, beans, and squash that come from these plants) to be sacrificed in order to sustain their young relatives, the Seneca. Alternatively, the Seneca might not understand the kinship relationship that Plains Indian people have with the buffalo, where they do little planting and do not have the same kinship relations with plants and the soil, but depend in a similar sense on the buffalo nation, *Tatanka Oyate*, sacrificing its members in order to sustain their little brothers and sisters, the Lakota people. The point is that these issues about the "naturalness" of certain activities ought not be understood as providing a basis for a universal ethic but rather should be understood as the expression of particular kinship relations and the obligations that arise from the creation of kinships.

Kinship has a regulative role similar to completeness. Kinship is not something that is automatic, like those who head to the wilderness to commune with their brother the bear or whatever. Kinship is something that must be established within a local community of beings (animals, rocks, and trees). Humans must find and establish their kinship relationships with those beings in order for the community to come together as a bottom-up unity. The general concepts of brother, sister, cousin, and so on are only metaphors of beginning—just as sacredness is only the starting place. Both sacredness and general kinship terms mark our attitude and approach to the search for our right path and right relationships.

Completeness also has a further regulative wrinkle in the expression of its layers of meaning. Just as the establishment of kinship creates a context for continual moral response, the completeness ideal requires continual examinations of the continuity of things, places, and so on. Deloria tells us that "spiritual aspect of knowledge about the world taught the people that relationships must not be left complete," and that in "stories about how the world came to be . . . the common themes . . . are the completion of relationships and the determination of how this would should function" (2001, 23). An Indigenous Hawaiian friend of mine told me a story about something that happened while he was doing construction on the big island. Just before his crew was about to begin breaking ground for a new housing complex, one of the elders from the local community asked to do a ceremony for the place. In this ceremony, he asks permission of the place to take on the housing of these buildings and the new lives of the people who would be there, but he also attempted in actions and prayers to connect the new shape this place would take with all the other shapes, events, rocks, plants, animals, and the like that were there and had been there. The continuity of relationships is embedded in the goal of completeness, and the continuity of relationships is the power of locality. All new relationships must be continuous with the other relationships that brought this new relationship into being. This is why when a singer is taught a song or a medicine person is given medicine, they always tell the people who taught them the song and where it comes from and its meaning or tell the people who gave them the medicine when they use the song or the medicine. This continuity of relationship is demanded by the goal of completeness. No relationship, meaning, or being can be ignored if we are to move forward with the greatest possible sustainable unity.

The Place of Kinship Relations in Western Environmental Ethics: The Future of Indigenous Morality in Locality

Regardless whether my readers are able to grasp the Native moral philosophies with all their nuances, there seem to be many surface-level conclusions that environmental ethicists might find useful. The issue of sustainability as a fundamental feature of epistemology and communities even before environmental policies might prove rather useful to thinking about what sustainability is and ought to be within the confines of Western environmental ethics. The spiritual or attitudinal approach to ecology might also prove inspirational. Native people do not place the emphasis of their thought of environmental ethics on the foundations of material resources. Recycling and resource management will never truly address what is really at issue in what we describe as our "environmental crisis." Of course, Native people understand that material resources can be depleted or that animals and plants can become extinct. However, their insight into the cause of these depletions and extinctions might prove insightful. For Native people, the disappearing of plants and animals is often the result of human treatment of these plants and animals, and just as the Ghost Dancers on the plains in the late 1800s believed in the return of the buffalo, Native people believe that these plants and animals might return if the people changed their attitudes and behaviors. The deeper insight is in the attitude of respect that Native philosophy puts much emphasis upon. It seems useful to think of the leaving of the plant and animal entities as a result of our disrespectful attitudes toward them. Even if one cannot see beyond the literalness of plants and animals being offended by our disrespect and going away, one surely can see that the root of the problems that cause extinctions brought about by humans is in the attitudes we take and in particular the lack of respect in our attitudes toward our relatives.

In addition to the debates regarding the importance and nature of value as it relates to the environment, Indigenous moral philosophy can provide helpful insight, I believe, into a number of other entrenched debates. One is the debate over the objects of environmental worth and relation. There has been great debate over just what sorts of things ought to carry the weight of moral worth and relation in environmental philosophy. There are those who argue that individuals are the primary objects of value. Nicholas Agar claims, for example, that the worth of a species is accounted for by the worth of the individuals that make up that species (1995). Holmes Rolston III argues that species are the foundation of worth since they carry biological potential and the possibilities even of individuals within a species (1975). John Rodman claims that an ecological community has a good of its own that is not based merely on the collective goods of its individuals (1977). In addition to these debates between holism and individualism, there are issues that arise with many of the attempts to define what makes an individual, species, or ecosystem valuable. If one defines this value in terms of being goal oriented, for example, critics will say that many machines are goal oriented (guided missiles, chess-playing computers, thermostatic heaters, and so on) but, whatever environmental value turns out to be, critics say that machines cannot have it.

In addition to the problems I have raised with placing the foundations of environmental ethics on the determination of object of value, there are important points that a relational or kinship ethics could make in regard to these debates. This point cuts across this field of issues: our relations are always to individuals or persons even when our relations are species and ecosystems. We do not have relationships to ecosystems as a collection of individuals; we have relationships to ecosystems as individuals. The point is that we have possible kinship relations to many sorts of individuals or relatives. One might be a particular plant in my backyard, one might be a particular mountain (made up of millions of individual plants, bugs, pieces of dirt, animals, fungal spores, and so on), one might be the coyote that roam the hills, but at each level of my relationships to these things and even things within things (the coyote may very well live on the mountain after all), I am relating to and understanding my kinship relation regarding an individual agent, however simple or complex that individual to whom I am relating is. A similar comment can be made about the worry that we might accidentally give machine or artificial items environmental value and thereby undermine our claim to such value: we relate to machines and artificial things too. Only if we worry about conforming to abstract categories of environmental object, simple objects, or artificial objects will any of these worries arise. One of the very important relatives in many Native localities is the drum. The drum forms the center and coming-together of people and sings the heartbeat of Mother Earth for the people. But this relative is made by human beings. This becomes a worry only if we are attempting to place categories of value on categories of things. If we take our relationship as the primary mode of moral reflection, we need not worry about any of these abstract categories under which the objects of our relationships might be subsumed. All our relationships can be an I/Thou. The relationship I have with my drum, the drum that I have made, is different, of course, than the relationship I have with animals or plants that provide me with food or with the relatives in my human communities that sustain me as well, but this does not change the fact that I do relate to it and so must treat it with respect as the relative that it is. I must understand how this drum is my kin and treat it with respect. I must approach my relationship with it and my understanding with this attitude of respect no matter what sort of thing it is. However, the thing it is helps determine what particular actions I ought to take in relation to it and in what particular manner is it my kin. This is not different for the drum, for tobacco, for the mountain I see to the north, or for the bear that teaches me about the Osha root medicine or can just as well eat me. The particulars of respect for any one of these kin are determined by our relationship and by all of the other relationships that go into any particular engagement within that kinship relationship. Future reflection on and further application of these concepts to other areas of environment ethics seem set to provide an interesting context for very different and perhaps very useful and insightful discussions about morality.

BIBLIOGRAPHY

Agar, N. 1995. "Valuing species and valuing individuals." Environmental Ethics
    17(4):397–415.

Alcoff, Linda Martín. 2007. "Mignolo's Epistemology of Coloniality."
    Centennial Review 7 (3): 79–101.

Alfred, Taiaiake. 2005. *Wasase: Indigenous Pathways of Action and Freedom.*
    Toronto: Broadview Press.

Almond, Brenda. 1986. *Moral Concerns.* Humanities Press.

Anderson, Hans Christian. 1949. The Emperor's New Clothes. New York:
    Houghton Mifflin Company.

Anzaldúa, Gloria. 1987. *Borderlands/La Fronteria: The New Mestiza.* San
    Francisco: Aunt Luta Books.

Aristotle. 2014. *The Complete Works of Aristotle: The Revised Oxford
    Translation.* Edited by Jonathan Barnes. Princeton University Press.

Arneil, Morag Barbara. 1992. "All the World Was America: John Locke and the
    American Indian." Dissertation, University College London.

Barlowe, Arthur. 2007. "First Voyage to Virginia 1584." In *American History Told by Contemporaries—Volume I: Era Of Colonization 1492–1689.* Edited by Albert Hall. Bushnell Bushnell Press.

Benson, John. 2000. *Environmental Ethics: An Introduction with Readings.* New York: Routledge.

Bernasconi, Robert. 1998. "Hegel at the Court of the Ashanti." In *Hegel after Derrida*, edited by Stuart Barnett, 41–63. London: Routledge.

Barreiro, Jose. 1995. "Bigotshtick: Rush Limbaugh on Indians." *Native Americas*, 12 (3): 40–43.

Black Hawk. 2008. *Life of Black Hawk, or Ma-ka-tai-me-she-kia-kiak: Dictated by Himself.* Penguin Classics.

Bodin, Jean. 1576. *Six Books of the Commonwealth.* Translated by M. J. Tooley. Oxford: Basil Blackwell.

Boyd, Richard. 1988. "How to be a Moral Realist." In *Essays on Moral Realism*, edited by Geoffrey Sayre-McCord, 187–228. Ithaca, NY: Cornell University Press.

Bracken, Christopher. 2014. "'In This Seperaton': The Noncorrespondence of Joseph Johnson." In *Theorizing Native Studies*, edited by Audra Simpson and Andrea Smith, 122–148. Durham, NC: Duke University Press.

Buber, Martin. 2014. *Between Man and Man.* Translated by Ronald Gregor Smith. Mansfield Centre, CT: Martino.

Buechel, Eugene, S.J. 1978. *Lakota Tales and Texts.* Edited by S.J. Paul Manhart. Pine Ridge, SD: Red Cloud Indian School.

Burkhart, Brian. 2016. "Theories of Coloniality and Indigenous Liberation through the Land: A Critical Look at *Red Skin, White Masks.*" *APA Newsletter on Indigenous Philosophy* 15 (2): 2–6.

Burkhart, Brian Yazzie. 2004. "What Coyote and Thales Can Teach Us: An Outline of American Indian Epistemology." In *American Indian Thought:*

Philosophical Essays, edited by Anne Waters, 15–26. Oxford: Blackwell.

Burrow, John W. 1966. *Evolution and Society: A Study in Victorian Social Theory.* Cambridge: Cambridge University Press.

Chinard, Gilbert. 1947. "Eighteenth Century Theories on America as Human Habitat." In *Proceedings of the American Philosophical Society* 91: 31.

Cajete, Gregory. 2000. *Native Science: Natural Laws of Interdependence.* Santa Fe, NM: Clear Light.

Cohen, Carl, and Tom Regan. 2001. *The Animal Rights Debate.* Latham, MD: Rowen and Littlefield.

"Cherokee Women Scholars' and Activists' Statement on Andrea Smith." 2015. *Indian Country Today,* July 17.

da Silva, Denise Ferreira. 2007. *Toward a Global Theory of Race.* Minneapolis: University of Minnesota Press.

Deleuze, Gilles, and Claire Parnet. 1987. *Dialogues.* Translated by Barbera Habberjam Hugh Tomlinson. London: Althone Press.

Deloria, Vine, Jr. 1969. *Custer Died for Your Sins: An Indian Manifesto.* New York: Macmillan.

————. 1970. *We Talk, You Listen: New Tribes, New Turf.* Lincoln: University of Nebraska Press.

————. 1994. *God Is Red: A Native View of Religion.* Golden, CO: Fulcrum.

————. 1998. "Intellectual Self-Determination and Sovereignty: Looking at the Windmills in Our Minds." *Wicazo Sa Review* 13 (1): 25–31.

————. 1999a. "Religion and Revolution among American Indians (1974)." In *For This Land: Writings on Religion in America.* New York: Routledge.

————. 1999b. *Spirit and Reason: The Vine Deloria, Jr., Reader.* Edited by Kristen Foehner, Sam Scinta, and Barbara Deloria. Golden, CO: Fulcrum.

————. 2001. *In the Light of Reverance.* Directed by Christopher McLeod. Performed by Vine Deloria Jr.

———. 2004. "Philosophy and Tribal Peoples." In *American Indian Thoughts: Philosophical Essay*, edited by Anne Waters, 3–12. Malden, MA: Blackwell.

Deloria, Vine, Jr., and Daniel Wildcat. 2001. *Power and Place: Indian Education in America*. Golden, CO: Fulcrum.

Dennett, Daniel C. 1996. *Darwin's Dangerous Idea: Evolution and the Meanings of Life*. Simon & Schuster.

Densmore, Chistopher. 1999. *Red Jacket: Iroquois Diplomat and Orator*. Syracuse, NY: Syracuse University Press.

Desbiens, Caroline. 2013. *Power from the North: Territory, Identity, and the Culture of Hydroelectricity in Quebec*. Vancouver: University of British Colombia Press.

Drake, Daniel. 1843. *Lives of Celebrated American Indians*. Boston: Bradbury, Soden.

Dussel, Enrique. 1993. "Eurocentrism and Modernity (Introduction to the Frankfurt Lectures)." *boundary 2* 20 (3): 65–76.

———. 2000. "Europe, Modernity, and Eurocentrism." *Nepantla: Views from South* 1 (3): 465–478.

———. 2013. "Anti-Cartesian Meditations: On the Origin of the Philosophical Anti-Discourse of Modernity." *Human Architecture: Journal of the Sociology of Self-Knowledge* 11 (1): 1–40.

Eastman, Charles. 1971. *Indian Boyhood*. Dover.

Eckel, Malcolm David. 1992. *To See the Buddha: A Philosopher's Quest for the Meaning of Emptiness*. San Francisco: Harper.

Eichstaedt, Peter H. 1994. *If You Poison Us: Uranium and Native Americans*. Santa Fe, NM: Red Crane Books.

Erdoes, Richard, transcriber. 2012. "Iktomi Farts Himself into Space (Rosebud Sioux)." nagualli.blogspot.com.

Ferrer, Amy. Leiter Reports: A Philosophy Blog. December 4, 2012. http://

leiterreports.typepad.com/blog/2012/12/what-can-we-do-about-
diversity.html (accessed December 9, 2012).

Fixico, Donald L. 2003. *The American Indian Mind in a Linear World*. New
York: Routledge.

Flanagan, Tom. 2008. *First Nations? Second Thoughts*. Montreal: McGill-
Queens University Press.

Foot, Philippa. 1995. "Does Moral Subjectivism Rest on a Mistake?." *Oxford
Journal of Legal Studies* 15 (1): 1–14.

Forbes, Jack D. 1998. "Intellectual Self-Determination and Sovereignty:
Implications for Native Studies and for Native Intellectuals." *Wicazo Sa
Review* 13 (1): 11–23.

Frazer, J. G. 1914. *The Golden Bough: A Study in Magic and Religion*. 3rd ed.
London: Macmillan.

Freud, Sigmund. 1950. *Totem and Taboo*. Translated by James Strachely. New
York: W. W. Norton.

Gleick, James. 1987. *Chaos: The Making of a New Science*. Viking Adult.

Grande, Sandy. 2000. "American Indian Identity and Intellectualism: The
Quest for a New Red Pedagogy." *International Journal of Qualitative
Studies in Education* 13 (4): 343–359.

Green, Joshua D. 2002. "The Terrible, Horrible, No Good, Very Bad Truth
about Morality and What to Do About it." Dissertation, Princeton
University.

Hare, R. M. 1989. "Moral Reasoning about the Environment." In *Essays on
Political Morality*. Oxford: Oxford University Press.

Hazlett, Allen. 2010. "The Myth of Factive Verbs." *Philosophy and
Phenomenological Research* 80 (3): 497–522.

Hegel, Georg Wilhelm Friedrich. 1975. *Lectures on the Philosophy of World
History: Introduction*. Translated by H. B. Nisbet. Cambridge: Cambridge

University Press.

———. 1977. *Phenomenology of Spirit.* Translated by A. V. Miller. Oxford: Oxford University Press.

———. 1991. *The Encylopeaedia Logic.* Translated by T. F. Geraets, W. A. Suchting, and H. S. Harris. Indianapolis, IN: Hackett.

Hilderbrandt, Walter, and Harold Cardinal. 2000. *Treaty Elder of Saskatchewan: Our Dream Is That Our Peoples Will One Day Be Clearly Recognized as Nations.* Calgary: University of Calgary Press.

Hobbes, Thomas. 1651. *Leviathan or The Matter, Forme, and Power of a Commonwealth Ecclesiastical and Civil.* London.

Hopi Tribe. 2014. Hopi Prophecy. June 5. https://www.welcomehome.org/prophecy/hopi1.html.

Howe, Craig, Lydia Whirlwind Soldier, and Lanniko L. Lee. 2011. *He Sapa Woihable: Black Hills Dream.* Saint Paul, MN: Living Justice Press.

Hursthouse, Rosalind. 1999. *On Virtue Ethics.* Oxford: Clarendon Press.

Jahner, Elain. 1983. "Introduction to Walker." In *Lakota Myth*, by James Walker. Lincoln: University of Nebraska Press.

Jennings, Francis. 1971. "Virgin Land and Savage People." *American Quarterly* 23 (4): 519–541.

———. 1976. *The Invasion of America: Indians, Colonialism, and the Cant of Conquest.* New York: W. W. Norton.

Kant, Immanuel. 1784. "Beantwortung der Frage: Was ist Aufklärung?" *Berlinische Monatsschrift* (December): 481–494.

Krech, Shepard III. 1999. *The Ecological Indian: Myth and History.* New York: W. W. Norton.

Laozi. . 2002. *The Daodejing of Laozi.* Translated by Philip J. Ivanhoe. Indianapolis, IN: Hackett.

Lassiter, Luke E. 1998. *The Power of Kiowa Song: A Collaborative Ethnography.*

Tuscon: University of Arizona Press.

Leopold, Aldo. 1949. *A Sand County Almanac, and Sketches Here and There.* New York: Oxford University Press.

Locke, John. 1821. *Two Treatisies on Government.* London.

———. 1975. *An Essay Concerning Human Understanding.* Edited by Peter H. Nidditch. Oxford: Oxford University Press.

Lugones, María. 1989. "Playfulness, 'World'-Traveling, and Loving Perception." In *Women, Knowledge, and Reality: Explorations of Feminist Philosophy,* edited by Ann Garry and Marilyn Pearsall. Boston: Unwin Hyman.

Lyons, Scott Richard. 2010. *X-marks: Native Signatures of Assent.* Minneapolis: University of Minnesota Press.

Mackie, J. L. 1977. *Ethics: Inventing Right and Wrong.* Harmondsworth, UK: Penguin.

Macy, Joanna. 1991. *Mutual Causality in Buddhism and General Systems Theory: The Dharma of Natural Systems.* Albany, NY: State University of New York Press.

Maldonado-Torres, Nelson. 2007. "On the Coloniality of Being." *Cultural Studies* 22 (2): 240–270.

Marshall, Joseph M., III. 2001. *The Lakota Way: Stories and Lessons for Living.* New York: Penguin.

McLuhan, T.C. 1972. *To Touch the Earth: A Self Portrait of Indian Existence.* New York: Pocket Books.

McNaughton, David. 1988. *Moral Vision.* New York: Blackwell.

Meadows, Donella H. 1972. *The Limits to Growth; a Report for the Club of Rome's Project on the Predicament of Mankind.* New York: Universe Books.

Mignolo, Walter D. 2000. *Local Histories/Global Designs: Coloniality, Subaltern Knowledges, and Border Thinking.* Princeton, NJ: Princeton University Press.

———. 2002. "The Geopolitics of Knowledge and the Colonial Difference." *South Atlantic Quarterly* 101 (1): 57–96.

———. 2009. "Dispensable and Bare Lives: Coloniality and the Hidden Political/Economic Agenda of Modernity." *Human Architecture: Journal of the Sociology of Self-Knowledge* 7 (2): 69–87.

Mills, Charles W. 1997. *The Racial Contract*. Ithaca, NY: Cornell University Press.

Moore, John H. 1998. "Truth and Tolerance in Native American Epistemology." In *Studying Native America: Problems and Prospects*, edited by Russel Thorton, 271–305. Madison: University of Wisconsin Press.

Naess, Arne. 1973. "The shallow and the deep, long-range ecology movement. A summary." *Inquiry* 16 (1): 95–100.

Neihardt, John G. 1932. *Black Elk Speaks: Being the Life Story of a Holy Man of the Oglala Sioux*. New York: William Morrow.

Newcomb, Steven T. 2008. *Pagans in the Promised Land*. Golden, CO: Fulcrum.

Nietzsche, Friedrich. 1954. *Twilight of the Idols*. Translated by Walter Kaufman. New York: Penguin.

Hull, David L and Michael Ruse (eds). 1998. *The Philosophy of Biology*. New York: Oxford University Press.

Ortega, Mariana. 2001. "'New Mesiztzas,' 'World Travelers,' 'Dasein': Phenomenology and the Multi-Voiced, Multi-Cultural Self." *Hypatia* 16 (3): 1–29.

Pagden, Anthony. 1987. *The Fall of Natural Man: The American Indian and the Origins of Comparative Ethnology*. Cambridge: Cambridge University Press.

Pinxten, Rik, Ingrid van Dooren, and Frank Harvey. 1983. *Anthropology of Space: Explorations into the Natural Philosophy and Semantics of the Navajo*. Philadelphia: University of Pennsylvania Press.

Quijano, Anibal. 2000. "Coloniality of Power, Eurocentrism, and Latin America." *Nepantla: Views from South* 1 (3): 533–580.

Ralston, Holmes. 1975. "Is There an Ecological Ethic?" *Ethics* 85:93–109.

Regan, Tom. 1983. *The Case for Animal Rights.* London: Routledge and Kegan Paul.

Ricoeur, Paul. 2004. *Memory, History, Forgetting.* Translated by Kathleen Blamey and David Pellauer. Chicago: University of Chicago Press.

Robinson, T.M, editor and translator. 1987. *Heraclitus: fragments.* Toronto: University of Toronto Press.

Rodman, John. 1977. "I. the liberation of nature?" *Inquiry: An Interdisciplinary Journal of Philosophy* 20 (1–4): 83–131.

Rolston, Holmes III. 1975. "Is There an Ecological Ethic?." *Ethics* 85: 93–109.

Rosenberg, Alex. Janurary 2, 2014. .cura te ipsum. 3ammagazine.com.

Said, Edward. 1978. *Orientalism.* New York: Vintage Books.

———. 1994. *Culture and Imperialism.* New York: Vintage Books.

Saldana-Portillo, Maria Josefina. 2003. *The Revolutionary Imagination in the Americas and the Age of Development.* Durham, NC: Duke University Press.

Schneewind, J. 1984. "The Divine Corporation and the history of ethics." In *Philosophy in History: Essays in the Historiography of Philosophy,* edited by R. Rorty, J. Schneewind and Q. Skinner, 173–192. Cambridge: Cambridge University Press.

Schroeder, Mark. 2005 "Realism and Reduction: The Quest for Robustness." Philosophers' Imprint, 5(1): 1–18.

Schuman, Rebecca. Feburary 3, 2014. Nasty and Brutish: A scandal in Colorado reveals that bullying bros still plague university philosophy departments. Slate.com.

Shafer-Landau, Russ. 2003. *Moral Realism: A Defence.* Oxford: Clarendon Press.

Silverblatt, Irene. 2004. *Modern Inquisitions: Peru and the Colonial Origins of the Civilized World (Latin America Otherwise)*. Durham, NC: Duke University Press.

Simpson, Audra. 2014. *Mohawk Interuptus: Political Life Across the Borders of Settler States*. Durham, NC: Duke University Press.

Simpson, Audra and Andrea Smith (eds). 2014. *Theorizing Native Studies*. Durham, NC: Duke University Press.

Singer, Peter. 1975. *Animal Liberation*. New York: Random House.

Smith, Andrea. 2014. "Native Studies as the Horizon of Death: Theorizing Ethnographic Entrapment and Settler Self-Reflexivity." In *Theorizing Native Studies*, edited by Audra Simpson and Andrea Smith, 207–234. Durham, NC: Duke University Press.

Smith, Linda Tuhiwai. 1999. *Decolonizing Methodologies: Research and Indigenous Peoples*. New York: Zed Books.

Smith, Michael. 1994. *The Moral Problem*. Oxford: Blackwell.

Spence, Mark David. 2000. *Dispossessing the Wilderness: Indian Removal and the Making of the National Parks*. New York: Oxford University Press.

Singer, Peter. 1990. *Animal Liberation*. New York: Avon Books.

Standing Bear, Luther. 1978. *Land of the Spotted Eagle*. Lincoln: University of Nebraska Press.

Stone, C. D. 1972. "Should Trees Have Standing?" *Southern California Law Review* 45: 450–501.

Sumner, L. W. 1996. *Welfare, Happiness, and Ethics*. Oxford University Press.

Taylor, P. 1986. *Respect for Nature. A Theory of Environmental Ethics*. Princeton, NJ: Princeton University Press.

Teuton, Sean Kicummah. 2008. *Red Land, Red Power: Grounding Knowledge in the American Indian Novel*. Durham, NC: Duke University Press.

Trowbridge, C. C. 1939. *Shawnese traditions: C.C. Trowbridge's account*. Ann

Arbor: University of Michigan Press.

Tully, James. 1997. "Rediscovering America: The Two Treatises and Aboriginal Rights." In *Locke's Philosophy: Content and Context*, edited by G. A. J. Rogers. Oxford, UK: Clarendon Press.

Turner, Dale. 2006. *This is Not a Peace Pipe: Towards a Critical Indigenous Philosophy*. Toronto: University of Toronto Press.

Varner, Gary E. 1998. *In Nature's Interests?: Interests, Animal Rights, and Environmental Ethics*. Oxford University Press

Walker, James. 1980. *Lakota Belief and Ritual*. Edited by Raymond J. DeMallie and Elaine A. Jahner. Lincoln: University of Nebraska Press.

Warrior, Robert Allen. 1992. "Intellectual Sovereignty and the Struggle for an American Indian Future." *Wicazo Sa Review* 8 (1): 1–20.

Wildcat, Daniel. 2005. "Indigenizing the Future: Why We Must Think Spatially in the Twenty-first Century." *American Studies* 46 (3/4): 417–440.

White Hat, Albert, Sr. 2012. *Zuya Life's Journey: Oral Teachings from Rosebud*. Salt Lake City: University of Utah Press.

Whitehead, Alfred North. 1920. *The Concept of Nature*. Cambridge: Cambridge University Press.

———. 1925. *Science and the Modern World*. Cambridge: Cambridge University Press.

Wilson, E. O. 1999. *The Diversity of Life*. New York: W. W. Norton.

Witherspoon, Gary. 1977. *Language and Art in the Navajo Universe*. Ann Arbor: University of Michigan Press.

Wittgenstein, Ludwig. 1953. *Philosophical Investigations*. Edited by G. E. M. Anscombe and R. Rhees. Translated by G. E. M. Anscombe. Englewood Cliffs, NJ: Prentice Hall.

Wolfe, Patrick. 2006. "Settler Colonialism and the Elimination of the Native." *Journal of Genocide Research* 8 (4): 387–409.

Yazzie, Robert. 2005. "Healing as Justice: The Navajo Response to Crime." In *Justice as Healing: Indigenous Ways*, edited by Wanda D. McCaslin. Living Justice Press.

Zhuangzi. 1994. *Wandering on the Way: Early Taoist Tales and Parables of Chuang Tzu*. Translated by V. H. Mair. New York: Bantam Books.

INDEX